THE POLITICS OF AGING

THE POLITICS OF AGING
Power And Policy

By

JOHN B. WILLIAMSON

Department of Sociology
Boston College

LINDA EVANS

Department of Sociology
Central Connecticut State College

LAWRENCE A. POWELL

Department of Political Science
Massachusetts Institute of Technology

In Collaboration With

Sharlene Hesse-Biber

Department of Sociology
Boston College

CHARLES C THOMAS • PUBLISHER

Springfield • Illinois • U.S.A.

Published and Distributed Throughout the World by
CHARLES C THOMAS • PUBLISHER
2600 South First Street
Springfield, Illinois 62717, U.S.A.

©*1982, by* CHARLES C THOMAS • PUBLISHER
ISBN 0-398-04608-5 cloth
ISBN 0-398-04609-3 paper

Library of Congress Catalog Card Number: 81-14568

Library of Congress Cataloging in Publication Data

Williamson, John B.
The politics of aging.

Bibliography: p.
Includes index.
1. Aged—United States—Political activity.
2. Aged—Government policy—United States.
I. Evans, Linda.   II. Powell, Lawrence A.
III. Title.
HQ1064.U5W5924   305.2'6   81-14568
ISBN 0-398-04608-5   AACR2
ISBN 0-398-04609-3 (pbk.)

Printed in the United States of America
SC-R-1

to Ithiel de Sola Pool

AUTHORS

LINDA EVANS

Associate Professor
Department of Sociology
Central Connecticut State College
B.A., Mount Holyoke College
M.A., Boston College
Ph.D., Boston College

SHARLENE J. HESSE-BIBER

Associate Professor
Department of Sociology
Boston College
B.A., University of Michigan
M.A., University of Michigan
Ph.D., University of Michigan

LAWRENCE A. POWELL

Department of Political Science
Massachusetts Institute of Technology
B.A., University of Minnesota
Ph.D. (Candidate), Massachusetts Institute of Technology

JOHN B. WILLIAMSON

Associate Professor
Department of Sociology
Boston College
B.S., Massachusetts Institute of Technology
Ph.D., Harvard University

PREFACE

Our goal in this monograph is to present an empirically based analysis of a number of theoretical issues that define the emerging field of political gerontology. Political gerontologists are concerned with the study of power relations as they concern the elderly. This includes analysis of the aged as a voting block and an interest group in the political arena, as well as interpersonal relationships of power and influence in everyday living.

The book is divided into three parts. In Part I we examine the available historical and cross-cultural evidence concerning the conditions under which the aged have had substantial power, as opposed to those conditions under which they have tended to have relatively little power. In Part II the focus is on the political arena in the United States during the twentieth century. Here we consider such issues as the rise of the pension movement during the 1920s, the political maneuvering that surrounded passage of the Social Security Act in 1935, and the rise of the aging movement during the 1960s and 1970s. In this section we also consider such issues as trends in voter participation and the political attitudes of the elderly. In Part III an effort is made to examine the issue of power in the context of the interpersonal relations of everyday living. In Chapter 7, for example, we consider the trajectory of power relations between husband and wife as they move through the life cycle. In Chapter 8 we analyze the mechanisms of social control used to regulate and constrain the elderly. These mechanisms range from mandatory retirement rules to the use of tranquilizers in nursing homes in order to manage "troublemakers." We conclude in Chapter 9 with an analysis of the possible consequences of present social and economic trends for the power the elderly will have in the years ahead. Will it be increasing or decreasing? If we have learned anything from the historical record to date, it is that the power of the elderly does not remain constant; it is in a continual state of flux.

Some gerontologists contend that the next fifty years will bring a marked increase in the political influence of the aged and tend to emphasize the importance of the demographic trend toward more old people. They argue that as the proportion who are elderly increases there will be a corresponding increase in their political influence. They point to the growth of the various organizations that speak on behalf of the elderly; some, such as the American Association of Retired Persons (AARP), have several million members. They also mention the growth of government bureaucracies (e.g. Social Security Administration, Administration on Aging, National Institute on Aging) as well as the increasing number of social workers, health professionals, program administrators, and planners, to say nothing of real estate developers and leisure industry workers who have an economic stake in government expenditures on programs for the aged.

Other gerontologists argue, to the contrary, that the elderly are not a significant political force today and that they are unlikely to become a significant political force in the forseeable future. The argument from this perspective is that the anticipated increase in numbers will not translate into political influence because most of the elderly will have other more important sources of political identification and loyalty, such as social class, occupational background, and ethnicity. Most of the elderly have had these other sources of identity much longer than they have had the identity of "elderly persons"; as a result, the influence of these other sources is stronger. Most people also feel more positive about these other sources of identity than they feel about their old age identity. The net result is that the aged tend to vote as they have voted in the past, and they are not likely to be mobilized around candidates who claim to represent the interests of the elderly. The same line of reasoning is used to argue that despite substantial increases in the number of old people that can be expected fifty years from now, there is no reason to believe that there will be a significant increase in the political influence of the elderly.

In this monograph the evidence with respect to each of these positions is analyzed. A number of strong arguments can be made on both sides of the issue, but we are not entirely satisfied with either of these polar positions. Our synthesis is not, however, simply a staking out of the middle ground. To us the evidence suggests that over the next several decades it would be reasonable to anticipate a marked increase in the *political resources* of the elderly. It is quite possible that this long run trend will produce an increase in the political influence of the elderly, but such an outcome is not inevitable. There are a number of counterbalancing factors, some of which tend to be triggered by the political gains the elderly make. This suggests a dialectical model of the political process. The greater the gains the elderly make, the greater the resistance from other age groups to further gains.

The Authors

ACKNOWLEDGMENTS

John Williamson is the primary author of Chapters 1 and 9 and is a coauthor of Chapters 2, 3, 4, 5, 6, 7, and 8. Linda Evans is the primary author of Chapters 2 and 8 and a coauthor of Chapter 1. Lawrence Powell is the primary author of Chapters 4, 5, and 6. Sharlene Hesse-Biber is the primary author of Chapters 3 and 7.

We owe a great deal to a number of people who have commented on preliminary drafts of parts or all of the manuscript and in other ways contributed to our thinking about the issues considered in this monograph. We have found the suggestions of John Donovan, Beth Hess, Elizabeth Johnson, David Karp, and Henry Pratt especially valuable. We are much indebted to Peter Bruce, Walter Dean Burnham, Lloyd Etheredge, John Hudson, Roger Hurwitz, Louis Menand, John Myles, Stephen Pfohl, Ithiel Pool, Lucian Pye, Roy Ross, Deborah Stone, and Sidney Verba. We are also indebted to Carroll Estes, Norval Glenn, Robert Hudson, and David Smith for agreeing to read and comment on substantial portions of the manuscript. While we wish to acknowledge our debt to those mentioned, we would not want to hold them responsible for any of our conclusions. A number of people have been of great assistance in the typing, editing, and other aspects of manuscript preparation. In this context we are particularly appreciative of the contributions of Gina Abeles, Lorraine Bone, Alice Close, Lori Girshick, Delia Johnson, Shirley Urban, Rick Werther, and Sara White. We also wish to thank Payne Thomas, Scott Thomas, Michael Thomas, Diane Enger, and William Bried of our publisher's editorial staff for their assistance and support throughout this project.

CONTENTS

EPILOGUE

THE POLITICS OF AGING

INTRODUCTION

Chapter 1

THE POLITICS OF AGE

Political gerontology is *the study of power as it involves the elderly*. This includes analysis of the power of the aged as a group and as individuals engaged in the persuasion, manipulation, and bartering transactions of everyday life. Put simply, we are interested in knowing the conditions under which the elderly tend to have more than their proportionate share of influence, both collectively and individually, and the conditions under which they have less.

Interest in the politics of aging has surfaced for a variety of reasons. One is the matter of sheer numbers. In 1900 there were approximately 3 million persons age 65 or over in the United States making up 4 percent of the population. By 1980 there had been a dramatic increase in this segment of the population to 24 million persons and 11 percent of the population. A demographic shift of this magnitude cannot occur without having profound political consequences. Furthermore, projections based on persons already born indicate that in the year 2030 there will be 50 million elderly persons making up 18 percent of the population (U.S. Bureau of the Census, 1979*b*).

The growth since the turn of the century has contributed to a substantial increase in the proportion of the federal budget allocated to income maintenance, health care, housing, and social services for the elderly. The political consequences of this increasing economic burden are very real today, and there is every reason to believe that the burden will be substantially greater in the years ahead (Derthick, 1979). This knowledge has triggered concern among gerontologists, journalists, and political analysts, as well as government planners and policymakers. How is a very substantial dependent population to be supported by a declining cadre of producers? How can the nation finance such a welfare burden and remain competitive in world markets? Beneath such concerns lie

3

questions about whether or not the elderly will be politically controlled by the rest of the population or will parlay their numerical strength into a formidable weapon for promoting self-interest.

Some analysts contend that the elderly have become a major political influence in this country or that they will become such a force in the years ahead (Peterson et al., 1976; Rose, 1965a; Butler, 1974). Others argue, to the contrary, that the elderly are not a significant political force today, nor will they become such in the foreseeable future (Maddox, 1978; Hudson and Binstock, 1976; Campbell, 1971). As will become evident in the chapters that follow, we do not feel entirely comfortable with either of these positions.

To us the evidence suggests that over the next half century the political resources (e.g. education) of the elderly will be increasing as they have since the turn of the century. It is likely, but by no means inevitable, that this increase in political resources will translate into an increase in political influence. We come to this conclusion because, in addition to a number of trends that should contribute to an increase in political resources, there are a number of others that will tend to neutralize these resources. There appears to be a dialectical relationship between programmatic gains for the elderly and the strength of the opposition to further gains from other groups. The more successful the elderly are in their claims on government monies, the less legitimacy they have when they (or their advocates) request additional programs or increases in funding for existing programs. The more they get, the stronger the resistance there is from other groups to further gains (Samuelson, 1978; Hudson, 1978).

HISTORICAL PERSPECTIVES

Before attempting to make projections about the possible influence of the elderly at some point in the future, we must thoroughly analyze the extent of their influence today. In turn, any such analysis of the power and influence of the aged calls for a consideration of what they have been in the past. For this reason we begin by discussing the historical evidence about the cultural and social structural factors that have tended to affect the relative power and influence of the elderly.

There is a great deal of cross-cultural evidence suggesting that the fate of the elderly has tended to improve as societies have moved from primitive economies based on fishing, hunting, and gathering, to more advanced economies based on agriculture (Simmons, 1960). As nomadic groups evolved into more stable societies, the elderly were often able to increase their status and power by obtaining control over important new social roles (Sheehan, 1976). As food supplies became more predictable, belief systems and rituals became more complex. In many societies the elderly came to control major political, legal, religious, and medical roles. Control of these key roles could often be used to improve one's position, with respect to tangible assets (Watson and Maxwell, 1977).

As societies grew more complex, the institution of private property emerged. In the context of a well-developed agricultural economy it became possible to accumulate assets. This greatly increased the influence of the elderly (at least for those who were able to acquire substantial assets); but not all of the elderly benefited from these changes. Those who were unable to accumulate assets did not experience a significant increase in power and influence. For example, elderly women tended to be excluded from the benefits of these societal changes. With the institution of private property came a concern among males with knowing who their heirs were. One theory is that they used their superior physical strength to establish patriarchal and patrilineal societies in which property was controlled and passed on through males, as opposed to the matrilineal alternative that was more common among the primitive hunting and gathering societies (Reed, 1981).

The institutionalization of property rights gave the elderly considerable control over those who were younger; particularly their children. But this power and control were not without costs, including intergenerational tensions and ambivalence toward the aged (Sumner and Keller, 1927). For example, in ancient Rome, fathers had almost unlimited power within the family, but at the same time they were unmercifully mocked on the stage. The theme of ambivalence toward the aged is not unique to ancient

Rome: it runs throughout historical and anthropological accounts of intergenerational relationships (Murdock, 1934; Simmons, 1945). The relative power and influence of the elderly reached its zenith in advanced agrarian societies such as ancient Rome and colonial America. In colonial America the elderly were venerated, and surviving to a ripe old age was interpreted in the Calvinist tradition as a sign of God's favor (Demos, 1978). The elderly had a great deal of influence in the major social institutions of the day, particularly the church. Clergy, schoolmasters, and judges typically held their positions until death; retirement was all but unknown. Fischer (1978) argues that at both a societal level and at the interpersonal level the influence of the elderly in America peaked just prior to the Revolutionary War.

This veneration of the elderly did not, however, extend to all who were old. The elderly poor without families able and willing to provide support were often treated with callous disregard, and some were run out of town for fear they would become dependent on the community for support (Jones, 1975; Keyssar, 1974).

The term *modernization* is often used in reference to the institutional and cultural changes associated with the transition from an economy based on agriculture, to one based in large measure on industry. According to the "modernization theory" of the status of the elderly, the power and influence of the elderly tend to decline as societies move from agrarian to industrial social systems (Frank, 1943; Watson and Maxwell, 1977). Modern societies place a high value on youth, vigor, productivity, and technical skills. This shift from the value orientation of traditional agrarian societies tends to undercut the power and authority of the aged.

While there do seem to be a number of cases that fit this theory (Cowgill and Holmes, 1972), there is also evidence that the process of modernization does not always lead to a reduction in the power and status of the elderly (Palmore, 1975).[1] Furthermore, in some instances such as that of the United States, there was a marked decline in the status of the aged prior to the onset of industrialization, urbanization, and other such changes associated with the

---

[1]Palmore has also presented a substantial amount of evidence that is consistent with the theory (e.g. Palmore and Manton, 1974; Palmore and Whittington, 1971).

process of modernization. For this reason we argue that the theory depends on a selective reading of the historical record.[2] Nonetheless, with appropriate specification and qualification, the theory can be useful for explaining historical shifts in the relative power and influence of the aged.

After the Revolutionary War the status and influence of the elderly began to wane. One interpretation is that the ideology of liberty and equality began to undercut the hierarchy of age (Fischer, 1978). The young no longer made an effort to look older than their years by powdering their hair or wearing wigs. The practice of giving the elderly the most desirable seats at the town meetinghouse and in church declined (Dinkin, 1968). Consistent with this trend was the legislation enacted in some states requiring judges to retire at a specified age; previously there had been no mandatory retirement.

This decline in the power and influence of the aged seems to have continued throughout the nineteenth century and well into the twentieth. Contributing to the decline was the rise of industrial capitalism and the urbanization accompanying this change. In a rural setting, the elderly who owned a farm usually were in a position to maintain considerable control over those children who stood to inherit substantial land holdings (Fischer, 1978). With the move to cities and factory work, adult children became less dependent upon their aging parents, and as a result, parents came to have less control over their children.

The long-term decline in the power and status of the elderly began to reverse with the rise of the pension movements in the 1920s.[3] At first it was primarily a movement of nonelderly social reformers working on behalf of the elderly. But by the early 1930s significant numbers of old people had become active in efforts on behalf of pension legislation. Analysts differ with respect to how much credit is given to the elderly and movements of the elderly in the enactment of the Social Security Act of 1935 (Hudson and Binstock 1976; Holzman, 1963; Pratt, 1976), but it is clear that this event did mark in a most unambiguous way the reversal of the

---

[2]See Chapter 3 for a full explication of this argument.

[3]See Chapter 4 for a discussion of the rise of the pension movement.

decline in power and influence of the elderly that had been taking place throughout the previous century.

The Social Security Act had the effect of undercutting the senior movement of the 1930s, because the movement had been so narrowly tied to the objective of obtaining a national old-age pension system (Pratt, 1976).[4] From the mid-1930s until the 1950s there was little evidence of any growth in the influence of the elderly. But, in retrospect, it is clear that the contemporary senior movement did in fact begin during the 1950s (Havighurst, 1963). By the early 1960s it was evident that the power and influence of the elderly in national politics was starting to emerge. Indicative of the change was the establishment of the Senate Special Committee on Aging (1961) as well as enactment of the Older Americans Act and with it the creation of the Administration on Aging (1965). Passage of the Medicare and Medicaid programs in 1965 was yet another significant indicator of the increasing influence of the elderly. The 1970s saw the enactment of much additional legislation favorable to the interests of the elderly, including the 1972 amendments to the Social Security Act making cost of living increments automatic, the 1974 pension reform law (Employee Retirement Income Security Act), and the 1978 legislation eliminating mandatory retirement for all federal government jobs, in addition to moving the minimum age of mandatory retirement for most jobs in the private sector up from age 65 to age 70.

By the 1960s many analysts were pointing out that the elderly constituted a significant and growing segment of the voting-age population. While the power and influence of the elderly were increasing during the 1960s and 1970s in the political realm, there was a similar trend in the context of the interpersonal relations of everyday living. Due to improved economic status, more of the elderly were living alone, as the trend was away from living with one's adult children (U.S. Bureau of the Census, 1979b; Kobrin, 1976). This trend was associated with an increase in autonomy and freedom from control by one's children, but it was also associated with a decline in control over one's adult children.[5]

----

[4]We will elaborate on this argument at several points, particularly in Chapter 4.

[5]See Chapter 7 for a more detailed discussion of this issue.

Improved economic status (U.S. Bureau of Census, 1979*b*; 1976) has done a great deal to increase the autonomy and influence of the elderly in the realm of everyday living. Similarly, the greater awareness that the elderly are a substantial and growing segment of the voting public has increased their influence in the political arena.

POWER AND POLITICS TODAY

As a foundation for an analysis of the political influence of the aged, it is useful to consider the evidence with respect to political attitudes, level of interest in politics, and how well informed people are on political issues, in addition to the evidence with respect to various forms of political participation. There are a variety of outcome measures that can be used to assess the efficacy of political activity by (and on behalf of) the elderly, such as the proportion of the federal budget allocated to programs for the aged; the success or failure of pro-aging legislative efforts; trends in spending and benefit levels associated with aging programs; trends in poverty rates and relative standard of living for the aged; as well as the allocation of campaign monies, staff, and time for courting the elderly vote by candidates for public office.

With respect to political attitudes, the evidence suggests that most people become more stable in their political orientations as they age, but they do not necessarily become more conservative (Foner, 1974).[6] On certain types of issues and under certain historical circumstances, people move politically to the left as they age. When circumstances suggest the need, older persons are willing to ignore any general conservative (or liberal) ideological predispositions they may have for the sake of pragmatic benefits that they perceive as in their interest as aged persons. Conservatism and attitudinal inflexibility would therefore be unlikely to constitute major impediments to the development of solidarity around pivotal elderly concerns.

A number of studies indicate that interest and information levels with regard to political affairs are consistently higher in old

---

[6]This is an argument we present in Chapter 5.

age than in earlier periods of the life span (Comstock et al., 1978). As education levels among the elderly continue to rise over the next several decades, these already high levels of political awareness can be expected to expand further, and this could increase the potential for mobilization around aging issues. New technological developments in mass communications may provide fresh opportunities to exploit these high interest and information levels to the political advantage of the aged. Particularly promising is cable television, which has the capacity to open up virtually limitless numbers of channels, thereby making possible age-specific programming for older people.

The increasingly interactive nature of new communications technologies opens up new possibilities for political organizing, information retrieval, electronic voting, and public opinion polling, which are not contingent on physical mobility. As such, emerging interactive communications technologies would eliminate a principle barrier to effective elderly political participation. On the other hand, the inherent commercialism of the broadcast industry could seriously thwart attempts by the elderly and their advocates to combat negative media stereotypes of old age.[7] As the principle transmitters of such images, the mass media of communication will play a pivotal role in determining whether or not a more positive group identity develops among older persons.

The continuing decline in identification with a particular political party and the increase in the extent of issue voting (Nie et al., 1976) suggest that traditional party loyalties may be less of a divisive factor among future generations of older people. Party-based splits, which have heretofore created diversity among older voters (often along socioeconomic lines), are likely to become less influential in the future. This could open up new possibilities for organization of an elderly coalition around age-specific issues.

Political alienation among the elderly stems in part from their marginal status vis-à-vis the "command" generation in predominantly productivity-oriented societies such as contemporary America (Martin et al., 1974). Since political alienation frequently

---

[7]With increased numbers, however, the elderly will become primary commercial targets. To the extent that they are targeted for a broader range of products, there may be a decline in negative stereotyping, particularly in advertising.

takes the passive form of "learned helplessness" or "powerlessness," continued high levels of alienation among the elderly may inhibit future political activity (Renshon, 1974).

Among the participatory behaviors of the elderly, the bulk of the research indicates that they maintain high levels of voter turnout well into old age, and that the level of participation in old age is especially impressive among those with high socioeconomic and educational backgrounds (Wolfinger and Rosenstone, 1980; Nie et al., 1974). Increases in education levels among future generations of the elderly will, no doubt, lead to higher rates of voting and other forms of political participation. With respect to elite participation, the evidence indicates that the most important political offices are often occupied by the oldest incumbents (Lehman, 1953; Schlesinger, 1966). Up to this point in time, however, aged incumbents within the American political system have generally been reluctant to identify with elderly concerns. If the number of the elderly voters in coming years increases as expected and if the negative stereotypes of old age become less prevalent, elderly political leaders will become more willing to identify themselves with older people and their concerns.

We will argue that "senior power" has been both overestimated and underestimated.[8] There is a tendency, particularly in the popular press, to overestimate the political influence that older people have today; but there is also a tendency to underestimate the potential influence the aged may have at some point in the future as a result of their increasing political resources.

The aged are often perceived to be more effectively organized than is actually the case. This perception has been encouraged in recent years by the high visibility of the Gray Panthers and other such aging activist groups. Also contributing is the visibility of certain advocates for the elderly in Congress such as Representative Claude Pepper and Senator Edward Kennedy. The media exaggeration of the political influence of the aged has led many to the conclusion that the elderly already constitute a powerful senior citizen voting block. In fact, such legislation as the Social Security Act, Medicare, and the Older Americans Act, which are

---

[8]See Chapter 5.

often interpreted as major victories for the aged, are largely the product of efforts of others on behalf of the aged, rather than being due to the political influence of the elderly themselves (Holtzman, 1963; Carlie, 1969).

To date, the political participation of the elderly has generally been analyzed from one of two theoretical perspectives: an interest group pluralism perspective or a social movement perspective. The most frequently used perspective is that of interest group pluralism (Binstock, 1972; Hudson, 1978a). With this type of analysis, public policy is viewed as the outcome of competition among a variety of groups, each seeking to articulate the interests of its constituents (Dahl, 1961). The social movement perspective derives from the collective behavior tradition (Blumer, 1971; Smelser, 1962). Proponents of this perspective point out that people often form mass movements for collective purposes that supersede narrow self-interest (Pratt, 1976). The senior movement has been analyzed in terms of a model that specifies a sequence of five stages through which social movements typically pass in the course of their development (Mauss, 1971; Ward, 1979).

In our analysis an effort is made to develop a "coalition formation" model incorporating the most useful aspects of both the interest group and social movement perspectives.[9] Our formulation goes beyond these alternatives and offers an explanation for the observation that old-age policy gains have typically occurred when the aging lobby has had the strong backing of other interest groups such as labor and the social welfare lobby. This coalition has been far more powerful than the elderly would have been if acting alone.

Earlier we mentioned a number of social program output indicators that can be used to assess the efficacy of political activity by and on behalf of the elderly. In this context it is of interest to consider the possible implications of recent trends toward increasing fiscal stringency in budgetary policy. Sweden has experienced economic pressures and perceptions of scarcity that are very similar to those experienced in the United States. But these pressures have not resulted in social program cutbacks on anything like the scale we are experiencing (Zetterberg, 1979). Why such a differ-

---

[9]For an alternative synthesis of the social movement and interest group perspectives see Pratt (1976:196).

ence in response? We argue that differences in political culture can produce different responses to essentially the same set of economic contingencies.[10]

American political culture with its ideology of individualism has helped produce a distinctive brand of old-age policies that differ in fundamental ways from those which have evolved in Sweden and other Western European nations. When comparisons are made with these Western European nations, there are sharp contrasts in the quality and extensiveness of programs designed to meet the needs of the elderly.

To this point our focus has been on the analysis of the power and influence of the elderly in the macropolitical arena. In this context we have considered historical trends, political participation, and public policy. It can also be informative to trace the consequences of macro-level political decisions for the micropolitics of interpersonal interaction in everyday living.

One context for such analysis is the politics of family living.[11] For example, enactment of Social Security legislation has had a profound impact on intergenerational relationships. Many of the elderly who in the past would have been forced to become dependent on their middle-aged children can now afford to maintain their independence and autonomy.

In recent years there has been a marked increase in the proportion of women employed outside the household. This in turn has implications for the relative power of women in the family (Scanzoni, 1979). Looking to the future we anticipate further shifts in marital power in a direction favorable to women. But we also note that the earnings gap between men and women does not seem to be closing. One likely consequence of this trend is a continued power advantage for elderly husbands relative to their wives. Continued poverty for many older women is another possible outcome.

While the elderly have as a group made a great deal of progress over the past fifty years with respect to economic status as well as availability of health care and social service programs, these gains

---

[10]See Chapter 6. High inflation and other symptoms of a faltering economy contributed to a marked shift to the right in the 1980 American Presidential election and an equally marked shift to the left in the 1981 French Presidential election.

[11]See Chapter 7.

have had their social costs, many of which have remained unattended
to by most analysts. Little attention has been given to the elaborate and pervasive mechanisms of social control that have evolved
in connection with these programs.[12]

Social Security led to an increase in autonomy, with respect to
intergenerational relationships, by making it possible for millions
of elderly Americans to remain economically independent of their
middle-aged offspring. But there has been a social cost to the
elderly in the form of an increased dependence on and control by
the state. With each new programmatic advance of the 1960s and
1970s on behalf of the elderly has come an increase in control by
federal and state planners and policymakers, social workers, program administrators, and other functionaries, over the lives of
those who have come to depend on these programs and agencies
for essential services.

Take the case of the Medicaid program. To become eligible,
people must first exhaust their personal assets. Many elderly
nursing home residents go through their life savings in a few short
years in the process of "spending down" to the point at which they
become eligible for Medicaid benefits. Once having exhausted
these assets most would find it all but impossible to live independently outside of the institution even if their health status were to
improve to the point at which this became a viable option. Sup-
pose that as an economy move a state decides to put a cap on
Medicaid spending; the nursing home operator is asked to provide
the best care possible, but on a reduced budget.[13] The patients are
trapped and the consequences for the quality of their lives are
potentially catastrophic.

THE MEANING OF POWER

In view of the centrality of the concept of power to much of our
analysis, it will be useful to discuss what we mean by the term and

---

[12]See Chapter 8 for an analysis of the social control aspects of social security and other social
programs.

[13]A spending cap may not call for an actual cut in the Medicaid spending, but it is designed
to limit future spending. In an era of substantial inflation this translates into reduced
allocations for future years.

how it differs from such related concepts as social control, authority, and influence.[14] (Much of the material to be discussed in this section is summarized in Figure 1-1. Those who are familiar with these concepts and the distinctions typically made among them can turn directly to Chapter 2 without significant loss of continuity.) Probably the most frequently cited definition of power is that proposed by Max Weber (1968:926): "In general, we understand by 'power' the chance of a man or a number of men to realize their own will in a social action even against the resistance of others who are participating in the action." The reference to action even against resistance implies that the power holder has the capacity to bring sanctions to bear if needed. Other analysts have been more explicit in their reference to the capacity to sanction noncompliance in their definitions of power (Bierstedt, 1974; Lasswell and Kaplan, 1950).[15]

In the present discussion, we will be making the case for a less-restrictive definition that has been proposed by Wrong (1980:2): "Power is the capacity of some persons to produce intended and foreseen effects on others." Note that in this definition there is no reference to the capacity to impose sanctions. The reason is that we want to include as instances of power relations certain cases in which the power holder is not in a position to sanction the power subject for noncompliance. Consider the case of the power holder who cannot sanction the power subject, but who is able to use persuasion to produce intended effects. We would also want to include the relationship between a power subject and an expert authority such as a physician. Patients typically comply with a

---

[14]In the discussion that follows we are much indebted to Dennis Wrong's (1980) exceptionally lucid analysis of many of these same concepts. In this section we provide a detailed analysis of power and related concepts. It is aimed at the reader who is not familiar with the extensive literature dealing with these concepts. We go into a number of issues in somewhat more detail than is essential for an understanding of the analysis in subsequent chapters. For example, a distinction will be made among five categories of authority, but this is the last time the reader will encounter separate terms for each of these subcategories. In subsequent discussion the appropriate subcategory should be evident from the context. It is important for the political gerontologist to be aware of these various subcategories, but it is rare to use separate terms to distinguish each.

[15]For example, Lasswell and Kaplan (1950:75) offer the following definition: "Power is a special case of the exercise of influence: it is the process of affecting policies of others with the help of . . . severe deprivations for nonconformity with the policies intended."

physician's commands even though the physician does not have the capacity to sanction noncompliance.

Power can be viewed as a subcategory of influence. A useful distinction can be made between *intended* and *unintended* influence. Power is equivalent to intended influence, but it does not include unintended influence (*see* Fig. 1-1). Unintended influence refers to the unanticipated effects of one's actions. For example, television commercials often present elderly persons in sick roles. The intended goal is to sell various health-related products to an older audience. But this advertising may in addition have the unintended effect of contributing to a negative self-image among older viewers and to negative health stereotypes about the elderly among younger viewers. To the extent that the intended effect is achieved, we would conclude that the influence is an instance of a power relationship (between the advertiser and those persons exposed to the message who purchase the product in response to it). But the unintended effects would not be considered instances of power relationships.[16]

Social control is also a subcategory of influence (*see* Fig. 1-1). Mutual (although in many instances highly asymmetrical) control is an aspect of all social interaction.[17] To the extent that the behavior of the aged is influenced by internalized social norms regarding appropriate behavior for elderly persons, we would consider it an instance of social control, but we would not consider this an instance of intended influence, as there is no clearly defined person or group that is the influence holder. With social control the source of the constraint on behavior may be internalized societal norms or even social institutions such as marriage and the family.

Social control is best viewed as a subcategory of influence because

---

[16]In making this distinction between intended influence (power) and unintended influence we are adopting Wrong's (1980:2–5) position. Some who have written on the topic would argue, in contrast, that influence is a subcategory of power or argue that neither is a subcategory of the other. Others such as Bierstedt (1974) would be unwilling to equate power with what we have called "intended influence" because such a designation would include a variety of forms of influence that he does not consider instances of power, e.g. authority based on expert competence and influence due to persuasion.

[17]A possible exception is the lack of any control on the part of the power subject in the context of certain forms of violence.

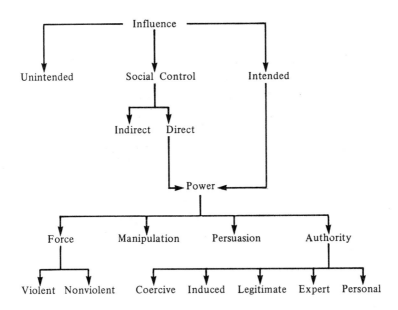

Figure 1-1. Typology of power and related concepts.

it tends to be restricted to instances of influence that involve constraint of the influence subject. But not all instances of influence involve constraint in the same sense. President Reagan is an elderly person who exercises a great deal of power and social control. One influence he has had on Americans has been to increase their consumption of jelly beans. This is a clear instance of influence, but it is not an instance of social control. The concept of social control is more specific than the concept of influence, and it includes a connotation of social constraint on behavior that is not present with all forms of influence.

A distinction can be made between two major categories of social control. The first we will refer to as *indirect* social control. It includes instances of social control in which there is no clearly defined person or group as control holder (agent of control). An example would be the social control of behavior due to internalized norms. This category would also include institutionalized rules and regulations that control the elderly such as mandatory retirement rules.[18]

The other category we will refer to as *direct* social control. In this case there is a clearly defined person or group as power holder. This is exemplified by the control exerted by the staff in a nursing home. If patients do not comply in response to efforts at persuasion, they will be forced to comply by various physical means. What we have referred to as direct social control is equivalent to intended influence or power (*see* Fig. 1-1).

A distinction can be made between *latent* power and *manifest* power.[19] As we noted earlier, in colonial America the (elderly) clergy had a great deal of influence. When they issued direct commands to their congregations and people responded to those commands, the interactions were instances of manifest power. When members of the congregation altered their behavior in anticipation of what the minister would command were he consulted, their action illustrated his latent power.

This distinction raises the more general question as to whether the belief that someone has power actually confers power. This is central to the debate between those who advocate the "reputational method" (Hunter, 1953; Bonjean, 1963) of studying community power and those who advocate the "decisional method" (Dahl, 1961; Wildavsky, 1964). Those who advocate the reputational method argue that if people believe a group has power, then it does have power. The advocates of the decisional method disagree. They argue that power is reflected in its exercise; one cannot tell how much power a group has unless one sees how successful it is in getting its way when important community decisions are made.

Wrong argues that a group has power if (1) others believe it has power; (2) those believed to be power holders are aware that others consider them such; and (3) those believed to be power holders use this knowledge by making commands they expect others to obey. But this group of persons believed to have power does not in fact

---

[18]This last example is less clear because a case can be made that it is often possible to locate an agent of control behind many institutionalized rules and regulations. In the case of mandatory retirement rules some would point to corporate owners, members of Congress, or an economic elite (big business). Only when these rules become widely accepted as fair and reasonable by the general population do they constitute instances of indirect social control.

[19]Sometimes the terms "potential" and "actual" are used in place of "latent" and "manifest."

have power if members of the group are unaware that others believe that they have power or do not believe it themselves regardless of what others think. Such persons are unlikely to make commands, and they do not expect compliance with their desires.

Earlier we mentioned that power relations are by definition asymmetrical; as Gerth and Mills (1953:193) put it: "When everyone is equal there is no politics, for politics involves subordinates and superiors." However, it is possible for there to be power differentials within different spheres even for the same two people. A husband may have more power with respect to the decision about the timing of retirement. His wife in turn may have more power with respect to decisions concerning whom the couple socializes with during their retirement years. In view of the possibility of considerable variation between couples in terms of who has more influence in each of a variety of different spheres, determination of who has how much power in a marital relationship and how it changes over the duration of the marriage can be quite problematic.

Bertrand de Jouvenel (1958) has suggested three dimensions for the analysis of power relationships: intensity, comprehensiveness, and extensiveness. *Comprehensiveness* refers to the number of spheres or aspects of the power subject's life that the power holder controls. Parents, for example, have very comprehensive power with respect to an infant.[20] They control the important decisions within most spheres of the infant's life. Similarly, the comprehensiveness of the control an adult child exerts over an aging parent tends to increase if that parent moves into the child's household. As a result of this move the adult child is in a position to control many more aspects of the parent's life. The comprehensiveness of power is low when it is limited to one sphere that is not of great importance to the power subject, for example, the ticket collector in a theatre.

Intensity refers to the limits on the power holder's control in those areas where there is control. In many primitive societies children had the right to abandon their infirm aging parents to a

---

[20]Illustrating the reciprocal nature of power, the newborn also exerts a great deal of control over the lives of its parents.

certain death due to starvation or exposure (Simmons, 1945). These infirm elders were often left behind to die when the group moved on to a new campsite. This illustrates greater intensity in the power of adult children over elderly parents than is the case in contemporary America. The intensity of a power relation is high when there are few if any limits regarding what the power holder can demand of or do to the power subject.

Extensiveness of power refers to the number of power subjects influenced by the power holder; it may range from one person (low extensiveness) to millions of people (high extensiveness). The male head of household in ancient Rome had the power of life and death over his children; his power was high with respect to comprehensiveness and intensity, but low in extensiveness. The President of the United States, on the other hand, has power over American citizens that is high in extensiveness, but relatively low in comprehensivenss and intensity. In general, the comprehensiveness and intensity of power tend to vary inversely with its extensiveness (Wrong, 1980).

Most analysts distinguish between force and authority as distinct categories of power. We can as Wrong suggests go a step further and add two other categories, "manipulation" and "persuasion" (*see* Fig. 1-1).[21]

We are using the term *force* to refer to both physical and psychological constraints on the freedom of the power subject. It includes the infliction of physical and psychological harm. It also includes the taking of property from power subjects against their will. We find it useful to make a distinction between two categories of force—violent and nonviolent.

Nonviolent force has been successfully used as a protest tactic. When a group such as the Gray Panthers organizes a sit-in by older people (sometimes including persons in wheelchairs) to protest cuts in social programs for the elderly, this is generally an instance of nonviolent force.

Violent force (violence) often involves the infliction of pain.

---

[21]Wrong (1980:23–24) is careful to point out that force, manipulation, and persuasion sometimes fail to meet the defining criteria of power relations. For example, they do not always involve reciprocal interaction between the power holder and the power subject.

There have been numerous reports of violence by aides in nursing homes directed against patients who do not (or cannot) comply with their demands (Stannard, 1973). Similarly, in recent years there have been increasing reports of physical abuse of the elderly by their children (Steinmetz, 1978).

There will always be examples of force that are difficult to classify as either violent or nonviolent. One example is verbal abuse. Up to a point the verbal abuse of the institutionalized elderly may be considered a form of nonviolent force (as would be the verbal abuse of political officials by elderly sit-in participants), but if pushed far enough verbal abuse can cause psychological harm. At this point it becomes a form of violence. Another example is the use of tranquilizers and physical restraints on institutionalized patients (Gubrium, 1975; Howard et al., 1977). In some contexts it is necessary to protect the patient and is clearly not a form of violence, but when such methods are used for purposes of patient management independent of medical need, they can be viewed as forms of violence.

When a power holder is able to influence a power subject to comply with his or her wishes without the power subject being aware of this intent, we have an instance of *manipulation*. Political propaganda and commercial advertising are two of the most frequently cited examples of manipulation (Wrong, 1980).

We include *persuasion* as a category of power because it is a means by which a power holder can get a power subject to comply with her wishes. In the case of persuasion the communication (command) is accepted on the basis of its content (as opposed to being accepted on the basis of the source) and only after independent evaluation by the power subject, taking into consideration his own needs and goals (and not taking into consideration possible sanctions for failing to accept the communication).

As a result of the increase in the minimum age for mandatory retirement from sixty-five to seventy, we are likely to find more effort on the part of employers to get older employees to take early retirement. These efforts may take the form of preretirement counseling, which includes information about such issues as sunbelt retirement communities, strategies for coping with inflation during retirement, Social Security benefits and regulations, health insurance options, and senior citizen discount travel packages. To the extent that the information provided paints a rosier picture of retirement than can reasonably be expected, we would describe such efforts when successful as instances of manipulation. To the extent that the presentation is fair and designed to address unfounded fears and misconceptions, such efforts can be considered instances of persuasion if they succeed in contributing to early retirement.

There is much debate about how to define the term *authority*. The most common definition is in terms of *compliance based on the voluntary consent of the power subject* (Parsons, 1969; Bierstedt, 1974; Gerth and Mills, 1953). Authority so defined is viewed as legitimate or institutionalized power and is often contrasted with "naked power," which corresponds to what we have referred to as force.[22] Those who make this dichotomy typically fail to emphasize the difference between power based on force and power based on the threat to use force. Both are grouped together and referred to as coercion, which is then contrasted with (legitimate) authority based on consent. Wrong makes a persuasive argument that this failure to distinguish between force and the threat of force tends to deemphasize the importance of coercion in the sense of a threat to use force in authority relationships.

We prefer a less-restrictive definition in which authority is defined as *the untested acceptance of another's commands or judgments*. In the case of authority (as contrasted with persuasion as described previously) it is not the content of the communication, but rather the perceived attributes of the communicator that induces compliance. A distinction can be made among five subtypes of authority all of which are instances of what Wrong would refer to as command-obedience relationships (*see* Fig. 1-1). The subtypes differ as a function of the motivation for obedience. In the case of legitimate authority there are shared societal norms that uphold the right of the power holder to command and the obligation of the power subject to obey. When the personnel director of a large

---

[22]Many commentators attribute to Weber (1968) the concept of authority defined as legitimate or institutionalized power. But Wrong (1980:36) points out that Weber does not define the term in such a way as to exclude compliance due to fear of sanctions for noncompliance.

corporation sends a notice to an employee informing her that she must retire one month after she turns seventy, the director is acting as a legitimate authority.

In the case of *coercive* authority, a person obeys because of the power-holder's threat to use force if he does not comply. Coercive authority depends on the power subject's belief that the power holder is capable and willing to use force.[23] The obedience of an elderly nursing home resident to the demands of an aide are in some instances responses to threats of force. When the resident believes that the aide is willing and able to use force, compliance is an instance of coercive authority.

When compliance is based on the promise of a reward (as opposed to the threat of punishment for noncompliance), we refer to it as an instance of *induced* authority. It is of interest to note that there is a tendency for relations of induced authority to be unstable and to shift to coercive authority. A wealthy grandmother may reward her grandchildren with lavish gifts on Christmas, birthdays, and other special occasions in return for their frequent visits (induced authority); but if at some point the grandchildren start coming less frequently despite these gifts, she may threaten to stop the largess altogether. To the extent that they have come to expect and to depend on these gifts, the relationship is transformed into one of coercive authority.

The category of *expert* authority is authority based on the special knowledge or skills of the power holder. Here the power subject obeys the communication because it is believed to be in her best interest to do so. When an elderly woman's physician tells her to take a specified medication to keep her blood pressure down and she follows this advice, it is an instance of expert authority. This is not an instance of legitimate authority because the patient does not obey out of a sense of obligation or duty. She can choose to refuse the physician's advice and take the consequences.

In a relationship of *personal* authority, compliance is based on the perceived personal qualities of the power holder. In this

---

[23]Force is often used to establish credibility and thus it contributes to future power relations based on a threat of force. A case can be made that force is less often used for the immediate effect on the victim than to establish a relation of coercive authority for the future (Wrong, 1980).

category we would include compliance with the demands of a friend or lover.

The various categories of power and influence that we have discussed (see Fig. 1-1) are most appropriately viewed as ideal types. While it is possible to come up with some relatively pure examples of each, it is important to realize that most instances of power and influence relationships are based on combinations of two or more of these categories.

It would be a mistake to conclude that politics is only concerned with the struggle to obtain power and influence. Equally relevant is the struggle by many to free themselves from the constraints imposed by the power of others. The issue here is *autonomy.* Many of the elderly are more concerned with maintaining their autonomy and independence than they are with the issues of power and influence. In general, those who have more power tend to have greater autonomy and to be less vulnerable to the demands of others. But it is also possible to have considerable autonomy while at the same time having relatively little power and influence over others. This is illustrated by the decisions of corporate executives who retire to Florida, leaving organizations and communities in which they had a great deal of power and influence. In their Florida retirement communities they typically have little power and influence, but a great deal of autonomy. The value the elderly place on autonomy is reflected in the strong preference shown for living independently rather than with their children. It is also reflected in the desire to avoid economic dependence on their children.

As we shall see in the next chapter, the desire on the part of elderly parents to maintain their independence and autonomy is not a new phenomenon. Throughout the ages people have been concerned with finding ways to assure as much autonomy as possible in old age, and the control of economic assets has proven particularly useful toward this end. Such assets have been important as a source of both power and autonomy.

PART I:
HISTORICAL AND
CROSS-CULTURAL PERSPECTIVES

Chapter 2

THE AGED IN PREINDUSTRIAL SOCIETIES

Perceptions of the elderly's power and prestige today are often based upon assumptions about their influence and treatment in the past.[1] Anthropologists have sought information about the official and unofficial roles occupied by old persons in different cultures. They have also attempted to link the power and prestige of the elderly to societal type, giving particular emphasis to differences in economic organization and level of technological development (Holmes, 1976; Press and McKool, 1972; Clark, 1971).[2] Historians have typically focused on a particular period in a specific society. For example, they have shed light on the fate of old persons within ancient China, Greece, or Rome; but very few historians have written about the elderly per se.[3] They have relied upon firsthand diary accounts, contemporary chroniclers of a period, and content analyses of popularly performed plays or widely read literature to discern what life as an old person was like within certain communities. By piecing sources together, they have been able to identify shifts in attitudes toward old people.

Although many points of disagreement persist among researchers, including such basic issues as when the premodern period ends and the modern period begins (Achenbaum and Stearns, 1978), some general patterns do emerge. While the past discloses neither unqualified approval nor utter disregard for old persons, their fate has nonetheless tended to improve as societies have moved from a primitive to an agricultural level of development. This improve-

---

[1]This is particularly evident in the literature on modernization theory, as we shall see in Chapter 3. For a review of early work relating to the decline in the status of the elderly with modernization, see Burgess (1960). For more recent work, see Cowgill and Holmes (1972) and Sheehan (1976). For a critical evaluation of this work, see Slater (1964), Lipman (1970), and Fischer (1978).

[2]See also Clark and Anderson, 1967; Arth, 1965; Spencer, 1965; and Holmberg, 1961.

[3]Achenbaum (1978a) and Fischer (1978) are noteworthy exceptions.

ment has been particularly applicable to males; when societies have generated surplus wealth the control of elderly men over these resources has tended to rise. This relationship between a society's surplus wealth and the relative status of the elderly holds up best for preindustrial societies. We will take up the effects of industrialization in connection with our discussion of modernization in Chapter 3. To set the stage for our analysis of modernization theory in the next chapter, the focus of the present chapter is on evidence concerning the power and influence of the elderly in primitive societies and preindustrial agricultural societies. When we use the term *primitive* we are referring to a society with little or no surplus wealth available for distribution among members. To the extent that a material cushion is often a prerequisite for the development of an elaborate culture, the term *primitive societies* roughly parallels what some authors refer to as "preliterate" or "tribal" societies.

Before beginning our analysis, it should be noted that certain methodological problems exist with anthropological and historical treatments of the elderly. For example, as anthropologists have become more accurate and scientific in their studies of primitive societies, these societies have dwindled in number. Much of the cross-cultural data available on old persons is based upon ethnographies written in the nineteenth and early twentieth centuries. Thus, in some cases, these tribes no longer exist as such, and use of the present tense can be misleading. Also, many of these early observers were "outsiders" who had language barriers to the cultures they were studying and were never privy to all aspects of group life. At times they failed to grasp distinctions between ritualistic deference ascribed to elderly treatment and actual interactions between generations (Lipman, 1970); at other times their very presence no doubt altered behavior somewhat. Perhaps of most importance is that all generalizations about elderly treatment were based upon those few individuals who made it to "old age." Since official timekeeping was loose, actual chronological age was difficult to determine, and we cannot always know how old the elderly were (Goody, 1976).

With respect to historical accounts of aging, we have already alluded to one of the most serious problems: the fact that information has been pieced together because chroniclers seldom focused on the status and power of the elderly. Since many documents used are secondary accounts, it is difficult to know whether authors were recording actual events or what they wanted to perceive and present. Historical accounts tend to focus on upper-class males, and for this reason, generalization to the poor and to women is often problematic.

To the extent that anthropological and historical data are sketchy or well-developed depending upon which society or tribe one is considering, much discretion exists for selecting certain cases in support of an argument. Similarly, in the present analysis, some tribes and societies have been selected as examples of general trends, but any such selection risks being somewhat arbitrary. Bearing in mind the methodological limitations of the available evidence, we now turn to a discussion of those factors that appear to have had the most impact on the power and status of the elderly.

SOCIETAL COMPLEXITY AND SURPLUS WEALTH

A major determinant of the elderly's power and control of resources throughout history has been the level of economic development.[4] By economic development we mean the degree of surplus wealth (or economic surplus) being generated. If Lenski (1966) is correct in saying that conflict over the distribution of surplus wealth increases as that surplus rises, the evidence suggests that the aged did well in this conflict during the preindustrial era.

In part, this improvement in influence and living standard with increased economic complexity is linked to the nomadic life-style typically required in simple hunting and gathering societies. While community members may agree upon how their meager food

---

[4]Throughout this discussion, "power" refers to the ability to influence others toward the direction of one's interests. At the macro-level, some kind of surplus is assumed—goods above those required for survival. At the micro or exchange level, some individuals presumably have more access to valued resources—land, wealth, skill, and know-how, as examples. This access can both reflect and expand their prestige or social value within the group. As a result of this access, an individual experiences autonomy (lack of dependence on others), which further enhances his or her power. See Dowd (1980a), as well as Lenski and Lenski (1978).

supplies are to be allocated, physical capacity is a prerequisite for participation. Tolerance for and indulgence of decrepitude tends to be low within these simple societies since strength is a major determinant of individual autonomy and group well-being. Sometimes conditions are so harsh that the enfeebled old are abandoned to starvation. To the degree that food-sharing practices are mandated within these simple communalistic societies, old persons can be sustained and protected to some extent.

When nomadic groups evolve into more settled and stable societies, the elderly have often managed to improve their bargaining position within the group. They have done this by garnering control over certain aspects of the emerging social structures. For example, as the predictability of food supply frees people up to develop belief systems and rituals, old persons have frequently occupied key positions within these more complex structures. They may control information about the environment and secret rites; they may benefit from food taboos imposed upon younger group members; and they may dominate judicial, administrative, and chieftain roles until severe physical and mental decrepitude undercut their authority.

The tendency for elaborate rites and traditions requiring deference toward the elderly to parallel the rise in their leadership roles is not accidental. Once old persons came to monopolize the secrets and ceremony of initiary rites, they were in a position to extend the associated taboos for their own benefit. For example, uninitiated boys could be denied access to young girls who were by custom not off limits to elderly men. And the choicest food morsels could be reserved for socially powerful adults as opposed to physically powerful initiates. Tradition thus replaced physical strength as the major determinant of status and power, and old persons became the guardians and enforcers of these traditions.

Essentially, old persons managed to gain responsibility for a valued communal resource and, in so doing, deference toward them increased along with their ability to remain independent. According to exchange theorists, individual autonomy is necessary for the exercise of personal power, and this in turn is provided by control of communally valued resources (Blau, 1964; Dowd, 1980a; Homans, 1961). Thus, expanded material resources at the macro-level have tended to be converted by the elderly into personal resources as well. To the extent that cultural resources get converted into personal material resources, elderly social power rises. Tribal chieftains, for example, might trade on their authority or knowledge to gain increased food allocations.[5]

While general improvement in societal stability enhances the elderly's status (Sheehan, 1976), their power has been particularly great when this prestige is underpinned with tangible assets, i.e. property (Dowd, 1975). Any resource that can be transmitted at will from generation to generation, such as information about food sources, knowledge of gods, and secret rites, abets favor and communal power for the elderly, but their intrafamilial position has been strongest with the emergence of private (as opposed to communal) property. A prerequisite for private property is a fairly developed agricultural economy. Whereas some primitive societies manage to live in one location and provide relative stability for members, a full-blown agricultural economy frequently permits individual accumulation of assets and eventually concern for the transmission of surplus holdings to offspring. At this point obligatory exchanges between family generations can have an economic basis as opposed to being based on custom or tradition alone.

Any demarcation between "primitive" and "agricultural" societies is necessarily somewhat arbitrary; for example, the Aztec and Inca cultures are often included in discussions of primitive societies, and yet their generation of surplus goods was sizable. For our purposes the Incas and Aztecs will be treated as links between the primitive and agricultural society types. Temporally, however, they existed long after ancient agricultural Rome and Greece and long before primitive societies of the twentieth century.

While we contend that the rise of agriculture was a significant boon for the elderly, this is not to say that abuse of the elderly is unknown in agricultural societies. To the contrary, the aged seem to have fared well in some hunting and gathering societies and quite poorly in some agricultural societies.[6] Despite the increase

---

[5]See Watson and Maxwell (1977) for a discussion of this process among the Samoans.

[6]As a relatively recent example, the homicide rate among old peasants in nineteenth century France reached the point where the state set up guidelines for transferrals of properties to offspring so that a parent's death would not prove to be such a boon (de Beauvoir, 1972).

in power and influence the aged experienced with the transition to agricultural economies, a profound ambivalence toward old people remained.

AMBIVALENCE TOWARD THE AGED

A recurring theme that emerges from anthropological and historical accounts of the elderly is that of resource control and power. Intergenerational relations have been (and still are) tinged with various mixtures of fear, affection, influence, respect, guilt, and coercion, and these commodities have flowed in both directions (Treas, 1977). Sometimes old people have been granted official respect and power while simultaneously being treated with cultural derision (Achenbaum and Stearns, 1978). At times this derision has been based on fear. In ancient Rome, for example, the father had total power within the family — he could kill, mutilate, or sell family members. But, at the same time, elderly father characters were mocked on stage as miserly, meddling, and competitive with sons for young women. Intergenerational anxieties ran in the other direction among the Gandu of Uganda, where the chief's first-born child (if a boy) was strangled so as to prevent his growing up and replacing his father (Murdock, 1934). As an example of parental manipulation of guilt, among the Chukchi a father who was displeased with his son sometimes asked to be killed and forced the son to carry out the execution (Sumner and Keller, 1927). Portnoy's complaint is not new.

The elderly, it seems, cannot win. If they control valuable assets and use these holdings as weapons, they risk sacrificing affection for coercive power. On the other hand, when they surrender holdings in pursuit of affection, they risk scorn at the least and possibly more, as King Lear so graphically depicts. Intergenerational tension over valued resources has existed throughout history.

A second theme that emerges from literature on the security and prestige of the elderly is their association with death and the connotations implied. As de Beauvoir notes, old persons have tended to be either glorified or disparaged in their portrayals; normalcy or nondeviancy eludes them. One interpretation is that

these schizophrenic images reflect the human quest for rejuvenation
on the one hand and perceptions of how the elderly are faring in
that quest on the other. When old persons have been rare, they
have sometimes been seen as defiers of death at least, if not
beneficiaries of rejuvenation. Medieval iconography depicted death
as a scythe and time (age), which is aligned with death, as an
enemy (de Beauvoir, 1972). The preoccupation with victory over
time has often meant that signs of age are to be shunned. Among
the Xosa, for example, men removed all gray hairs and took on
young wives so as to get by proxy new freshness, bloom, and
protection against age (Simmons, 1945).

This common association of old age with death was symbolized
within both the ancient world and the middle ages by blindness.
Blindness was an exile to which those who lived too long were
confined, and presumably this exile represented a limbo between
life and death where spiritual insights in preparation for death
were possible. It is interesting to examine this symbolism in terms
of the idea that boundaries of acceptable behavior are identifiable
by those rule-breakers who get labeled as deviants or devalued
persons (Durkheim, 1947, 1958; Erikson, 1964). Clearly this depic-
tion of old persons as blind (deviant) places them at the outer
boundaries of what is to be considered human and represents a rite
of transition into a devalued role—the near dead. This ever-
present linkage of old age with death has made it possible for old
age to be envied within various societies in terms of age-related
resource control and yet be loathed as an experience. Enviable
resources that have always been available to youth are their youth
and their strength. Viewed from the perspective of exchange theory, time is a finite and irreplaceable resource available to youth.
While youth may not explicitly exercise it as a basis of power with
elders, the fact that they will probably outlive them toughens their
bargaining position (Dowd, 1980a).

WOMEN AND THE POOR

While the decrepitude associated with growing old has never
been envied, the increase in resource control has. However, not all
segments of the aged population benefited equally from these

changes in patterns of resource control. In particular, the elderly poor and elderly women were almost uniformly excluded from the benefits of these changes.

So far we have emphasized the advantages of increased economic stability for the elderly to the point where it sounds as though social class inexorably rises with age. But there have always been poor old persons and neither they nor women have experienced improvement in a relative sense. A second factor upon which most anthropologists and historians can agree is that the onset of settled agriculture that did so much for old men seriously weakened the power of old women. Thus the process that gave rise to the great agrarian civilizations of ancient Greece, Rome, and China also launched major class differences and the subjugation of women. Even within primitive societies, the more secure the food supply and elaborate the social structure, the less well-off are women in terms of status and power (Simmons, 1945). Their standard of living may rise absolutely, but the resources and social deference they can command fall. Some attribute this demise to the presumably arduous labor required in the performance of farming tasks and a decreasing contribution made by women toward basic survival needs (O'Kelly, 1980). A second and more sophisticated explanation is that with the accumulation of an economic surplus made possible by farming techniques, the institution of private property became more prevalent.

With private property came a concern among males about knowing who their heirs were. Toward this end, they used their superior physical strength to establish patriarchal communities in which property was passed through males as opposed to the matrilineal practice found more frequently within hunting and food gathering societies (Reed, 1981). A double standard of sexual behavior was thus imposed (Sherfey, 1973). Essentially women became property themselves with this "dawn of civilization"; a peasant and slave class were simultaneously created (Bottomore, 1966). It is important to stress that while elderly men who owned property shared the prerogatives of their gender and class, elderly women experienced the subordinated status of all women. As the lot of elderly males rose, conditions deteriorated for old women and the elderly poor.

FOOD TABOOS AND SECRET KNOWLEDGE

The mechanisms of resource control in the simplest of primitive societies tend to differ from those in more complex primitive societies. In the simpler societies food-sharing customs and food taboos were important as mechanisms of resource control; in more complex societies secret knowledge was much more important as a source of power.

Although primitive societies vary a tremendous amount in organizational structure, they can be divided into three groups: (1) nomadic semipermanent bands; (2) basically geo-permanent populations living in villages and bound by presumably common ancestry; and (3) peasant communities supported by agriculture or animal husbandry (Sheehan, 1976). Among geographically mobile populations, real property (if it exists) is confined to the likes of lean-tos and temporarily used pastures. The elderly have few if any resources they can accumulate or control. Indeed, conditions are often so harsh that old persons are relatively rare and, by western standards, often middle aged as opposed to old. These mobile bands, which are egalitarian and youth-oriented, provide no particular status to the elderly on the basis of age.

The one practice that can offer some measure of security to the old is food-sharing. Old people tend to fare best among fishers and collectors when it comes to communal food practices and less well among hunters and herders. Because decrepitude is frequently not tolerated among the mobile, much unevenness in treatment of the aged results. For example, among the Tasmanian islanders (who were hunters) the sick and infirm were given a little food and left behind to die. Within certain Eskimo families, the aged were left in a hut or out in the open to freeze to death; some were sent out to sea on an ice floe or in a kayak (Freuchen, 1931). Conversely, the Aleuts who gained their livelihood by fishing treated their old well and indeed viewed long life as a reward (de Beauvoir, 1972). Hottentot hunters of Africa also cared for their old in every way, but those who were poor or suspected of witchcraft were left behind to die (Murdock, 1934). Earlier we spoke of the fear versus respect playoff that has prevailed in attitudes toward the old, and their vulnerability to charges of witchcraft reflects this ambivalence. The same ascribed properties that demand respect can just as easily provoke fear and contempt.

Food-sharing practices become most useful to the elderly when they are underscored by taboos, and these in turn are usually part of rituals or belief systems that appear with a more settled life-style. As ancestry worship, rites of passage, and magic evolve, the elderly have frequently managed to corner the market and secure a prestigious position for themselves. Religious beliefs and super-stitions give rise to associations between eating habits and disas-ters; thus elaborate food taboos can result. Among the Polar Eski-mo, eggs, lungs, livers, and young seals went to old men, and Omaha youth were told their arrows would twist as they shot if they were to eat certain choice morsels thought to be harmless only to the elderly (Simmons, 1945). The Chukchi of Siberia, who claimed reindeer milk caused impotence in young men and flabby breasts in young women, reserved this source of nutrition for the old. Food taboos are widespread within primitive societies, particu-larly those with secret initiatory rites controlled by senior members.

Most anthropologists do not go so far as to say the elderly have invented these food taboos for their own purposes, but some suggest that once in place these taboos are manipulated to elders' advantage (Webster, 1932). The primary justification often comes in the form of threats, such as sores, retardation, disease, and death, which will result if the rules are violated. Because these rulemakers are often the gatekeepers to adult society and genuine participation within community life, these threats are onerous indeed.

Knowledge of initiation secrets is a powerful resource in itself. Information regarding skills, ceremonies, and medicines has always been a valuable asset among preliterate groups, and control of this asset has contributed to the elderly's reputation as "wise" within some communities. The elderly in such situations appear to have a sense of where their self-interest lies and a determination to establish monopolies over valued resources. They are adept at using secrecy to increase the value of information that they hold.[7] Even when old people occupy no political offices other than advisory

---

[7]See Goffman (1959) and Young (1965) for discussions of information control and the virtues of secrecy.

ones, as was the case among the Congo's Lele tribe, they control vital information for the smooth running of affairs (de Beauvoir, 1972). For example, Lele elders kept the secrets of rites and held detailed knowledge of debts and marriage bargains. Among the Tiv of Nigeria old men were viewed as sages who knew tribal geneologies, could heal the sick, and protect the earth's fertility. Often ancestry worship and rites of passage were closely related in that only the initiated could make sacrifices to ancestral spirits. Sometimes old persons can not only control the rites but due to their age proximity claim to have an inside track with the feared ancestral spirits.

Ancestral worship presupposes some concern with descent, and as communities expand their agricultural techniques and become more economically secure, property holdings can move from intangibles, such as knowledge, to tangibles, such as crops and animals. At this point, rights of inheritance and marriage exchanges take on more complexity. Family and kin networks come to govern every aspect of life, and familial obligations can be underpinned by subtle or not-so-subtle economic coercion. As was noted earlier, with the introduction of real property as the basis of exchange, the relative advantage of women in hunting societies is completely reversed; they often become property themselves to be bartered. Elderly women of course share in this decline in power and influence. Whereas old persons may have counted upon communal hospitality obligations for survival in the past, old men now can drive economic bargains with their offspring.

Among the Mafulu, men controlled their holdings till death. Banks Islanders were known to hide a portion of their wealth and reveal it to a son only if he performed his filial duties appropriately. Trobrianders held tightly to their lands, only releasing access in degrees and for a considerable price. As Simmons (1945:46) notes in discussing these tribes, a "firm hold on the strings of a fat purse was one effective compensation for declining physical powers" even in primitive societies. The exchange aspect of intergenerational power dynamics is vivid here. Not only do these old persons want to exercise personal autonomy, but they willfully try to keep offspring in a dependent and therefore less-powerful position.

Because of the collectivistic nature of Aztec and Inca civilizations, old persons did not have to rely on exchange with their children per se. These cultures were agriculturally advanced and in many respects more on a par with the ancient civilizations of China and Greece than with the primitive tribes so frequently studied by anthropologists. Even though their warrior values precluded any honor for death from old age or natural causes, the elderly were well provided for. Aged Incas received food and clothing from the public storehouse, and those who were infirm could count on neighbors tilling their soil and attending to their needs (Simmons, 1945; Vaillant, 1950). Essentially these societies provided systematic old-age assistance. Unlike their ancient counterparts who stressed private property and familial descent, these civilizations emphasized collectivism and group responsibility.

It should be noted that all societies discussed thus far, whether dependent upon gathering, fishing, hunting, or agriculture for survival, are physically demanding, and for this reason formal positions occupied by the elderly have tended to be either religiously or politically based. As we have seen, elders have controlled spiritual information and rites, and they have frequently served as group sages, advisors, and chiefs. But economically based status only surfaced in more advanced societies, along with tangible property. To some degree this "overrepresentation" of the elderly among religious and political leaders has continued through today. Of more importance is the fact that with the development of elaborate agricultural societies, old men often headed all three realms (the economic, religious, and political)—a combination that made them formidable.

In agriculturally based primitive societies the aged came to have more power than they did in hunting and gathering societies. This trend was magnified in the ancient agricultural societies of Greece, Rome, and particularly China. In these civilizations the power and influence of the elderly (or more precisely wealthy elderly males) reached what seems to have been an historical peak.

ANCIENT CHINA, GREECE, AND ROME

Advanced agriculturally based civilizations have ranged from the labor-intensive rural kind of ancient China, through the mixed rural and commercial type of Greece and Rome, to the feudal variety of the Middle Ages. Colonial America represented one of the final outposts of this kind of economic organization within western societies. We shall look at these cultures in turn to see how their elderly fared.

Probably no civilization has placed as much authority in the hands of old men as China. Confucius paved the way by equating old age with the possession of wisdom and establishing a strict system of relations between inferior and superior (Chandler, 1949). The linchpin of this society-wide hierarchy was the family, and within the family the father had life and death powers over his children. Daughters were sometimes eliminated at birth; sons were obligated to obey their fathers. The patriarch's authority did not diminish with age, and even women acquired some "power" in old age by tyrannizing their daughters-in-law. All old persons were respected, and some individuals falsely added years so as to share in this deference to age.

Although very old men were few, those who lived to be seventy relinquished their official positions to the eldest son(s) so as to prepare for death. But such practices involved the transmission of property and authority only upon the father's death or at a time when the eldest son was about fifty years of age himself. Unlike some societies in which the formal power of the elderly was either circumvented or ridiculed, Chinese offspring submitted to this ironclad authority; for many, suicide was the only means of avoidance. This absence of ridicule suggests that the patriarch's power was unqualified, i.e. he did not have to be accountable for how he used his power. Respect for the aged was so ingrained that a law remained into the nineteenth century requiring a "lingering death" for anyone guilty of patricide and decapitation for the schoolmaster who had instructed the offender (Gray, 1878).

It should be noted that while the young sometimes cursed their oppression in literature and operas, old age itself was never bemoaned. This is in sharp contrast with western civilizations where old age is repeatedly depicted as a burdensome experience which reflects a failure to rejuvenate and defy death. The Chinese also put a high value on not dying, but old age symbolizes success in this feat, not failure.

Unlike the power of old Chinese men, which remained stable for centuries, the fortune of Greek old persons varied (Richardson, 1933). Prior to about 800 B.C. elderly Greek males were invested with wisdom and granted honorific positions (Homer, 1950), but the feudal aspects of the society precluded their exercising real power. A characteristic of feudal societies is the appropriation and defense of property by force. Rather than laws, arms are used to secure and protect holdings. This of course places the elderly somewhat at the mercy of younger and stronger allies. Nonetheless, by the seventh century B.C., a number of old persons held land and formed oligarchies to oversee the industrial, commercial, and financial changes occurring in an attempt to stop many of them. Age became a qualification for holding offices, and the interests of property merged with those of old age. Old men enacted laws protecting their land rights. As long as regimes were aristocratic and conservative within Athens, for example, old men fared well, but when a democracy was instituted, intergenerational conflict became manifest. This link between democracy and power among youth will appear two millenia later within colonial America.

Old persons retained some power and were able to interpret the laws. They also served as judges in cases where children were accused of assault or neglect against their parents. Children were responsible for their parents and could go to prison or forfeit citizenship if found guilty. But the very existence of these clashes between generations was a testimonial to ambivalence in the treatment of old persons. While fathers could certainly exercise economic power over their offspring by withholding inheritances, cultural derision of the elderly increased. Aristophanes' (1967, 1961) comedies are examples. Old men are presented as wanton and ridiculous, lacking in good sense, and threatening to use economic power as a weapon in competition for young women. Again the fear versus respect aspect of intergenerational relations emerges. Whereas Plato (1941) dwelled on children's duty to their aged parents, Aristotle (1946) associated age with degradation, not progress. One attempted to legitimize control by the elderly; the other rationalized the supplanting of one generation with another. This theme also resurfaces two millennia later in America, as we shall see.

Interestingly, just as the elderly of Athens suffered a demise in power with the implementation of democracy, so did women.[8] Women were confined to the home at all times except during certain festivals and funerals. And within the home they were confined to the women's quarters. Patriarchy at this point was so developed that married Athenian women were viewed as broodmares whose sole function was to produce children for inheritance purposes. Women beyond childbearing age had no discernible asset. The condition of old people and women was superior in Sparta. Old persons could hold political positions for life, while women capitalized on the absence of male warriers to enjoy a level of civic participation unheard of in Athens (Pomeroy, 1975).

Although the Greeks practiced infanticide, there is no evidence that they killed their old. Among the Romans, however, there is some indication that certain old persons may have been drowned, particularly poor ones (de Beauvoir, 1972). The contrast in circumstances between rich and poor old persons was huge in both ancient Greece and Rome. But as Roman institutions became firmly established and the authority of the *paterfamilias* firmly entrenched, a spillover effect occurred for the elderly poor. Infanticide continued to be practiced right through the republic, but old people's lives became untouchable.

Land constituted the basic property form in Rome, and a peasant emphasis upon continuity permeated the society. Ancestral worship involved major obligations. This traditionalism along with heavy property concentrations among the elderly resulted in sizable power. Indeed the senate was comprised of rich land owners and remained powerful and conservative for centuries. Members made all military appointments, conducted diplomatic missions, and managed government finances. These same elderly elites owned their families as well as their lands, but they were somewhat more reticent in exercising this life-and-death power than their Chinese counterparts. In theory, the *paterfamilias* could do anything to his family, but public opinion seemed to have discouraged cruelty. The mocking on stage of elderly characters

---

[8]This relationship between democracy and a decline in elderly status is also addressed by Achenbaum (1978*a*) with respect to American society.

suggests that the elderly's control was not ironclad (Haynes, 1963). Again the themes of fatherly miserliness or wanton competition with sons provide evidence of intergenerational skirmishes. The period during which Rome was patrilineal, patrilocal, and patriarchal ranged from about the eighth century B.C. to the end of the second Punic War (202 B.C.).

Then the Republic began to give way to the Empire, and military prowess rather than lineage and age became the basis of power. The authority and legal rights of women, which had always been superior to those of Greek women, were noticeably expanded (O'Kelly, 1980). In part, this was because Roman women refused to forfeit roles and responsibilities they had assumed while the men had been at war. Another reason was that known paternity for inheritance purposes was no longer so "political" in its consequences. But the very condition that helped enhance the position of women (i.e. military-based power) was a disadvantage for the traditional old guard. Emperors were young and ruled in spite of the senate, not because of it. Not coincidentally, as the senate's powers were contained, so were those of the *paterfamilias;* fathers could no longer kill either a child or a slave.

One of the uniting features of these ancient Chinese, Greek, and Roman cultures was a double message regarding what constituted appropriate behavior for an old person. In all instances enormous economic and political power entrusted to (or acquired by) the elderly was accompanied by philosophical and literary suggestions that disengagement from worldly concerns was the best way to deal with aging. For example, while Chinese patriarchs had the power to rule their families indefinitely, Taoism simultaneously encouraged their withdrawal from the grasp of materialism to pursue spirituality. Stoicism and epicurianism also urged a less worldly life-style for the aged. As has been noted, Chinese operas as well as Greek and Roman theatre addressed issues of oppressive parental control and withholding of resources from offspring. This ambivalence, of course, related to the fear versus respect tradeoff which has always characterized intergenerational relations. History suggests it continued through the Dark Ages, the Middle Ages, and into colonial America (Coffman, 1934; de Beauvoir, 1972).

MEDIEVAL EUROPE AND COLONIAL AMERICA

With the collapse of the Roman Empire and the onset of the Dark Ages, quality of life declined for all age groups. Life expectancy dropped, and old people almost disappeared from the chronicles of power.[9] However, as Christianity began to change from a youthful cult to a full-blown institutionalized religion, older persons began to assume leadership positions, and by the late medieval period the papacy was controlled by elders. Contract law, which developed in the thirteenth century, helped protect the old's economic power. Also, as the vassalage system expanded with feudalism, seigneurs, as their title suggests, tended to be old and prosperous. Old knights were protected for life by their lords, but due to the militaristic nature of the society, physical strength counted for a lot. Unlanded elderly knights were ignored more than mistreated. The elderly poor received their usual disparaging treatment. Even though rich old men were faring well in terms of economic resources, they were the butts of literary ridicule just as their predecessors had been. Whereas old men were mocked in part for their power, old women were mocked for their powerlessness.

In seventeenth-century America, life expectancy was not much greater than it had been in ancient Rome, and persons reaching seventy years of age were still a rarity by today's standards. In many respects, conditions for colonial America's old paralleled those of their Roman counterparts. Laws were in place, and agricultural stability and prosperity prevailed. Although land constituted an important intrafamilial power base for American patriarchs, just as it did for Europeans in the seventeenth century, hostility towards them never reached the depth that it did in Europe (Fischer, 1978). In part, European sentiments may have reflected centuries of feudal and religious control by seniors, but religious beliefs imported to America unquestionably contributed to the elderly male's prestige and authority. Authority, as opposed to economic coercion, was the cornerstone of their lofty status, though in time control of other resources was generated.

---

[9]Charlemagne (742–814 A.D.), who ruled until he was seventy-two was one exception.

Just as the Roman *paterfamilias* benefitted from ancestor worship and was thought to be closest to the dead gods, so were American elders beneficiaries of Calvinist doctrines appropriated by the Puritans. Calvinism taught that only a few had been saved by Jesus for an afterlife, and believers understandably looked for signs that they were among the chosen. The rarity of old age no doubt contributed to its selection as a "sign." Old men were ascribed with godly overtones, described as looking like God, and implicitly assigned closer proximity to God than other mortals. In the matter of proximity to God, they were akin to the elderly Romans (and Chinese), but as is true among some primitive societies, this ascription of otherworldliness could (and did) slip into charges of witchcraft at times, particularly for older women (Demos, 1970).

The prestige commanded by elderly males was easily converted into leadership positions within the state, the church, and the family. Age underpinned sizable inequalities, and clergymen, school teachers, and governors stayed at their jobs until they died. Whatever wisdom ancient philosophers might have attached to disengagement, early colonists would have no part. They also kept tight control over their children and often used land holdings and inheritance powers coercively. To the extent that criticisms were made against the old, they tended to focus upon miserliness, greed, and abuse of parental authority—the same charges made throughout history by the young. Unquestionably, this was an era when Plato's call for respect (or at least deference) for one's elders was heeded; indeed some persons tried to look old so as to partake of this ascribed authority, as the ancient Chinese had sometimes done (Fischer, 1978).

By the late eighteenth and early nineteenth centuries, Aristotle's claim that the young are better equipped to lead than the old was restated in very similar terms. As Americans fought for independence and news of French assaults on inequality drifted across the ocean, age—a major basis for inequality—came under fire. Just as elderly Greeks suffered a major loss of power with Solon's implementation of a democracy, so did colonial septuagenarians take it on the chin with cries of "liberty." Rather than increased democratization resulting in extension of old men's prerogatives to the elderly poor and women, old men began a descent in prestige which material assets could not stop. Thoreau mirrored Aristotle when he wrote: "Age is no better, hardly so well qualified for an instructor as youth, for it has not profitted so much as it has lost . . . I have yet to hear the first syllable of valuable or even earnest advice from my seniors. They have told me nothing and probably cannot teach me anything . . . (Thoreau, 1942:33)."

Even though these kinds of sentiments are popularly associated with modernization, these words were written in the full-bloom of America's agricultural economy. As we have seen, treatment of the elderly has varied within and among agricultural societies across time, and ambivalence has been the rule rather than the exception. While agricultural-type societies have proven significantly more favorable for elderly power than primitive ones, at no point in economic development have old persons experienced either a utopia or an abyss. A mixture of affection, resentment, fear, envy, and guilt has informed intergenerational relations. Even today in a basically modern world, characteristics usually associated with an idealized agricultural past persist in some societies. By a "basically modern world" we mean one where values conspire to promote rapid change, weakened kinship ties, pursuit of work different from one's parents, and emphasis upon achieved roles. All of these features are in contrast with the traditionalism of agricultural civilizations, and collectively they suggest a segregation of the elderly from a society's mainstream.

CONTEMPORARY PREINDUSTRIAL SOCIETIES

There are a number of societies in existence today where agriculturally rooted values continue — sometimes in conjunction with rapid change. We shall examine some of these to see what forms a trade-off between the old and new can take and with what result for elderly prestige and power.

An often heard criticism of modernization is that its emphasis upon change and geographical mobility promotes a conversion to nomadic life-styles (Sheehan, 1976). While primitive and modern societies are fundamentally different, they do share an orientation toward mobility and individualism, which is in sharp contrast to the stability and traditionalism fostered within agricultural societies. Today throughout the world youth are frequently encouraged to forsake the knowns of village life and seek their fortunes in megalopolises. Acculturation and the strains between young and old it creates are regular topics addressed by anthropologists. What is perhaps more interesting are the variations in adaptation that take place when value confrontations occur and the resiliency of some traditions to survive in relatively hostile environments.

As has been true throughout history, today the experience of growing old appears to be perceived negatively throughout the world, but the elderly themselves are still highly valued in some societies. To the extent that community residence remains fairly stable, old people do well (Fennell, 1977). They tend to stay integrated within the world of work and, through lifetime interactions with other villagers, repel facile stereotyping about their obsolescence (Benet, 1971).[10] Old persons also do well where they are highly valued, hold assets, or participate in kin-tribe networks. As a general rule, these advantages tend to dissipate with increased infiltration of the community by urban values, but even within such a modern society as Israel, ethnic traditions can serve as buffers for the old. In spite of similar living conditions, for example, old Israelis from Asian-African backgrounds are less isolated (and less suicidal) than their European-American peers. This is thought to result from their extended family forms (Schichor and Bergman, 1979). To further support these arguments, we will consider the situation of the elderly in three contemporary societies: the centenarians of the Andes, the rural mainland Chinese, and the Pueblo Indians of New Mexico. In each case traditional values prevail to one degree or another, and retirement is rare.

For many years Vilcabamba, Ecuador, a rural community in the Andes, has been cited by gerontologists for the extreme longevity of its people (Davies, 1975; Leaf, 1973). Recent reports have called the evidence of unusual longevity into question (Sullivan, 1978). However, regardless of how many of these people actually live to become centenarians, it is clear that being very old is a highly valued status. Not only have the elderly managed to defy time — the eternal quest — but they also have attracted researchers who lavish attention and show interest in the life-styles of all age groups.

Then, too, tourism has been modestly spurred by rumors of these death-defying people.

Life in this region is characterized by much stability—the rhythms of daily life being determined by the rising and setting of the sun. Diets are comprised primarily of vegetables and fruits, and much physical exercise is required in attending mountainside crops. While pollution-free air, activity, and diets low in animal fat are prevalent among all known groups of centenarians and are believed to be relevant (Keelor, 1976), so are a capacity to relax and a satisfaction with one's work. A key characteristic of the old in Vilcabamba is the juxtaposing of autonomy and communal integration. Many of the old live on the mountainside while their offspring live in the village, so dependence of the old upon the young as we think of it is rare. No one expects the elderly to be different, and forced tilling of the soil is regarded as normal, not punitive.

A major exception to this glowing picture of elderly well-being is the situation for women. Peasant traditionalism, which has served old men so well throughout history, continues to serve women poorly in Vilcabamba. They are expected to reproduce about as regularly as cattle, and the differential power of the sexes is best exemplified by the relatively short lives of married women in comparison with single ones. This discrepancy may reflect religion-based mores as much as anything else, since women of rural China—another society with patriarchal traditions—are approaching a par with men today. But then China has been permeated much more thoroughly by antitraditional ideologies than has the Andes region.

Whereas Vilcabamba's old are seen as a communal asset, rural Chinese often hold assets that serve them well within the family.[11] Some are tangible, others are not. Even though agriculture has been collectivized in China, and the authority of age was systematically undercut by Mao's youth-oriented reforms, parents continue to hold sizable control over offsprings' economic well-being. They do this through traditional customs of matchmaking, controlling the family purse strings, and exercising inheritance options. All of these tasks presuppose intergenerational proximity and economic

---

[11]This account is based on Treas (1979).

interdependence—conditions that do exist in part because of economic austerity.

There is no formal retirement within communes, and old people usually participate in local workshops where they make repairs or sew, or they may tend grazing animals. Although these purposefully light chores merit low incomes, they do enable the purchase of radios or bicycles for families. Multigenerational families are commonplace, and here too old persons perform necessary functions such as garden tending and child care.

In spite of legal prohibitions against arranged marriages, the tradition persists. Parents not only find partners for their children but also provide dowries or gifts (also illegal) to help establish the couples in housekeeping. And because the old still retain ownership of homes in some instances, an offer to share such an abode is eagerly sought. Family residences are preferred by many over a more communal-type dwelling. In opposition to the ancient tradition of eldest son inheritance rights, children share equal inheritance rights. If disputes arise, children who have best performed filial obligations are supported in law. As we can see, some of these intergenerational practices are legally based; some are traditionally based. But, unquestionably, economic circumstances have underpinned the continuing authority of the old.

Among the Pueblo Indians of New Mexico, respect for the elderly is based upon their tribal integration as well as their extended family position (Rogers and Gallion, 1978). The Pueblos live in small villages, raise crops, and place a high value on traditional ways of doing things. Thus it is not surprising that the old who are associated with tribal continuity are also highly regarded. They are viewed as the "keepers of the culture" and are relied upon to relay traditions, legends, and the native language to children. As is true in Vilcabamba and rural China, no official retirement exists, and old people spend their time working the land, caring for grandchildren, gardening, watching television, and making crafts. These tasks are often divided by sex (men till; women care for grandchildren) and some, such as craftmaking, are income-generating. As exposure to English-spoken television programs might suggest, the Pueblos straddle cultures in a major way, and tomorrow's old will no doubt be farther down the road to modernization than today's.

What does this perusal of elderly conditions within primitive, ancient, and contemporary agricultural societies tell us? First, we have seen similarities which cross-cut society type. For example, old people are frequently associated with death, though this proximity can carry either positive or negative connotations. Where ancestral worship occurs or age signifies God's favor, the elderly command much social power. When old age is depicted as a limbo between life and death, it has often inferred enhanced spirituality but has been accompanied by social ostracism as well.

Typically, the elderly's power has risen as societies have become settled and generated a surplus. Old people in primitive societies have used their control of rituals as a vehicle for embellishing food taboos to their advantage. Older American colonists parlayed their presumed proximity to God into political and clerical positions and from there helped reinforce a property system that gave fathers a lifelong grasp on children. Rural Chinese elders are still able to choose mates for offspring partly because of a traditional respect for old persons, but also because they have accumulated a property edge with which to sweeten their children's "marriageability."

We have seen persisting ambivalence in the parent-child relationship regarding what constitutes a fair exchange between generations. Since the law has proven of immense importance to the elderly in underpinning their property holdings, it is clear that intergenerational "affection" is not sufficient old-age insurance. On the other hand, to the extent that parents withhold inheritances and keep adult children in a child-like status, they are perceived as omnipotent, greedy, and oppressive. Old people appear to seek a balance between commanding duty and engendering love from their offspring. Some authors argue that an imbalance in reciprocity is a prerequisite for a relationship to continue; if there is no imbalance, there is less stability in the relationship, because neither party has a real need for the relationship to continue (Sahlins, 1972). Since the parent-child balancing act has yet to be perfected, prolonged future interaction between the two may be predicted.

For better or worse, old persons have fared best in stable societies where the past has meaning and where formalized power is
centralized—often within their hands. During the preindustrial
era neither rapid social change nor democratic forms of government served their interests particularly well.

We have found that the power and influence of the elderly tends
to increase as a society's surplus wealth increases. This relationship holds up well for preindustrial societies, but it must be
qualified when we take into consideration advanced industrial
societies. We will explore this qualification in connection with our
discussion of modernization in Chapter 3.

Chapter 3

MODERNIZATION AND
THE STATUS OF THE ELDERLY

Accd:ording to the modernization theory of the status of the
elderly, in premodern societies older people were respected
members of their communities holding positions of prestige, power,
and authority (Cowgill and Holmes, 1972). The image is of a
preindustrial society, a rural and agricultural community in which
the authority and prestige of the elderly derive from their position as heads of families (not only of the nuclear family, but also of
the larger extended family) and from traditions of respect and
subordination to their greater experience and wisdom. A similar
contrast emerges in comparisons between industrial societies and
contemporary preindustrial societies in which the elderly are
accorded the respect and deference appropriate to their status as
wise elders and chiefs (Laslett, 1971).

Embedded in these comparisons between the old and new
worlds is a nostalgia for simpler times and cultural values that
stress family and kinship ties and the wisdom that comes with
the experience of a long life. As societies have modernized,
many traditional values have been lost, including those that affect
attitudes toward the elderly. Modern industrial society puts a
premium on youth, vigor, change, productivity, technological
skills, and newness. Under the impact of the changes accompanying modernization, the power and prestige of the elderly have
declined.

What we refer to as "the modernization theory" has been widely
used for five decades as a descriptive and explanatory framework
for analyzing the changes in the status and power of the elderly as
societies move from agrarian to industrial social systems (Epstein,
1931; Frank, 1943; Simmons, 1945, 1952, 1960; Cottrell, 1960; Cowgill
and Holmes, 1972; Press and McKool, 1972; Watson and Maxwell,

51

1977). A wide range of long-term developments such as increased life expectancy, urbanization, industrialization, and bureaucratization are considered important determinants of the diminished influence of the elderly.

Despite its wide acceptance, we are going to argue that the theory's explanation for the elderly's status depends upon a selective reading of the historical record and on a number of questionable methodological assumptions. Our interpretation of the evidence suggests that, contrary to what this theory would have us believe, the process of modernization does not always lead to a reduction in the power and status of the elderly. A major thrust of the present chapter is to critique the work of those who use the theory uncritically. A second thrust is to defend the theory against the attacks of those who suggest that it be rejected. With appropriate qualification and specification the theory is useful to those who seek to explain historical shifts in the relative power of the aged.

THE MODERNIZATION THEORY

According to the modernization theory, the status and power of older people decline with increasing modernization. Before getting into an analysis of the validity of this theory we need to explicate what we mean by the term *modernization.*

Most of those who write about modernization avoid any attempt to provide an explicit definition of the term and those who do make an attempt often get into trouble. Dore (1969), for example, defines modernization as " . . . the transformation of one's own society or segments of it in imitation of models drawn from another country or society." In a similar vein Lerner (1968) defines modernization as " . . . the current term for an old process — the process of social change whereby less developed societies acquire characteristics common to more developed societies." Cowgill (1974*a*) is correct in pointing out that many such definitions are too tautological to be of much use. Less problematic is Berger's (1976:35) definition of modernization as " . . . the institutional and cultural accompaniment of growth."

Theories used to explain the vast wealth inequality between

rich and poor nations can be divided into two competing paradigms: the theory of modernization and the theory of imperialism. As Berger (1976:11–12) points out, each paradigm has its own set of "clue concepts"[1] and each has a "pejorative vocabulary for the respective rival, and a conceptual apparatus designed to liquidate intellectually whatever definitions of the situation emerge from that tainted source." Some theorists consider "modernization" and "growth" value-free concepts, in contrast to "development," which is not considered value-free because it refers to instances of economic growth and sociocultural modernization that are considered desirable (1976:35–36).

There is a tendency for economists, political scientists, and sociologists to come up with definitions of modernization that reflect a rather narrow disciplinary perspective. Economists have tended to define modernization in terms of level of economic development, with particular attention to the stage Rostow (1963) characterized as that of "self-sustaining growth." For example, Levy (1966:11) asserts that a " . . . society will be considered more or less modernized to the extent that its members use inanimate sources of power and/or use tools to multiply the effects of their efforts."

Political scientists, in contrast, tend to define modernization in terms of the development of political institutions with a focus on such issues as the emergence of nationalism, the concentration of power in a central government, and the participation of citizens in an electoral process (Weiner, 1966; Lerner, 1958; Nettl, 1968). The assumption that modernization involves an imitation of the political institutions of western democracies underlies most definitions that have been offered by political scientists.

Sociologists have tended to emphasize institutional differentiation and more generally a functionalist perspective (Eisenstadt, 1966; Parsons, 1964). As Cowgill (1974*a*:126) points out, they have pointed to " . . . the increasing separation of the major social institutions from each other—familial, economic, political and reli-

---

[1] Some of the "clue concepts" of the modernization paradigm are "development," "modern," "economic growth," "institutional differentiation," and "nation building." Some for the imperialism paradigm are "dependency," "exploitation," "neocolonialism," and "liberation" (Berger, 1976:11).

gious." Some have emphasized shifts in attitudes and values (Inkeles and Smith, 1974; Armer and Schnaiberg, 1972; Stephenson, 1968).[2]

Historians disagree concerning when the process of modernization took place for different presently modern societies. This is in part due to variation between societies with respect to the timing of the changes in various components of modernization (Achenbaum, 1978*a*). Furthermore, changes commonly thought of as aspects of modernization may actually serve to reinforce and uphold traditional attitudes and values. For example, in some societies the introduction of modern medicine, a modern military force, or the transistor radio may represent modernization in the sense that each is associated with modernity. However, whether or not such "modernization" implies eventual acquisition of the entire package of modernity is problematic. The introduction of modern medicine, for instance, may only serve to compound the poverty by increasing population pressure. The transistor radio may be used to reinforce traditional values, and a highly sophisticated military may be in the service of a very reactionary regime. In short, selective modernization may only strengthen traditional institutions and values; the rapid social change a society experiences in one sphere may serve only to prevent change in another (Tipps, 1973).

The definition of modernization that follows is in many ways a synthesis of the various conceptions considered to this point. It comes as close as any we have been able to find to specifying the concept of modernization that we will be critically evaluating in this chapter.

> Modernization is the transformation of a total society from a relatively rural way of life based on animate power, limited technology, relatively undifferentiated institutions, parochial and traditional outlook and values, toward a predominantly urban way of life based on inanimate sources of power, highly developed scientific technology, highly differentiated insti-

---

[2]Most of the literature on modernization deals with the phenomenon at a macro or societal level. Inkeles and Smith, by contrast, focus on the consequences of these changes at the individual level. They come up with a profile for the modern individual as an informed participant citizen who has a marked sense of personal efficacy, who is highly independent and autonomous, and who is open-minded and cognitively flexible (Inkeles and Smith, 1974:290).

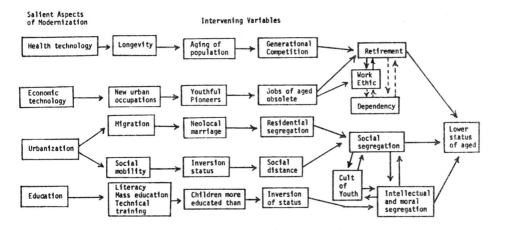

Figure 3-1. Aging and modernization. From Gubrium, Jaber F.: *Late Life,* 1974.
Courtesy of Charles C Thomas, Publisher, Springfield, Illinois.

tutions matched by segmented individual roles, and a cosmopolitan outlook
which emphasizes efficiency and progress (Cowgill, 1974a:127).

The preceding definition is used in the theory as formulated by
Cowgill and Holmes (1972) in their fifteen nation cross-cultural
study of modernization and the status of older people. Their
theory has subsequently been revised (Cowgill, 1974a), and it is
this revised version that is summarized in Figure 3-1. While we
will focus on this particular formulation of the theory, the arguments we make apply equally well to most other formulations of
the modernization theory.

Advances in economic technology and the resulting new occupations demand highly educated workers with updated skills. The
younger worker has a decided advantage, for the older worker is
often less well educated and his or her job skills are often obsolete.
In addition to these structural disadvantages for the older worker,
there are informal disadvantages that reflect the general "youth
cult"[3] of modern society. Older workers are sometimes harrassed
about their advancing years by younger workers. Blau (1973) has

---

[3]Cowgill (1974b:15–16) defines the "cult of youth" as the prevalent value system which
glorifies youth as a symbol of beauty, progress, and vigor and discriminates in favor of youth
in employment and the allocation of societal resources.

described a form of systematic hazing in some factories in which the younger workers jeer at the older workers with comments such as "How old are you today, Grandpa?" and "Old man, when are you going to quit?" She tells us of a birthday party given to a sixty-seven-year-old worker, as described by a young mill hand in South Chicago: "We painted up a big sign with 'Happy Birthday' on it ... then on the other side we drew one of those old tire company ads showing a youngster holding a candle and saying 'time to re-tire.' We all thought it was funny. But the old man didn't see the joke" (Blau, 1973:135).

Urbanization's contribution to the diminished status of the elderly is linked to the age segregation it produces. In modern industrial societies, workers often move to where the jobs are, and jobs tend to be concentrated in urban areas. Because of this, families are geographically separated and emotional ties are weakened. Social relationships in rural neighborhoods have traditionally been centered around kinship ties, and grandparents have had clearly defined roles and have enjoyed relative power and authority. Urban life reduces reliance on family and kinship ties, which become less important than ties based on occupational interests and activities in the urban setting. Family ties of course remain but are secondary in importance. Older persons are thus devalued in family relations as well as in the work world, and there is no new realm of influence that fosters a continued sense of importance in the lives of older family members (Burgess, 1955).

Advances in health technology have led to a longer life span for the elderly and thus an increase in their number. The expansion of the aged population combines with a lowered demand for older workers, placing the elderly worker and the young worker in competition for fewer positions. To reduce unemployment, retirement practices are instituted. Given society's emphasis on the work ethic,[4] which defines status in terms of the work one does, the worker who retires loses status and identity along with the job (Harlan, 1950).

---

[4] Cowgill (1974b:15) treats the work ethic as a factor "which has thus far conditioned and modified the effects of modernization on the status of the aged, but not as an essential ingredient of the modernization process itself."

The system of education in a modernized society also affects the status of the elderly. Modern educational systems focus mainly on the younger age groups, a development that undercuts the traditional view of elders as repositories of sacred knowledge and the wisdom of past generations. As knowledge becomes increasingly specialized, traditional knowledge and the role of the elder as transmitter of information becomes devalued. Although modern society still acknowledges the knowledge and experience accumulated over time, there is also the view that they become obsolete because of rapid technological developments. The importance and usefulness of the elderly's experience is thus diminished, and the process of aging further loses the value that it once represented (Bengtson, Dowd, Smith, and Inkeles, 1975; de Beauvoir, 1972).

There are empirical studies that tend to support the theory's basic tenets. Notable among supporting studies are two by Palmore and his colleagues. The first compares the status of the aged in the United States at two different times in history; the second is similar to Cowgill and Holmes' approach in comparing the status of the aged in societies that differ in their level of modernization. Palmore and Whittington (1971) found that the status of the elderly declined in the United States between 1950 and 1969 in terms of relative income, employment, education, and residential density. Palmore and Manton (1974) conducted a thirty-one nation cross-cultural comparison categorizing societies as modern or developing based on the society's gross national product, the percent of labor force in agriculture, change in the percent of labor force in agriculture, and the level of education (percent illiterate). The status of the elderly was found to be lower in modern societies than in developing societies.[5]

The modernization theory has a strong appeal, in that it appears to provide a reasonable explanation for the relative status of the elderly in preindustrial and modern societies. Yet, there remain numerous problems with this theory that become increasingly evident the more closely it is examined. The most glaring of these is its reliance on an overly simplified view of historical development.

---

[5]Status is measured by an Equality Index based on employment occupation and education (Palmore and Manton, 1974).

WERE THEY THE "GOOD OLD DAYS"?

The preindustrial period in America has been referred to as the "Golden Age" for the elderly. It is the period between the late 1600s and 1780, when the status of the elderly relative to other age groups is said to have been at its zenith. The image is of a general "exaltation of age," with the elderly enjoying positions of power, authority, and prestige. It is said that the attitudes exalting the aged were even reflected in styles of dress, a situation that contrasts directly with the present-day emphasis on appearing young. People even emulated the old by powdering their hair and wearing clothes cut to flatter the figures of elders (Fischer, 1978). This image of the "Golden Age" for the elderly is partly drawn from historical record, but the record also indicates that attitudes toward the elderly were not exclusively those of veneration and respect.

Smith's (1978) study of life in a preindustrial English colony in Hingham, Massachusetts, reveals that their values stressed able performance and the good of the group over respect due age. Fathers both crushed and aroused hostility in their sons before they were also obliged to help them to get a start in life.[6]

It appears that respect for the elderly was restricted to the wealthy and powerful; the poor among the aged often suffered considerably. The wealthy elderly, while commanding respect, also generated resentment because of their wealth and power. Most preindustrial communities lacked sufficient resources to satisfy all, and the atmosphere of scarcity generated conflict. The elderly, whether poor or rich, were not always well treated, although "ritual" deference may have been accorded. One historian has concluded that there was never a Golden Age for the elderly, that old age was physically as well as psychologically painful, and that the elderly received "respect without affection, honor without devotion, veneration without love" (Fischer, 1978:224).

Age per se may never have been the basis of respect and status, but rather it was wealth and knowledge. To the extent that these may accumulate with age, as among higher socioeconomic groups,

---

[6]Smith (1978) also noted that before 1780, Hingham was dominated not by the old but by the middle aged.

it may appear that the aged enjoy a favored status. But the evidence suggests that the determinants of status have more to do with socioeconomic factors than with advancing age itself. For example, Harlan's (1964) study of three preindustrial Indian villages did not support the hypothesis that the elderly would be found in positions of leadership in the village councils. The elderly were in fact underrepresented; in general, membership in organizations was inversely related to age. The two factors most closely associated with village leadership were socioeconomic status and education. No men of lower income groups held memberships, compared to 50 percent of those of the two highest income groups. This evidence suggests that in studies of modernization and its impact, the status of the aged should be based upon representative sampling of all socioeconomic levels (Harlan, 1964).

It may be that researchers have misread the "ritual deference" elderly people received in traditional societies as indications of power and status. According to Lipman (1970), a more realistic appraisal of the position of the aged in preindustrial societies would show that their actual power and status were often low. In fact, Lipman notes that throughout preindustrial and industrial society there is a tension between the ideals of the society and the reality—a tension that continues in the modern era. He compared the prestige of the aged in a preindustrial rural community with that in an industrial urban community—both in Portugal. He found two distinct dimensions in the attitudes of the respondents toward the status of the aged. The first dimension was "ritualistic deference," which posits that old people are to be treated as if they were wise and respected, on the basis of their age alone. The second dimension was "realistic appraisal," which calls for an objective appraisal of the aged's wisdom and resources. Lipman concluded that prestige and authority in the traditional community were not related to age per se, but rather to individual attributes and resources. These factors were relevant for young and old alike. However, he did find that the aged as a group were accorded ritual deference. Realistic appraisal of the elderly's condition showed an increase in status as one moved from the rural to the urban setting, the opposite of what would be expected on the basis of the modernization theory. Lipman (1970) suggests this more positive appraisal of the elderly's situation in urban industrial societies is a reflection of a rising standard of living and of old age being less of a handicap.

It appears that life in the "good old days" was not quite the way modernization theory suggests. The historical record does not justify the theory's assumption of an ideal status of the elderly in preindustrial societies, but instead indicates that the elderly's status was much more complex. We cannot state conclusively that their status was either idyllic or dreadful.

THE IMPACT OF MODERNIZATION

The variety of societal changes that constitute modernization has not had the predicted impact on the status of the elderly. Instead, many of these changes, such as urbanization and industrialization, have touched the elderly only peripherally; others have affected the elderly in ways that are distinctly different from the theory's predictions. And, due to the range of factors contributing to the status of the elderly at any one time, some aspects of their status decreased as others increased in response to the same societal changes.

According to the modernization theory, industrialization negatively affects the economic status of the elderly by undermining their position in society as their jobs become obsolete. Achenbaum (1978) challenges this claim and notes that in the United States the most dynamic changes accompanying increases in economic technology passed the elderly by. Their skills did not become immediately obsolete because many were able to remain in agriculture or traditional crafts and many had a large stake in property ownership (Achenbaum and Sterns, 1978). The percentage of the elderly in the labor force before 1890 declined very slowly. Between 1840 and 1890, for example, the percentage employed for elderly whites only slightly declined. In 1840, some 38 percent of all white people over 65 were gainfully employed compared with 37 percent in 1890 (Achenbaum, 1978a:69). It has been only during the last eighty years, in fact, that there has been a withdrawal of older males from the work force, and it is unclear that industrialization per se has accounted for this decrease. New retirement plans and alternative sources of income have also made it financially possible for the elderly to quit work.

Some practices in the workplace can benefit the older worker, a factor often overlooked by modernization theorists. Perhaps the most outstanding illustration of this is the seniority system in the U.S. House of Representatives: Between the years 1880 and 1910, several practices diminished the Speaker's ability to designate a committee chairperson, requiring the appointment of those who had served the longest term. Congress started the seniority system in order to reduce the Speaker's prerogatives and to bureaucratize operations, not to honor its elderly members. Yet, as a result of this new system, the House leadership was soon populated by comparatively older individuals who increased their power the longer they remained in office.

Other developments associated with the modernization theory, such as advances in modern medicine and urbanization, did not affect the status of the elderly in the direction one would expect on the basis of the theory. Advances in medicine, for instance, did not initially increase the numbers of elderly as the theory would suggest. Achenbaum (1978a) notes that between 1790 and 1830 the proportion of Americans who were elderly increased very little. This does not mean to imply that the elderly population stopped growing. However, with respect to the relative number of all Americans considered old, the dramatic increase occurred during the twentieth century. It is only within the last five decades that we have witnessed the development of a relatively large population over the age of sixty-five who are not employed and must depend on family and public sources for financial assistance.

Urbanization, it is alleged, separates the aged from their families and creates social isolation and a decline in their status within the family unit (Cowgill, 1974b). This viewpoint is challenged by several empirical studies that demonstrate that the elderly are far from isolated and living apart from family and friends. Instead, they interact frequently and live in close proximity to their children, although they do not commonly share the same household (Shanas et al., 1968; Litwak, 1960; Adams, 1968; Rosow, 1967). One recent survey found that among older Americans with living children, 80 percent had seen them within the past week and over

half within the past day (Harris, 1975). Based on national probability samples in each of three industrial societies, Shanas et al.
(1968) noted that 84 percent of the elderly live within one hour of
at least one child and 85 percent saw one of their children within
the past week.

If we accept the modernization theory's claim that urbanization
separates the aged from their families, we must also accept the
implicit assumption that there was a "before" time when the elderly lived together with their children. Recent empirical evidence
tends to cast doubt on this generalization (Kobrin, 1976). Laslett's
(1976, 1979) research on the family structure of preindustrial English society suggests that the extended family was not the dominant
form of family organization and concludes instead that the elderly
preferred to live independently, but close to their families. This
was a situation not unlike the current family structure of contemporary society. What parents wanted in the preindustrial world
was a place of their own, with help in their house, with access to
their offspring, and within reach of support (Laslett, 1976; Kobrin,
1976).

Thus far, our examination of the modernization theory suggests
that the status of the elderly in premodern societies is much more
varied than the theory asserts. There is little empirical evidence
that totally supports the theory, and our closer examination of its
basic tenets reveals a different picture. We have noted that there is
no common status for the aged in either premodern or modern
societies. We have suggested that status itself may be a multi-
dimensional concept that consists of "ritual deference" on the one
hand and a "realistic appraisal" of the elderly's status on the other.
We further noted that the theory's reliance on a linear "cause and
effect" relationship between status and aging is questionable; there
are instances where modernization has had no impact on the
elderly's status and some instances where the status of the elderly
actually increased. A closer look into the cause and effect assumptions of the theory will serve to underscore this point.

THE PROBLEM OF CAUSALITY

Perhaps the most revealing flaws in the theory of modernization
come to light when we examine a number of the theory's causal

assumptions. It is not clear that those factors deemed to affect the status of the elderly have in fact done so; some of these developments have even occurred after the decline in the elderly's status. Fischer (1978) notes, for example, that the social status of the elderly in American society began to decline during the years 1770 to 1840, prior to industrialization and urbanization—the two changes that the modernization theory purports to be associated with the decline in the elderly's status. He documents this conclusion with a range of evidence: Fischer notes that during this time the basis for seating in meeting houses began to shift from age to wealth, as seats were auctioned off to the highest bidder. Mandatory retirement laws were instituted, beginning with judges in New York State in 1777. Clothing and hairstyles began to be patterned after youth, not age. The hierarchical, vertical composition of family portraits depicting an old man towering above his family gave way to more egalitarian or horizontal compositions. The abolition of primogeniture saw eldest sons losing their economic advantage over younger brothers. Children were less frequently named after their grandparents. A pattern of reverse prejudice became evident in the census in the nineteenth century as individuals underreported their age; a notable change from the eighteenth century, where the opposite tendency prevailed (Fischer, 1978).[7]

Other research questions the causality of the relationship between modernization and the elderly's status by pointing to a reversal in the relationship in the later stages of modernization (Palmore and Manton, 1974; Palmore, 1976). These researchers suggest that the pattern is J-shaped rather than linear; that is, the relative decline in the status of the elderly (in terms of health, occupation, income, and education) bottoms out and begins to rise as societies become increasingly modernized. Palmore (1976) attributes this to a slowing down in the rates of change for the younger population. The dramatic rate of improvement in health and longevity that was

---

[7]Not all historians, however, accept Fischer's analysis. For example, Stone (1977) takes issue with Fischer's analysis. He asserts that the range of evidence Fischer employs to support the argument that there was a "deep change" in the elderly's status at this time is ambiguous and subject to alternative interpretations. He notes, for example, the change in seating customs in Massachusetts meeting houses could also be explained by an ideological change, from deference to democracy and a realization of the fact of increased economic inequality.

achieved in the beginning of this century has decreased. Purchasing power and the massive shifts from rural to urban occupations and from the lower to higher status occupations have leveled off. Educational attainment has also tapered off (Palmore, 1976). Palmore notes that these diminished rates of change for the younger cohorts have the effect of reducing the discrepancies between older and younger generations.

Some support for the turnaround in the elderly's status with increasing modernization comes from a recent study conducted by the Harris (1975) polling organization, which showed that attitudes about the aged are improving. This survey noted that the public recognizes that the elderly of the 1970s represent a more resourceful and independent group (they are perceived as better educated, healthier and wealthier) than older Americans in the 1950s and 1960s. The public is also aware that the elderly of today enjoy greater longevity and are more likely than previously to live out their longer lives in their own households.

A particularly interesting challenge to the modernization theory is the case of Japan. The status of the elderly remains high in Japan in spite of its rapid industrialization (Palmore, 1975). The Japanese continue to have a strong cultural tradition of respect for the old that derives from an age-grading system whereby the younger generation defers to the old. Attitudes of filial piety based on Confucian precepts and the ancient practice of ancestor worship continue to reinforce respect for elders. Japanese custom continues to enforce deference to elders through a number of practices: elders are shown respect and affection on a daily basis by honorific language, bowing and practices such as priority of the elders in serving, seating, bathing, and so on. Popular sayings, special celebrations on one's sixty-first birthday, as well as the national observance of Respect for Elders Day and the National Law for Welfare of the Aged also reflect the high status accorded the elderly (Palmore, 1975).

From the foregoing, it appears that the web of causality linking modernization and the elderly's status is more complex than the modernization theory can accommodate. Cultural factors, such as tradition of longstanding respect for elders, appear to have an independent impact in determining the value of the elderly in modern Japan. This interpretation of the elderly's situation runs counter to the modernization theory's more economic emphasis whereby individual status is determined by one's relationship to the means of production. An economic interpretation does not appear to be valid in the Japanese case because the high degree of industrialization and the elders' lower level of employment (compared to agricultural societies) have not led to low status for the elderly. On the contrary, their relatively high status lends support to an analysis which argues for the inclusion of cultural factors and their independent impact on the social status of the elderly (Palmore, 1978).[8]

OTHER CRITIQUES OF THE THEORY

Many researchers feel that a large part of the distortion derives from the modernization theory's ideological bias.[9] Critics claim that it is an ethnocentric concept which implies an evolutionary model of progress that is entirely western (Grew, 1977; Tipps, 1973).

Modernization theory judges the progress of nations by their nearness to western institutions and values. The theory derives the attributes of "modernity" from a generalized image of western society and then procedes to posit the acquisition of these attributes as a criterion of modernization (Tipps, 1973). This thinking has led to a theory of modernization, which has dichotomized history into two periods: the premodern (or preindustrial) and the mod-

---

[8]There are, however, alternative interpretations for some of this evidence. Palmore (1975) tends to view the status of the elderly in Japan too optimistically by only concentrating on the overt aspects of respect such as honorific bowing and preferential seating. An alternative interpretation is that there was simply a slower rate of decline in the elderly's status in Japan than modernization theory would have predicted. Some support for this position comes from comparative research into the suicide rates of Japanese elderly. Wen (1974) found an unusually high suicide rate for Japanese elderly compared to United States data. He hypothesizes that the rapid social and economic changes taking place in Japan have weakened the norm of filial piety. The expectation that the young will take care of the old still prevails, but is now often unrealistic. As a result, the elderly feel disappointed, and this disappointment may trigger their suicide.

[9]The strongest ideological critiques comes from Marxists who tend to reject the modernization paradigm entirely and to propose instead a competing theory of imperialism (Berger, 1976).

ern. Yet, these two stages of historical development are only an *ex post facto* ordering of history that is based on a particular place, time, and value system. The most diverse types of societies are combined together in the same category. These premodern social structures share little more than the label "traditional" and the obvious fact that they are not modern (western) nations. At times it is impossible to know whether to place a society into one category or the other. Tipps (1973) underlines this problem in his analysis of the colonial experiences of new states. He notes that as a result of having modernization superimposed on them by conquest, new states have become hybrid societies — neither traditional nor modern. The dichotomized terms employed by modernization theorists are inadequate when dealing with these hybrid societies. They ignore the complexities in the range of developments between societies and lead to oversimplification of the elderly's status within societies.

There is a tendency for modernization theorists to ignore important differences between preindustrial and industrial societies. In the case of preindustrial societies we have noted that modernization theorists paint a rosier picture of the "good old days" than appears to be warranted by a close examination of the historical record. This stems, in part, from a climate of strong ambivalence toward industrialism on the part of many western intellectuals. This ambivalence manifested itself in a nostalgic sense of paradise lost that pervaded many characterizations of the traditional past leading to romanticized visions of a traditional past in which people who were poor by today's standards led simple, contented lives (Tipps, 1973). Modernization theory's portrait of life in preindustrial societies masks the social, economic, and political differences among nations, which help account for the variation among them in the status of the elderly.

The tendency to see the world divided into two categories (premodern and modern) leads to an oversimplified portrait of the elderly's condition in the modern world. A case can be made that there are three different modern periods: early, modern, and postmodern, and that there are three different positions on the validity of the modernization model depending on which period one is referring to (Fischer, 1978). The range of different and apparently contradictory findings concerning the status of the elderly in modern societies stems, in part, from the fact that modernization theorists are working only *within* one of these periods and then making generalizations that many interpret as applying to all three. Theorists working in the early modern era (1500–1800) are in agreement that the modernization model requires major revisions, while students of modern history (1800–1945) generally accept the model as is (Fischer, 1978). Scholars working in the contemporary period (1945–present) tend to apply the model in reverse, noting that with increasing levels of modernization (i.e. postindustrial society) the status of the elderly begins to rise (Palmore and Manton, 1974).

The modernization theory gives little attention to the importance of the social and economic variation in the elderly's status within a given society. Too often, modernization theorists generalize about the elderly as though they were a homogenous group. However, research has demonstrated that trends in the status of the aged are highly variable, depending upon such factors as sex and socioeconomic status. We noted earlier, for example, that age per se did not necessarily determine the elderly's status in preindustrial societies (Harlan, 1964; Maddox, 1970). What is often missing from modernization models are controls for such factors. The necessity for such controls becomes even more apparent when we take into consideration the evidence from longitudinal studies, which indicates that variability in many social, psychological, and economic characteristics becomes more pronounced as people age (Maddox and Douglass, 1974).

We know that there are important sex differences in the status of the elderly with respect to social, economic, and health factors. For instance, widowed women are more likely to have contact with their children and are more likely to live with their children. Widowed men tend to live alone or in an institutional setting. Men earn more than women, and there is no indication that the income gap between the sexes is decreasing (Palmore and Maddox, 1977). Others have noted that as societies modernize, elderly women may gain in status and prestige compared with their positions in preindustrial society.

The impact of urbanization and industrialization may affect

each sex differently. For example, the patriarchal organization of a traditional society is often vulnerable to even glancing contact with modern ways, while the unofficial matriarchy one notes in some traditional societies may survive the transition to modernization (Gutmann, 1977). Gutmann theorizes that since cities are settled by the young who are liberated from the stifling control exercised over them in the small community by the elderly, city living represents an outcome of a revolution against male gerontocracy. In this situation, the patriarch loses status in the city and hitherto other disadvantaged groupings, including women, may find their freedom.

There is a marked increase in life expectancy for women brought about by modernization. Increased female longevity is accompanied by a corresponding shift in the patterning of affectional ties. Social ties in the city tend to be strongest between mothers and their daughters. These bonds are eventually sources of economic assistance and social support to aged mothers (Gutmann, 1977).

There are socioeconomic differences among the elderly that contribute to the variation in status for both preindustrial and modern societies. In industrial society those individuals within the lower socioeconomic classes tend to have poorer diets, substandard housing, and tend to visit physicians less frequently. As a result their health suffers more, they are more likely to be disabled, and they have higher death rates (Palmore and Maddox, 1977).

These differences in terms of sex and socioeconomic status illustrate the need to qualify any generalizations about the relationship between modernization and the status of the elderly. The theory's failure to account for the effects of sex, socioeconomic status, and other such factors is a serious flaw.

SHOULD THE THEORY BE REJECTED?

Does the weight of the criticisms that we have considered imply that one would best reject the modernization theory? While some critics believe the theory should be rejected on the grounds that it does little to advance our knowledge and understanding (Tipps, 1973) this is not our position. Despite its limitations (and as we have pointed out there are many), the theory does make an important contribution to an understanding of factors affecting the elderly's status. Particularly important in this context is the observation that large-scale changes such as urbanization, industrialization, and mass education do influence the elderly's power and status. The exact nature of modernization's impact on the status of the elderly continues to be a subject of debate, but this does not justify a total rejection of the theory. In fact, many of the limitations that we have mentioned could be taken into account by modernization theorists. In addition, the exceptions to the theory's predictions of a decline in the elderly's status with modernization (e.g. the case of Japan) serve the important function of specifying the conditions under which the theory is or is not applicable. This counter evidence could be used to modify (qualify) the theory, rather than simply being used to reject it.

There are a number of steps that could be taken to deal with flaws in the modernization theory. Given the variations in the timing of modernization and its impact in different spheres, it would appear that the theory could be strengthened if the major components (e.g. health technology, economic technology, urbanization, and education) were separated and studied individually; each of these components may have a different impact on the power and status of the elderly. If we found that all of these factors were operating in the predicted direction, then we would feel comfortable referring to the process as modernization. One might, on the other hand, hesitate to refer to the process as modernization if it involved only one of these factors; were this the case it might be better to refer to the change in status or power as being due to a specific component (e.g. urbanization) rather than being due to the more general process of modernization.

Just as there are various components of the process of modernization, there are also a variety of configurations the process can take in different societies. It appears more reasonable to design a conceptual model that allows for several major stages of modernization, rather than just the dichotomy of traditional (premodern or preindustrial) versus modern. In this way, one could incorporate the historical evidence that the process of modernization neither occurred simultaneously in all societies nor dramatically overturned the existing social order. Instead, modernization affected specific aspects of a given country's social and economic structure at different points in time and had a particular impact on the elderly's status (Achenbaum and Sterns, 1978). Such a perspective allows us to better understand the differing impact modernization has had on the power and status of the elderly from one society to another.

As we noted earlier, the empirical evidence relating to the modernization theory is contradictory. In the beginning stages of modernization there is a decline in the status of the aged (Fischer, 1978) while at the later stages—postindustrial society—there is some evidence that the elderly's status begins to rise with increasing levels of modernization (Palmore and Manton, 1974). Viewing the process of modernization in continuous rather than discrete terms enables one to reconcile these conflicting results. This explanation for these apparently contradictory findings serves to enhance the model by specifying the conditions under which modernization will increase, decrease, or have no impact on the elderly's status.

We have had two major goals in this chapter. The first has been to call into question the work of those who use the modernization theory uncritically as an explanation for historical shifts in the relative status and power of older people. The evidence with respect to the theory is far from conclusive; it calls out for qualification and specification. Our second goal has been to defend the theory against those who would have us reject it entirely because of its limitations. We have argued that with appropriate qualification and specification the theory can be useful. It does point to a number of factors that must be taken into consideration by those who seek to explain historical shifts in the relative position of the aged.

The primary application of the modernization theory will, most likely, continue to be in historical accounts of change in the power and status of the elderly in western nations. However, with appropriate modification and qualification the theory can be used to analyze the impact of changes associated with the modernization process in third world nations today and in years to come. The theory can also be used to analyze the likely impact of technological innovation on the future status and influence of the elderly in western nations. Will technological breakthroughs in communication, mass media, transportation, and health technology lead to greater influence and autonomy for the elderly, or will such changes lead to new mechanisms of social control? We will return to this important question in later chapters, but so as not to get ahead of ourselves we will first consider the historical origins of what is today referred to as the "senior movement."

PART II:
POWER, PARTICIPATION, AND POLICY

Chapter 4

SENIOR POWER: SOCIAL MOVEMENT, INTEREST GROUP, OR COALITION?

The twentieth century has witnessed a great deal of political activity by or on behalf of elderly Americans. Groups such as the Fraternal Order of the Eagles, the Townsend Movement, and the Gray Panthers have organized to promote the causes of older citizens. Some groups have achieved impressive successes; others have exerted little permanent impact on policy. In recent decades the political interests and demands of the elderly have gradually become institutionalized. Voluntary organizations such as the American Association of Retired Persons, the National Council on the Aging, the National Association of Retired Federal Employees, and the National Council of Senior Citizens have come to play an important role in this context.[1] These organizations have served as focal points for elderly concerns and have actively promoted age-related causes through congressional lobbying, media exposure, and electoral pressures. In addition, the promotion of age-related interests has increasingly become an integral part of the established legal and policymaking structure itself, via such legislation as the Social Security Act, Medicare, and the Older Americans Act and through the creation of bureaucratic structures such as the Social Security Administration, the Administration on Aging, and the National Institute on Aging.

Most of those who have described the historical emergence of old age as an important political concern have analyzed the evidence from one or the other of two major theoretical perspectives. The first of these is the "interest group pluralism" perspective

---

[1]Today the National Retired Teachers Association (NRTA) and the American Association of Retired Persons (AARP) function as one organization in national politics; it is referred to as NRTA/AARP, or simply AARP.

(Binstock, 1974; Hudson and Binstock, 1976). Stemming from the political science tradition of "group theory" (Bentley, 1908; Truman, 1951; Latham, 1952; Hagan, 1958; Dahl, 1961; 1971), this model portrays attempts to articulate elderly interests and influence policy as taking place within a competitive bargaining environment in which antagonistic "interest groups" vie with each other for access to policymakers and policymaking structures. Public policy is seen as the outcome of pluralistic competition among societal groups, each seeking to articulate the private interests of its membership by gaining access to legislative and administrative processes.[2] The group's particularistic demands, as "inputs" into the formal legislative apparatus of the political system, become realized when an interest group manages to exert sufficient "pressure" vis-à-vis competing groups (in the form of lobbying and electoral threats) to effectively influence societal "outputs" (target legislation).[3] Some of the more recent theorists have pointed out that in a pluralistic, zero-sum bargaining environment of this sort organized special interest groups representing "private power" with extensive financial resources tend to effectively dominate the formulation and implementation of American public policy (McConnell, 1966; Lowi, 1971; Binstock, 1972).[4]

A second approach looks at these twentieth century political developments in senior power within the broader rubric of an ongoing "social movement." The sociological tradition of "collective behavior" research, represented in the work of Smelser (1962), bypasses some of the assumptions of the "interest group pluralist"

---

[2]A thorough explication of the major strengths and weaknesses of political science group theory literature can be found in a review article by Greenstone (1975). Other informative overviews include Almond (1958), Balbus (1971), Connolly (1969), Dahl (1971), Downs (1957), Golembiewski (1960), Hagan (1958), Kariel (1961), Key (1964), Mansfield (1970), Olson (1965), Rothman (1960), Salisbury (1969; 1970), Weinstein (1962), Zeigler (1964), and Zisk (1969).

[3]See Easton (1953, 1965). Eastonian "systems analysis" depicts the dynamics of political systems as involving input processes (demands, supports), conversion processes (policymaking, conversion of inputs into appropriate legislation), and output processes (resultant legislation, policy).

[4]Schattschneider (1960:31–32) notes that the business or upper class bias of the pressure system shows up everywhere. Similarly, Connolly (1969:17) points out that this upper class bias in interest group politics inhibits some segments of society from efficacious involvement in the balancing process.

model by recognizing that persons often mobilize in large numbers to form mass movements for collective purposes, which go significantly beyond narrow self-interest, in response to some larger societal need (Carlie, 1969). Building on previous conceptualizations by Fuller and Myers (1941a, b), Blumer (1951), Brinton (1952), and Smelser (1962), Mauss (1971) outlined a sequence of five stages through which social movements typically pass in the course of their development: incipiency, coalescence, institutionalization, fragmentation, and demise.[5] While these abstract stages are merely ideal types, and no concrete movement follows them precisely, they are nevertheless useful in tracing the general progression of movements, such as the old-age movement (Ward, 1979).[6]

Both the "interest group pluralism" (Dahl, 1961; Lowi, 1969; Binstock, 1972) and "social movement" (Blumer, 1952; Mauss, 1971; Pratt, 1976; Ward, 1979) perspectives possess certain explanatory advantages for understanding the growth of senior power in this century. But each approach also leaves important questions unanswered. In the present chapter we present a synthesis that goes beyond both of these interpretations. Age-related political developments are discussed in terms of the various individual "interest groups," which have sought to articulate elderly concerns and gain access to decisionmakers and the policymaking process. At the same time, these isolated old-age struggles are placed within the broader explanatory perspective of an ongoing

---

[5]Early attempts at tracing the evolution of social movements included Troeltsch's (1931) study of the transformation of religious sects into churches and Brinton's (1952) study of the development of revolutions. The concept of successive stages in the developmental progression of a social movement has also been explored in works by Hopper (1950), Heberle (1951), Hoffer (1951), King (1956), Lang and Lang (1961), and Killian (1964). The notion of the "natural history" of a social movement was developed in work by Fuller and Myers (1941a, b), Blumer (1951, 1971), and Mauss (1971, 1975). Blumer (1951, 1971) has suggested a five-stage model of the natural history of a social movement, and Reissman (1973) posits three stages (identification, shaping, and disappearance).

[6]Carlie (1969) and Ward (1979) have discussed the development of senior power trends since the 1920s in terms of this broader "social movement" approach. Carlie (1969) compares the relative historical explanatory power of "social movement" versus "interest group" perspectives, concluding that the social movement approach yields a better explanation. Ward (1979) was the first to apply the Mauss (1971, 1975) model of the "natural history of a social movement" to the historical development of old-age struggles.

"social movement," tracing its evolution through stages of incipiency (1920–1950), coalescence (1950–1965), and institutionalization (1965 to present). Based on this, we develop a "coalition formation" interpretation that incorporates the most useful aspects of "interest group pluralist" and "social movement" perspectives, but which also goes significantly beyond both. A "coalition formation" perspective offers a more compelling explanation as to why old-age policy gains have usually occurred in conjunction with the gains of other interest groups such as labor, minorities, and the poor. As we shall see, the formation of flexible coalitions with other groups whose interests have, at least temporarily, been related to those of the aged has made possible a combined political strength far beyond that which the aged could conceivably have wielded alone.[7]

HISTORICAL PRECONDITIONS TO
THE AMERICAN SENIOR MOVEMENT

When aging emerged as an issue in politics during the early decades of the twentieth century, processes of modernization had for some time been separating older persons from the mainstream of American social life. Processes of rapid change accompanying industrialization and urbanization in nineteenth century America produced common frustrations and chronically unsatisfied needs. These accumulated dissatisfactions were later to surface as the objective basis for mass action and the development of a senior movement. Among these shared grievances tolerated by the elderly were inadequate or nonexistent pension coverage, high medical care expenses, their devalued social status, unemployment, and poor housing conditions (Achenbaum, 1978a).

In Europe these issues associated with aging had appeared much earlier. Germany, for instance, had initiated a compulsory old-age insurance system in 1889, half a century before the passage of the American Social Security legislation. The United States was slower

---

[7]Holtzman (1963) notes that the labor movements of the late nineteenth and early twentieth centuries and the socialists were in large measure responsible for modern national old-age programs and policies in many nations. Similarly, Carlie (1969) comments that those working for old-age reforms represented many groups, most of which were non-aged based and had only a partial interest in the welfare of the elderly.

in responding to the economic and political dilemmas of its older citizens for a number of reasons. There were comparatively fewer unemployed elderly persons concentrated in American urban areas due in part to the existence of the frontier and the persistence of a substantial population of self-sufficient farmers. In comparison with European countries, the United States maintained a higher proportion of immigrants, and persons over sixty-five comprised a smaller percentage of the total population. The prevailing ideology of laissez faire liberalism was considerably more hostile to intervention by the public sector in the life of the individual than was the case in Europe during the same period (Lubove, 1968).

To be sure, indigence and unemployment had emerged as salient problems among the elderly by the later decades of the nineteenth century, especially in the more densely populated urban centers of the industrial Northeast (Achenbaum, 1978a). But a massive system of Civil War pensions temporarily camouflaged the severity of the problem by providing many with support in old age. Nearly a million Americans were supported by Federal veteran's pensions during the 1901–1905 period (Fischer, 1978). In addition, some persons received benefits from the states. Ironically, many of the same Americans who vehemently denounced old-age pensions as "European," "socialistic," and contrary to the spirit of atomistic individualism were themselves being supported by one of the most extensive socially provided pension systems then in existence.

A confluence of events in the first decade of the twentieth century upset this superficially harmonious state of affairs. The percentage of the elderly in the population, which had gradually risen during the nineteenth century, now began to grow at an unprecedented rate (Burgess, 1960; Hauser and Vargas, 1960).[8] These demographic pressures took place at a time when the

---

[8]Lubove (1968) notes that the proportion of the American population 65 and over rose from 2 percent in 1850, to 4 percent in 1900, and 6 percent in 1920. In each decade of the period between 1900 and 1930 the rate of increase in the elderly population was greater than that for the nation as a whole. The most rapid increase occurred between 1920 and 1930. Between 1900 and 1929 the figures for average life expectancy at birth increased from 48 to 58 years for males, and from 51 to 61 years for females.

unpredictability of the American economy, based on a national economic philosophy of laissez faire capitalism, was a source of growing discontent. Unemployment rates had increased sharply during the depression of the 1890s, with approximately 20 percent of the work force unemployed in 1894. After a brief return to normalcy, economic conditions again worsened in the panic of 1907. Unemployment rates among men over 65 reached more than one third of all eligible elderly workers (Achenbaum, 1978*a*). Moreover, these developments occurred concurrently with a shrinkage of the Civil War pension system.

It was within this historical context that age-specific concerns began to be addressed by reformers. There were three distinct schools of reform that arose during the first decade of the twentieth century, representing different proposed solutions to the economic and political woes of the aged (Pratt, 1976). The first group, adhering to the nineteenth century individualist approach, consisted largely of settlement house managers, social workers, and charity organizers. Using the National Conference of Charities and Corrections as their organizational vehicle and communicating their appeals through Paul Kellogg's *Survey* magazine, they defined old age problems in terms of "poor relief" and advocated voluntary charity as the solution. Their most prominent spokesperson was Jane Addams.

The approach of a second group of old-age reformers was corporatist in emphasis. Working through the American Association of Labor Legislation (which had been established in 1906) the group consisted largely of economists and other social scientists, among the most prominent of whom were John Commons (University of Chicago), Richard Ely (University of Wisconsin), and Henry Farnum (Yale University). The corporatist recipe for reform involved the creation of industrial pensions through a process of collective bargaining between labor and employers, subject to regulation by the government.

A third group of reformers during this period was socialist in ideology and collectivist in its approach to old-age pension reform. Abraham Epstein, Isaac Rubinow, and Stephen Wise headed this faction. Advocating the implementation of a system of compulsory old-age insurance on a nationwide basis, they viewed this goal as linked to the larger issues of expansion of public sector activities and the reduction of social inequalities through redistribution of income.

During the first decade of the twentieth century these individualistic, corporatist, and socialistic factions actively promoted their ideas in public forums, competing for the attention of elected officials and the general public. But the number of adherents remained relatively small, and their political influence proved to be minor (Fischer, 1979). American political representatives continued to be adamantly opposed to any form of old-age pension system that would be administered by the public sector.[9] The only state legislature in which an old-age pension bill was passed prior to 1914 was Arizona, and the state supreme court declared the law unconstitutional shortly thereafter.

INCIPIENCY: 1920-1950

According to Mauss (1971),[10] social movements originate with a period of "incipiency." In this embryonic stage, a "concerned public" (in this case the elderly and those working on their behalf) gropes toward the establishment of a shared identity based on a perception of threat to their common interests. Activities by the concerned public may include the expression of grievances, needs, and demands in the media; writing letters to political representatives; and the holding of *ad hoc* meetings. The most difficult task at this stage for the concerned public is the coherent delineation of their concerns and the forging of a common identity. In particular, it becomes necessary at some point to define boundaries that separate the interests of those concerned from the interests of the societal mainstream.

The larger society's response to these expressions of discontent

---

[9]The American opposition to the provision of old-age pensions was in stark contrast to the European experience during the same period. Denmark, for example, established a nationwide pension system in 1891. France initiated an optional pension system in 1897, which became compulsory in 1910. England adopted a national pension system in 1908 and New Zealand adopted one in 1898 (Lubove, 1968).

[10]For a later and somewhat more elaborate statement of the theory of successive stages in the "natural history" of social movement, see Mauss (1975).

may consist of cooptation, repression, or some combination of the two strategies. Cooptation involves appeasement, attempts to restore societal equilibrium through compromise and consensus, and attempted absorption of the movement's momentum. Repression is most likely to be invoked as a solution if political elites perceive the budding movement as dangerously subversive or as harboring an alien ideology (Mauss, 1975). Either type of societal response— cooptation or repression—if employed effectively, will tend to arrest or at a minimum delay the social movement's development into successive stages.

The incipiency stage of the American senior movement occurred roughly between 1920 and 1950. By the 1920s the social atmosphere in the United States had become ripe for the emergence of old age activism. American legislators had already demonstrated their unwillingness to endorse public old-age pension systems by rejecting proposals put forth by early twentieth century reformers. Pension plans provided through the private sector were also slow to develop, and very few persons were covered by them. Overall, by 1914 less than 1 percent of American workers could rely on any form of pension to provide security in old age (Fischer, 1979). For the vast majority of American elderly, the only alternatives available in old age were family support, accumulated savings, or residence in an almshouse (Achenbaum, 1978a). Concurrent with these trends, available statistics document an increase in elderly unemployment. The percentage of males over 65 in the labor force steadily declined from 70 percent in 1890, to 56 percent in 1920, and eventually to 42 percent in 1940 (Achenbaum, 1978a). Predictably, the incidence of pauperism among older Americans grew rapidly. The percentage of those over 65 forced to depend on some form of public relief for their subsistence increased from 23 percent in 1910, to 33 percent in 1920, and to 40 percent in 1930 (Fischer, 1978). The prevalence of these economic conditions among the aged provided a dramatic backdrop for reformers' appeals for old-age pension support, allowing such appeals to take root and develop into a viable political movement.

The origins of a "senior movement" are traceable to several groups who campaigned on behalf of old-age pensions in the 1920s. The first of these was a national brotherhood called the

Fraternal Order of the Eagles. Organized into an "Aerie" in every state, the fraternal order held a Grand Aerie at the national level on an annual basis. At a time when the economy was in a worrisome post-World War I slump, national Eagles leader Frank Hering persuaded the organization's rank and file to devote a substantial portion of the Eagles' resources to the establishment of old-age pensions. Initiated in the Indiana State Aerie in 1921, the measure was endorsed by the Grand Aerie in the same year. The Eagles, equipped with a preexisting organizational framework on local and national levels, enthusiastically drafted pension bills, organized community pension clubs, and launched extensive lobbying campaigns in state legislatures. Tangible results were forthcoming. Pennsylvania, Montana, and Nevada adopted old-age pension schemes in 1923, and a majority of the remaining states followed suit within the next decade. Despite these encouraging developments, pension amounts remained skimpy, and eligibility requirements were inordinately strict. Moreover, the plans were usually voluntary rather than compulsory. Thus, as late as 1930 over 95 percent of elderly Americans continued to be without pension assistance. Still the Fraternal Order of the Eagles had managed to achieve an expansive breakthrough for the burgeoning senior movement by initiating in a majority of the states the precedent of public responsibility for security in old age (Lubove, 1968).

The inspiration provided by the Eagles stimulated similar attempts in the 1930s when the Depression drove home the vital need for societal-level solutions to the economic problems of older Americans. During this period, California emerged as a nexus of old age activism. Elderly unemployment rates there were substantially higher than the national average. Furthermore, in many California towns the percentage of the population over 65 was twice that for the nation as a whole. In this environment various old-age pension schemes began to be proposed at an unprecedented rate (Fischer, 1978).

A prominent example was a program put forth by Upton Sinclair in 1933 designed to "end poverty in California" (EPIC). Sinclair's EPIC plan proposed a 12-point reform package, including a $50 per month pension to all Californians over 60 who had resided there for 3 years or more (Achenbaum, 1978a). Having established himself as an author of muckraking novels urging humanitarian reforms, Sinclair rose to power in California's Democratic party, capturing its nomination for governor in 1933. In the bitter 1934 gubernatorial campaign that ensued, however, his opponents—a coalition of conservative Democrats and Republicans—claimed that EPIC really stood for "end poverty, introduce Communism" (Fischer, 1979). The red-baiting cost Sinclair the election, and his political fortunes declined thereafter, precluding attempts to implement the plan.

Another of these proposed plans was put forth by the "Ham and Eggs" group. The organization was initiated by Robert Noble, whose endorsement of EPIC had cost him his job as a radio announcer. Noble's "California State Pension Movement" adopted the slogan, "25 dollars every Tuesday" and called for unemployed persons over 50 to receive a weekly payment in scrip. Stamped with a specified expiration date to ensure prompt spending, the scrip would lose its value after a period of one year. Prompt spending by the elderly was intended as a measure for stimulating the Depression economy by increasing circulation of currency (Pratt, 1976). The Ham and Eggs group eventually fell into the hands of Willis Allen, who altered the slogan to "30 dollars every Thursday." The concept gained widespread popularity, and the Ham and Eggs group was soon boasting a following of 300,000 adherents. Although it eventually folded, the Ham and Eggs group's rallies, radio programs, and mass marches left an indelible imprint on subsequent California old-age struggles (Fischer, 1979).

By far the largest and most influential mass organization during this period of incipiency was the Townsend Movement. Emerging in California during the early 1930s, and named after Dr. Francis Townsend of Long Beach, California, the movement put forth the "Townsend Plan." The plan proposed that all United States citizens over 65 receive $200 per month ($150 in an earlier version) under the conditions that recipients refrain from participation in the labor force and that recipients spend the pension amount within thirty days (Holtzman, 1963; Altmeyer, 1966). Revenues for the plan were to be derived from a universal 2 percent sales tax on all business transactions (Achenbaum, 1978a). By opening up new jobs and expanding the purchasing power of older Americans,

Townsendites claimed that the measure would stimulate the economy and thereby hasten recovery from the Depression, as well as provide some measure of relief from suffering among the elderly.

Spearheaded by the charismatic Townsend, the movement at its peak attracted followers in every state, over one million nationally. The potential political muscle of such groups became evident when Long Beach supporters of the Townsend Plan undertook to oust an incumbent congressman whom they considered indifferent to elderly concerns. Townsendites nominated their own candidate, seventy-two-year-old John McGroarty, who went on to win the election. The electoral victory was an unmistakable indication of the political leverage that older Americans were capable of exercising as a voting bloc if sufficiently provoked by lack of attention to their needs on the part of incumbent officials. Once in Washington, McGroarty introduced a bill calling for adoption of the Townsend Plan, which was voted down by a margin of four to one (Fischer, 1979).

Although the Townsend Plan was defeated, governmental officials had been forced to recognize the increasing political salience of elderly interests and demands, and the Long Beach election proved that the latent political clout of elderly voters could become a powerful weapon. President Roosevelt, however, had his own ideas as to how old-age security could best be provided. He emphasized in his message to Congress that he preferred a contributory system of social insurance to one that would entail increases in general taxation (Altmeyer, 1966).

The impact of the Depression on many older Americans was devastating: elderly unemployment was consistently higher than the national average; personal savings of the elderly—meager even in good times—proved grossly inadequate during the Depression; nor could many of the elderly rely on any substantial family assistance, since most Depression families experienced great difficulty in providing for even their immediate members (Achenbaum, 1978a). A combination of fear of electoral consequences and genuine concern about a pressing national problem, which had become increasingly visible, led to old-age security being placed higher and higher on the federal legislative agenda.

Although the Townsend Movement had a negligible impact on

the design of the subsequent Social Security Act, it had a great deal to do with the urgency with which the task was undertaken by political elites.[11] Reacting to mounting dissatisfaction, President Franklin Roosevelt chose Secretary of Labor Francis Perkins to head a cabinet committee that would draft a national social insurance program (Sanders, 1973; Booth, 1973). A social security bill was promptly submitted to Congress (within 6 months) and passed in 1935.

As a governmental response to pressures that had been slowly mounting for several decades, the Social Security legislation was, at least in one sense, a major turning point in the history of old age struggles for economic security in the United States. The establishment of some form of nationally administered social insurance system marked a victory for the old-age pension movement, even though it was much more modest in scope than Townsend, Epstein, Rubinow, and others had hoped for. While it may not have been evident at the time, the act represented a pivotal shift in the administration of welfare functions from voluntary institutions to the public sector, as well as from local to federal levels. By so doing, it established legal and ideological precedents that made possible subsequent amendments to the Social Security Act by raising benefit levels, adding survivors' and dependents' benefits (1939), adding disability insurance (1956), introducing Medicare for the elderly (1965), incorporating automatic benefit adjustments for inflation (enacted in 1972, implemented 1975), and initiating indexing of earnings (1977) (Schulz, 1980).

In another sense, however, the Social Security Act was a major disappointment for many. As an act of political accommodation by the established political order designed to defuse the growing fury of constituents, its success was primarily political rather than social or economic. It succeeded politically by taking much of the wind out of the sails of the old age protests of the day; all but

---

[11]There is considerable disagreement regarding the nature and extent of the influence exerted by the Townsend Movement on the subsequent Social Security Act. The strongest case for substantial influence is argued by Holtzman (1963:87), who suggests that "the inclusion of an old-age insurance provision within the act represented *a direct response* to the Townsend pressure" (emphasis added). In contrast, Schlesinger (1958), Altmeyer (1966), Cohen (1970), and Pratt (1976:23) have tended to downplay its importance.

putting an end to a senior movement that had been heavily organized around this one issue. While the rhetoric of the act promised sweeping reforms in the circumstances of elderly workers, an equally important objective was to get the elderly out of the labor force in order to create jobs for younger workers. The act was consciously designed to avoid redistribution of wealth and adhered strictly to the equity principles of private insurance. The act omitted government contributions, with eligibility and benefits closely tied to the extent of contributions by workers. The tax system upon which it was based was so regressive that it had the net effect of *increasing* income inequality (Lubove, 1968; Fischer, 1979).

These and other deficiencies of the act immediately came under attack by prominent reformers and spokesmen of the senior movement, who had long advocated much more comprehensive coverage with fewer restrictions. For a time Dr. Francis Townsend ascended to even greater heights of popularity as a result of popular reaction against some of the shortcomings of the act (Fischer, 1979). Also disappointed with the provisions of the act was reformer Isaac Rubinow, who protested that he had not devoted himself tirelessly to the advocacy of social insurance for thirty-five years "in order now, at this late date, to abandon my ideal for the sake of a somewhat glorified system of public relief" (Lubove, 1968:176). The most adamant critic of the new legislation, however, was Abraham Epstein. Epstein was infuriated by the conspicuous failure of the Committee on Economic Security to consult either himself or Rubinow in drawing up the act. Rubinow complained that Francis Perkins had treated Epstein "shabbily" in excluding him from the decision-making process.

Rubinow and Epstein were essentially in agreement in their assessments of the basic limitations of the act. Both felt the legislation was incapable of providing genuine financial security to the elderly, since it did not entail any significant measure of redistribution of income to the aged.[12] Also, both considered the exclu-

---

[12]Recall that Upton Sinclair's EPIC Plan called for a pension of $50 per month, the Ham and Eggs Plan called for $30 per week, and the Townsend Plan called for $200 per month; but the actual Social Security old-age pension, which did not start until 1940, paid only $271 per year.

sion of health insurance to be a fundamental defect. Both reformers maintained that only government contributions with their
redistributive consequences would make economic security a reality for the elderly (Lubove, 1968). Epstein distinguished between
"social insurance" and "private insurance" and insisted that the
Social Security Act was a federally administered example of the
latter. Social insurance, according to Epstein, did not advocate
"individual protection according to ability to pay" but entailed
instead "a socially adequate arrangement which will protect all
workers as well as society from certain social hazards" (Epstein,
1938:762). He complained that the Committee on Economic Security, from whose deliberations he had been excluded, had con-
fused governmental social insurance with private insurance.

   This burst of criticism of the act by old-age reformers like
Townsend, Rubinow, and Epstein was short-lived. The Social Security legislation had the long-term effect of taking much of the
force out of the senior movement. By cooptation of its key issues
and the temporary appeasement of many of the involved constituencies, it proved possible to absorb the movement's momentum.
Key issues of the movement were defused without significantly
modifying the distribution of wealth or abandoning fundamental
value tenets of individualism, self-reliance, and free enterprise.
This cooptative societal response delayed the further development of the old-age movement for several decades, but did not
entirely arrest its development into further stages.

   In the wake of the Social Security legislation, the Townsend
Movement and other strands of the senior movement lost momentum and fell into disarray, having lost much of their prominence
on the national scene. The dormant period that followed in the
1940s and early 1950s has been described by Pratt (1976) as the
"dismal years" of the senior movement. During these years of
relative quiescence the only significant old age activity was George
McClain's "Citizens Committee for Old-Age Pensions," which at
one point claimed hundreds of thousands of participants in California and managed to achieve increased state expenditures on
elderly concerns. As Fischer (1979) points out, the "dismal years"
of the senior movement corresponded with the "baby boom,"
which occurred in the 1940s and early 1950s. These changes in

fertility rates altered the age composition, decreasing slightly the percentage of older Americans in the general population. This demographic shift may have contributed to this period of relative inactivity in the old age movement.

COALESCENCE: 1950-1965

In the second stage of a social movement, which Mauss (1971) terms the *coalescence* stage, the rather diverse organization and sentiments of the "incipiency" stage begin to congeal into more permanent organizations. Activity at this stage typically consists of the formation of alliances, caucuses, and *ad hoc* committees, in addition to the organization of local and regional formal associations. A social movement may be hastened into the coalescence phase by perceived failures of the society to respond adequately to previous demands and expectations, or in response to overt governmental attempts at repression.

The coalescence phase of the senior movement can be traced to events that occurred in the 1950s (Pratt, 1976). The period of relative quiescence that had characterized the 1940s proved deceptive. The quiet political mood masked an underlying sense of dissatisfaction with Social Security provisions, which remained in need of reform. In the 1950s these dormant, largely unresolved old-age issues reemerged onto the national political scene with renewed vigor. In the 1940s senior citizens centers had begun to form throughout the United States, and in the 1950s the number of these senior clubs grew rapidly. While their primary purpose was as social and self-help groups, they also provided a forum for political discussion, thereby promoting a sense of communality and political consciousness among the old. By 1960, about 250,000 older persons were members of senior clubs (Havighurst, 1963).

Common expressions of dissatisfaction with existing Social Security provisions naturally flourished in these forums. Social Security had imposed an arbitrary definition of old age on older Americans and forced them to retire at a fixed age. By 1960, 71 percent of American men over 60 were no longer participating in the work force (Achenbaum, 1978a). Among elderly Americans there was a growing sense of relative deprivation and frustration, as well as an increasing expectation that it was the duty of society to provide economic security and health care in old age. Social Security had eased problems of economic insecurity among the elderly, but had never solved them. Inflation and growing costs of medical care heightened this sense of anxiety among many of the aged (Fischer, 1979).

This increasing awareness of relative deprivation, social injustice, and shared political identity among the aged was accompanied by the emergence of influential national organizations. In 1950, the National Council on the Aging was formed, followed in 1958 by the American Association of Retired Persons. Both groups quickly grew to formidable proportions.[13] Other groups, such as the National Retired Teachers Association, the National Association of Retired Federal Employees, and the United Auto Workers retiree organization joined the swelling tide of influential senior groups with nationwide clienteles and lobbying arms in Washington.

These political pressures on behalf of the elderly were greatly enhanced by the formation during this period of a coalition between old age interests and American labor organizations. Between 1958 and 1965 the AFL–CIO became active in efforts to get Medicare legislation enacted, and this was a reflection of labor's increasing attention to the needs of retirees (Marmor, 1981). Earlier in the century, old age and labor struggles had frequently arisen together and sought after the same goals. Such issues as disability insurance, workers compensation, unemployment, pensions, and medical insurance involved a substantial overlap between the interests of workers and the elderly, since younger workers wanted security in old age and older workers found themselves affected by employment (and unemployment) policies (Lubove, 1968). During the coalescence period from 1950 to 1965, Charles Odell of the UAW became a prominent figure promoting the common issues of these two interests as a combined force to achieve increased political leverage. Another emergent leader during this period was Ethel Percy Andrus of the National Retired Teachers Association/ American Association of Retired Persons.

The 1960s saw unprecedented growth in the senior movement,

---

[13]Today NRTA/AARP has over 9 million members.

in legislation responding to the special needs of the aged and in organizations concerned with the needs of the elderly. The decade began with the important political precedents of the 1960 Senior Citizens for Kennedy organization, the first White House Conference on Aging (1961), the formation of the Senate Special Committee on Aging (1961), and the founding of the National Council of Senior Citizens (1961).

An important turning point in the political clout of the elderly occurred when "Senior Citizens for Kennedy" was established by the Democratic party as a campaign organization in 1960. Until the late 1950s, Republican candidates had usually taken the traditional association of elderly voters with their party for granted. A majority of older voters had consistently voted for Republican candidates since the 1948 election (Survey Research Center, 1965; Pratt, 1976). The pattern had apparently been set during the New Deal-Fair Deal period when the Democratic party became associated in the minds of voters with inflation and high taxes—economic realities that were particularly stressful to aged persons living on reduced incomes.

When the mood among older voters began to shift in the late 1950s, the Democratic party was quick to seize on the opportunity by establishing "Senior Citizens for Kennedy," within the broader umbrella organization, "Citizens for Kennedy." Campaign-related activities undertaken by the national headquarters of Senior Citizens for Kennedy included recruiting, generating media publicity, support for Kennedy's personal campaign effort, lobbying, and "educational" work within the party. While establishment of the Senior Citizens for Kennedy organization represented a critical juncture in the history of old-age political activism, the primary impact was not in persuading elderly voters. Fewer elderly voters shifted from Republican to Democratic during the 1960 election than was the case for the electorate as a whole (Survey Research Center, 1965; Pratt, 1976). Rather, the primary impact was in persuading Democratic politicians that the elderly were a significant electoral constituency. This recognition that older voters were a force to be reckoned with led to enlarged efforts by both parties in subsequent elections to court older voters.

By the mid-1960s the cumulative pressures of nationwide senior interest groups with demonstrable lobbying power in Washington, growing recognition of potential electoral leverage, and substantial support from labor organizations all combined to produce an influential "gray lobby." Partly due to the liberal political climate of the times and partly due to these cumulative political pressures, this coalition of interest groups was able to successfully take on taxpayer groups over Social Security, the American Medical Association over medical insurance for the elderly, and major corporations over mandatory retirement provisions. The mid 1960s produced landmark legislation such as Medicare (1965) and the Older Americans Act (1965), which established the Administration on Aging as a permanent fixture within the federal bureaucratic structure.

Such advances did not come easily in the American political climate; the struggle to achieve a medical insurance program for the elderly is a case in point. The Medicare bill, which was enacted in 1965 and which went into effect a year later, was the product of a long and difficult struggle for Social Security health insurance, which spanned the administrations of Roosevelt, Truman, Eisenhower, Kennedy, and Johnson. The Germans had provided health insurance coverage for elderly workers in the time of Bismarck (1883), and the British had adopted health insurance for low-income workers as part of a social security pension program in 1911. By 1940, every government in western Europe was providing a national health insurance program for at least its low-income citizens (Stevens and Stevens, 1974; Schottland, 1970). Enactment of Medicare in 1965 reflected America's late entry into compulsory health insurance, and its restriction to the elderly was quite different than the pattern established in other industrial countries (Marmor, 1969).

In the American context, the first serious consideration of the possibility of old-age health insurance came when Roosevelt's advisory Committee on Economic Security briefly considered the issue. But Roosevelt felt that the government health insurance issue was much too controversial to include in the Social Security bill, fearing that its inclusion would endanger both the passage of the bill and Roosevelt's upcoming bid for reelection. An account by Edwin Witte, executive director of the committee, indicates that

Roosevelt's political instincts were on target:

> When in 1934 the Committee on Economic Security announced that it was studying health insurance, it was at once subjected to misrepresentation and vilification. In the original social security bill there was one line to the effect that the Social Security Board should study the problem and make a report to Congress. That little line was responsible for so many telegrams to members of Congress that the entire social security program seemed endangered until the Ways and Means Committee unanimously struck it out of the bill (Anderson, 1951:90).

When the issue resurfaced as a serious consideration in the early 1960s, ideological polarization over the merits of the proposed Medicare legislation rapidly set in. Within the Congress an alliance was quickly formed among conservative Southern Democrats and Republicans in opposition to the "entering wedge of the socialized state." Testifying in 1963 before the House Ways and Means Committee, the president of the AMA claimed that socially provided medical insurance for the elderly was "unnecessary" and "dangerous to the basic principles underlying our American system of medical care" (Marmor, 1969:21).

Senior power lobbies alone could never have countered such powerful opposition from organized special interest groups. Instead, support for the bill came from a *coalition* of organized labor (by far the most influential pressure group), social workers, and old-age lobbies. The formation of a broad-based coalition of individual pressure groups whose interests significantly overlapped those of the elderly provided the key to a winning legislative strategy.

The issue was clearly a "redistributive" one in terms of its potential consequences for the allocation of benefits and burdens among socioeconomic groups. The pattern of interest group alignments therefore reflected a rare degree of ideological polarization (Marmor, 1981:112):

INTEREST GROUP COALITION FOR MEDICARE	INTEREST GROUP COALITION AGAINST MEDICARE
AFL–CIO	American Medical Association
American Nurses Association	American Hospital Association
Council of Jewish Federations and Welfare Funds	Life Insurance Association of America

INTEREST GROUP COALITION	INTEREST GROUP COALITION
FOR MEDICARE (continued)	AGAINST MEDICARE (continued)
American Association of Retired Workers	National Association of Manufacturers
National Association of Social Workers	National Association of Blue Shield Plans
National Farmers Union	American Farm Bureau Federation
The Socialist Party	The Chamber of Commerce
American Geriatrics Society	The American Legion

The ensuing battle, based on this extreme ideological polarization, represented a classic case of class conflict between the haves and the have-nots, between money-providing and service-demanding sectors of society, which assumed the form of an idealistic debate over socialized medicine versus the voluntary "American way" (Marmor, 1973; Lowi, 1964). The bill, which finally passed Congress in 1965, was a scaled-down version of hospital insurance for the aged, reflecting compromises designed to satisfy some of the economic demands imposed by hospitals and insurance companies in the course of the development of the legislation.[14]

Almost from the moment it went into effect the Medicare program encountered problems of administration and implementation. Ironically, those who had been the most vehement opponents of the legislation became some of its chief beneficiaries. Providers of medical services for the elderly were quick to discover ambiguities in the statute and use them to their advantage in the implementation phase of the legislation. Physicians' fees rose consistently at an annual rate of 5–8 percent in the wake of the passage of Medicare (Somers and Somers, 1967). Hospital prices rose by an unprecedented 22 percent between July 1966 and July 1967 in anticipation of additional Medicare-related revenues (Marmor, 1969; Rice and Horowitz, 1968).

While the Medicare issue was capturing the spotlight in 1965, the passage of a far less publicized measure, the Older Americans Act (OAA), went virtually unnoticed. The initial appropriation for the OAA was a thousand times less than that for Medicare

---

[14]For an elaborate account of the political atmosphere surrounding the passage of Medicare, see Marmor (1969, 1973), as well as Stevens and Stevens (1974).

(Pratt, 1976). Yet the long-range impact of the OAA, in providing an ongoing framework for the coordination and enlargement of federal programs benefitting the aged, may prove to be even greater than that of Medicare. The OAA's establishment of the Administration on Aging (AoA) as a federal agency within the executive branch (Department of Health, Education, and Welfare) did much to legitimize and formalize involvement of senior interest groups within the policymaking structure itself. This establishment of an entrenched federal bureaucracy from which to promote and expand elderly interests constituted an important first step toward the "institutionalization" of the senior movement.

INSTITUTIONALIZATION: 1965 TO PRESENT

When established political institutions officially recognize a social problem or movement and begin to devise a series of routine measures for dealing with it, we can speak of the movement as having reached the stage of "institutionalization" (Mauss, 1971).[15] In the institutionalization phase, a movement is characterized by a broad-based, highly coordinated organizational network, a large membership, substantial economic and political resources, and sophisticated division of labor. These attributes are utilized to launch periodic "thrusts" into the political process in the form of lobbying and electoral pressures. This stage typically marks the high point with respect to the influence of a social movement. The mass media and elected representatives take its demands seriously and begin to compete for its favor. Its major spokespersons become frequent speakers at rallies, universities, meetings, and in other public forums.

In an effort to solve the social problems articulated by the movement, governmental representatives introduce and pass legislation. Some or most of the objectives put forth by the movement may become a part of established institutions through the adoption of the movement's proposed programs of reform or through the establishment of entrenched government agencies

---

[15]It should be kept in mind that this process of institutionalization of the movement does not automatically imply the concomitant institutionalization of its proposed program.

representing the interests of the movement's constituency. A social movement at this stage of development is at its point of greatest power, having graduated from being an "input" into the policy-making process to a "withinput" (Easton, 1965; Heisler and Kvavik, 1974).

The current senior movement can most accurately be described as being in the institutionalized phase. Beginning with the 1971 White House Conference on Aging, American leadership elites began to officially recognize and thereby legitimize the right of old-age mass membership groups to receive a sympathetic national forum for their interests and grievances. The 1971 White House conference represented a clear-cut break from the decision-making patterns of earlier years. The conference accelerated the pace of "institutionalization" of elderly interests in several important respects: (1) The conference provided a national forum for *coalition formation* among diverse groups interested in legislation impacting the elderly; (2) the conference *heightened the visibility* of elderly concerns to federal officials and lawmakers; (3) heightened visibility also *increased the level of awareness among elderly persons* in the general public, exposing them to the potential benefits of participation in nationwide, mass-membership senior citizens organizations; and (4) official recognition, opportunities for nationwide coalition formation, heightened visibility, and direct access to policymakers constituted resources that *increased the political leverage* of the elderly (Pratt, 1976; Ward, 1979).

The 1971 White House Conference on Aging generated a wide variety of recommendations for improvements in the status of older Americans in such areas as income maintenance, health services, housing, nutrition, and employment. These included proposals for a 25 percent increase in Social Security payments, enlargement of the Medicare program, the development of housing, transportation, and nutrition programs specifically for the aged, employment training programs for elderly workers, and federal subsidies to support gerontological research. This unique confluence of political pressures on Congress led to the enactment of a number of the conference's suggestions over the next several years. Social Security benefits were increased by 20 percent in 1972, a special nutrition program was initiated, and Medicare was expanded. The watershed of old-age-related legislation that occurred in 1972 was portrayed by Senator Frank Church as ranking in importance only behind 1935 when Social Security was enacted and 1965 when Medicare became law (Fischer, 1979). There is evidence that the National Council of Senior Citizens (NCSC) was very influential in getting the 1972 Social Security Amendments passed; this substantially increased benefit levels and added a provision for automatic cost-of-living adjustments (Pratt, 1981).

The beginnings of the institutionalization phase can be traced back to the establishment of the Administration on Aging in 1965. Location *within* the federal bureaucracy itself gave the senior movement an entrenched niche from which to organize, propose, and consolidate old-age policy advances. The facilities that are available to federal agencies and the monopoly on technical information gave the promotion of many elderly concerns a "withinput" status in the policymaking process, which improved its leverage (Pratt, 1976).

Other evidence that portions of the interests and demands of the senior movement are beginning to become institutionalized can be found in expenditure levels. Following the 1971 White House Conference on Aging, expenditures devoted to the solution of problems related to old age rose at a rate that was without precedent in the history of American old-age policy. Between 1970 and 1976, Social Security expenditures increased from $36 billion to $90 billion. Further evidence of the growing institutionalization of many elderly concerns can be seen in the establishment of automatic Social Security increase mechanisms which insulate such expenditures within the secure budgetary category of relatively uncontrollable costs (Fischer, 1979).

Present senior associations are far more effective than were their forerunners during the incipiency and coalescence phases. Ward (1979) attributes this enhanced effectiveness to several pivotal changes:

1. The needs and demands of the elderly have received wider public acceptance than was the case in the 1930s and 1940s. For example, one study found that 80 percent of a national sample felt there is a real need for people to join together to

work toward improving the conditions and social status of people over 65 (Harris, 1975).

2. Elderly concerns have also achieved wider official acceptance and legitimacy in recent years, exemplified by the 1971 White House conference as well as the establishment of the National Institute on Aging.

3. Senior associations are considerably more sophisticated organizations than was the case earlier in the century (Pratt, 1976). They have larger memberships, better intra-and interorganizational coordination, more extensive economic resources, and are more bureaucratized than was true of earlier senior organizations, such as the Ham and Eggs group and the Townsend Movement. As such, they tend to be less dependent on continuous guidance from individual charismatic leaders for their survival.

FRAGMENTATION AND DEMISE?

Mauss's classification scheme defines two final stages in the "natural history" of a social movement: "fragmentation" and "demise." The irony of social movements is that their success at getting movement objectives incorporated into the established legal framework of society tends to create the conditions for fragmentation and eventual decline. Perceived policy advances with respect to the issues that were central to the concerned public, even if only partial and largely symbolic, tend to undermine support for the movement due to the perception that things have really improved, which may or may not actually be the case. Hard-core activists who insist that fundamental movement objectives remain unrealized will be labeled "extremists" by both the general public and elements of the movement (Ward, 1979). Smelser (1962) describes this process as "the devisive effects of institutional accommodation." Thus "purist" and "reformist" factions are likely to result within the formerly cohesive movement, fighting among themselves over the actual extent of achieved objectives and over strategies for future action. The "demise" stage represents the logical consequence of the "fragmentation" stage, with critical elements of the movement's program, leadership, and membership having been effectively coopted by established political institutions.

Given widespread public knowledge of the problems still faced by many of America's aged, the fragmentation and demise stages are not likely to occur in existing old-age associations in the near future. Due in part to the nature of competitive interest group politics in the American context (Lowi, 1964; Olson, 1965; McConnell, 1966), few *fundamental* changes have been forthcoming within societal institutions impacting the elderly. Despite scattered symbolic victories and a great deal of minimally funded token legislation, the senior movement's goal of a comprehensive national aging policy that would ensure every aged American a comfortable level of economic, medical, and interpersonal security is not yet widely perceived as having been accomplished (Lubove, 1968; Marmor, 1973; Stevens and Stevens, 1974; Estes, 1979). This perceived distance from sought-after policy goals can be expected to fuel the "institutionalized" phase of the movement for some time to come, perhaps interrupted periodically by temporary periods of what Mauss terms "quiescence"—similar to that which occurred in the 1940s. Indeed the point of peak activity within the institutionalized phase may be still to come, as elderly Americans begin to make full use of their acquired political muscle to push for additional and more comprehensive reforms.

There are many who claim that the aged are unlikely to become a significant political force in the foreseeable future (Campbell, 1971; Hudson and Binstock, 1976). They argue that strong political identification with population subgroups defined by such attributes as religion, ethnicity, and social class make political identification with others based on the attribute of old age unlikely. Middle class, college-educated elderly, for example, would have substantially different political preferences than poor Mexican-American elderly. It has also been argued (de Beauvoir, 1972; Rosow, 1974) that since the elderly are a subgroup based on a negatively valued attribute, the stigma attached to old age in American society will present serious barriers to the sense of group solidarity necessary to develop a substantial group consciousness among older Americans.

There is some truth in this analysis. But being heavily influenced by the "interest group pluralist" tradition, it tends to overemphasize the importance of diversity and crosscutting cleavages among the elderly population. Such differences do in fact exist, but they do not necessarily present insurmountable barriers to effective organization on behalf of senior interests. In recent years, for example, the black and women's movements have managed to thrive and achieve positive group identities despite substantial intragroup heterogeneity.

Moreover, in the past, American old-age struggles have not arisen in total isolation. They have arisen alongside the struggles of concurrent movements such as those of labor, minorities, the handicapped, and other welfare constituencies. They have frequently shared in the political momentum generated by such parallel concerns and have thrived on flexible coalitions based on overlapping interests. In the case of the drive to achieve passage of Medicare, for example, labor and old-age groups effectively combined forces around medical insurance legislation, which they perceived to be to their mutual benefit.

The emphasis on interest group pluralism and heterogeneity has tended to lead to pessimistic predictions as to the future of old-age struggles. But those who discuss senior power as if there were already a full-blown "senior movement" with a substantial "age consciousness" and a developing "subculture of the aged" (Rose, 1965*a*, *b*) have tended to exaggerate in the opposite direction, generating naively optimistic projections. It should be kept in mind that much of the activity that gets described as "the aging movement" has been conducted by persons acting *on behalf of* the aged, not by the aged themselves.[16] Moreover, in forming flexible coalitions with labor, minorities, and other disadvantaged constituencies, the elderly have benefited from their proximity and momentum. The major aging legislation of the 1960s and 1970s was in large measure shaped by forces other than organized aging groups (Harootyan, 1981). The elderly, as a *separate* social move-

---

[16]There are, of course, important exceptions to this generalization. In some cases it is the aged themselves who organize and put pressure on government officials. For example, in 1975, seniors in Arizona were able to get the state legislature to pass a law making it illegal to rent or sell property in "adults only" subdivisions to persons with minor children (Anderson and Anderson, 1981).

ment, have yet to develop a mature "age consciousness." Even if they should do so in the near future, they will probably continue to find it highly advantageous to form flexible *ad hoc* coalitions with groups who have overlapping interests on specific issues, in order to maximize their political leverage within the American political system.

In attempting to assess the likely impact of the senior movement in coming years, the political climate of the early 1980s must be taken into consideration.[17] For at least the next several years the strength of the aging movement will be measured more by its ability to resist cutbacks than by its ability to obtain new programs and expanded benefits from existing programs. Its strength will be measured relative to that of other welfare constituencies as all such groups attempt to resist government attempts to cut back on the growth of the welfare state. The gains of the 1960s and 1970s do make the elderly somewhat vulnerable as they undercut their legitimacy as a policy constituency (Hudson, 1978*a*). As the perceived aggregate well-being of the elderly improves relative to other segments of the population, there emerges a dialectical response from these other policy constituencies. Such a response is particularly likely in a "zero-sum society" of the sort that Lester Thurow (1980) has described. Such a dialectical model would lead us to anticipate that the stronger the old-age constituency becomes, and the more successful it is in efforts to obtain an increasing share of societal resources (such as the federal budget), the stronger and more well organized will become those constituencies that oppose this trend. This in turn will tend to reduce the relative power of the elderly, particularly with respect to further increases in their claim on societal resources.

---

[17]During the decade of the 1970s a number of old-age programs shifted from being very politically popular to being sources of much discord. Particularly noteworthy in this context is the Social Security program. As the system has matured, it has become increasingly expensive. This, combined with a weak economy, has made the program much more controversial than anyone imagined it would ever be (Derthick, 1979).

Chapter 5

POLITICAL ATTITUDES AND PARTICIPATION

During the past few years the question of how much power the elderly are capable of wielding as a cohesive political force has begun to draw serious attention from social scientists, as well as government officials. The low fertility rates of recent years are contributing to what will eventually become a dramatic increase in the proportion of elderly in the American electorate. Population projections indicate that by the year 2030 persons over age 65 will constitute 17 percent of the population and 20 percent of the eligible voters (U.S. Bureau of the Census, 1975; Binstock, 1976; Califano, 1981). The trend toward earlier retirement will contribute millions more who identify with elderly issues (U.S. Bureau of the Census, 1976; Binstock, 1974). Moreover, by the beginning of the next century biomedical advances could lead to a significant increase in life expectancy (Rosenfeld, 1977).[1] These possibilities have led scientists and planners to ask whether, or under what conditions, such demographic changes might translate into an increase in political power for the aged—through voting, interest group politics, or continued expansion of social service programs, health delivery systems, and other aspects of the "aging network" (Estes, 1978).

One group of analysts worries that the elderly will come to wield excessive power and influence. Their primary concern is that an essentially unproductive coalition of elderly interests may demand more social welfare benefits than a shrunken work force can bear. The anticipated increase in income transfers from productive workers will, it is feared, create an enormous burden on an already sluggish economy in coming decades.[2]

---

[1]For more discussion of these trends, see Morrison (1979), Peterson et al. (1976), Ragan and Dowd (1974), as well as Bengtson and Cutler (1976:150–156).

[2]Concern over the economic consequences of declining birthrates and a dwindling working population is not just an American phenomenon; the same issue is very much on the minds of government planners in a number of European nations as well (Painton, 1981).

A different group of analysts (typically more oriented toward liberal reforms for disadvantaged groups) worry that in the 1980s a growing public perception of energy and resource scarcity, together with signs of a more general decline in the American economy, may lead to a serious taxpayer backlash against social programs for the elderly. They fear that the political power of the aged may prove insufficient or too poorly organized to counteract these forces. They warn that in an unsympathetic social climate of this sort elderly needs for basic necessities such as adequate nutrition, heating in winter, and medical care may be compromised. These analysts point to harbingers of this trend in the "taxpayer revolt" of the late 1970s and predict that the trend will continue or even expand over the next several decades.[3] In keeping with this line of reasoning a *New York Times*/CBS News poll conducted in late 1979 found that 71 percent of Americans favored social program cutbacks to combat inflation.[4]

Before attempting to assess whether this combination of demographic and economic changes is more likely to produce an increase or a decrease in the political influence of the aged, it is relevant to first examine the current situation with respect to political attitudes, behavior, and influence.

In the present analysis we argue that "senior power" has been both overestimated and underestimated as a political force. There has been a tendency to overestimate the actual political influence of the aged today, while at the same time there has been a tendency to underestimate the potential for an increase in influence in years to come.

The elderly are perceived as being more effectively organized than they are. For example, the Gray Panthers organization has been given a great deal of visibility by the media, but in reality there is little grass roots political organization behind it. Many

---

[3]A sense of the substantive issues involved in the clash of viewpoints between these two groups of policy analysts can be found in Cook (1979), Hudson (1978a:436–439), Broder (1973), and Binstock (1976). Particularly revealing is an exchange that occurred in the *New York Times* between researchers Rabushka and Jacobs (1980) and chairman of the House Select Committee on Aging, Claude Pepper (1980).

[4]The *New York Times*/CBS News poll was based on telephone interviews of 1,385 voting-age Americans from October 29, to November 3, 1979 (*see New York Times*, 1979).

people, particularly in the popular press, assume that the elderly constitute an influential senior citizen block of voters, but there is little evidence that the "gray power" movement has been able to exert substantial impact on public policy. One of the conclusions of the previous chapter was that the elderly have for the most part made their programmatic gains in coalition with other more powerful groups. The programs for the elderly of the 1960s and 1970s were due more to the power and influence of advocates on behalf of the elderly than to the influence of a "senior vote."

Conversely, there is a tendency to underestimate the potential political power that could emerge in the future. This tendency to underestimate the elderly's potential for political influence stems largely from misconceptions about the political attitudes and political behavior of the aged. Existing evidence suggests that the elderly are much more flexible in their attitudes and more interested and involved in political affairs than is often assumed. Evidence concerning the predispositions of the aged toward politics points to a potential for sustained political involvement, once an issue becomes perceived as salient. Whether this potential will in fact translate into concrete gains in elderly political clout is, however, much more difficult to predict.

In coming years the elderly may very well remain the relatively weak political force that they are today. On the other hand, a plausible case can be made that they could come to possess considerably expanded power and influence. A number of social, economic, and political changes are expected to take place over the next fifty years that would greatly increase the probability of this latter outcome, although they do not ensure its occurrence.

The tendency to underestimate potential elderly influence is related to a number of common misconceptions and stereotypes about the political behavior of older adults. In the present analysis we shall look at what is known about the political attitudes of the aged and their political behavior (participation) to see to what extent and under what conditions it would be possible for the elderly to become a major political force. Among the political attitudes of the aged, we will examine evidence with regard to levels of political interest, information, party identification, and alienation. We will also look closely at the stereotype of the elderly as inherently more conservative than other age groups.

POLITICAL ATTITUDES OF OLDER PERSONS

Aging and Conservatism

During the late 1960s, a popular expression among disenchanted youth was, "Don't trust anyone over thirty!" It was accepted as an article of faith among young people that "old" and "conservative" were synonymous terms. So strong was this belief that when radical Yippie leader Jerry Rubin reached the age of thirty he promptly altered the slogan to, "Don't trust anyone over forty!" rather than risk being identified as a conservative (Rubin, 1970). This view of older persons as inherently conservative has hardly been limited to the 1960s radicals. The theme can be traced back at least as far as the ancient Greeks and Romans.

Many of our assumptions about the political attitudes and behaviors of older people are a product of broader societal stereotypes that portray the elderly as "set in their ways." As with most stereotypes, these have at least a partial basis in reality. Also, like most stereotypes they can breed serious distortions, which become justifications for social prejudices and discriminatory practices directed against older persons.

Aging does not necessarily lead to more conservative political attitudes and behaviors. Under certain circumstances and on certain types of issues the opposite clearly holds true, with persons becoming more liberal and even radical as they age. To portray the elderly as simply becoming more conservative obscures both the diversity and the complexity of political attitudes among older persons.

Most studies of the political attitudes and orientations of older people have focused on those issues for which the elderly do in fact tend to be more conservative, often ignoring more liberal elderly stances or treating them as exceptions. Not surprisingly, such investigations have usually concluded that there is a tendency toward increasing conservatism with age.[5] This dispropor-

---

[5]An example of this selective research strategy is Glamser (1974:549–554). In a multivariate analysis of the relationship of age to conservative opinions, Glamser chooses race relations, patriotism, and law enforcement as the component issue domains for construction of his conservatism scale.

tionate emphasis on the conservative traits of the elderly has contributed to the perpetuation of popular stereotypes that portray them as stubborn, rigid, old-fashioned, and unwilling to change politically.

Research conducted in a variety of western societies has suggested that the aged are at least marginally more conservative in the aggregate than are their younger counterparts. This pattern has been found to apply not only to their ideological stances toward politics in general, but also to their positions on a number of specific issues, e.g. housing integration, abortion, and government intervention in the economy. If one looks at older persons' preferences for a conservative party as indicative of underlying conservative attitudes, it is possible to cite additional evidence. Several studies have found stronger Republican party identification among older-age groups in the United States than among younger ones (Campbell et al., 1960; Crittenden, 1962; Riley and Foner, 1968). Evidence of a similar relationship between aging and conservative party preference exists for other western nations such as France, Italy, Germany, and Great Britain (Lipset, 1959; Rose, 1964; McKenzie and Silver, 1968; Butler and Stokes, 1971). In most cases this relationship continues to hold when both socioeconomic status and educational level are controlled. Taken at face value, the above evidence would seem to suggest that there is a "conservative" tendency for persons to drift toward the "right" as they age, which holds across cultural contexts in a variety of western industrialized nations.

Studies of the stability of political orientations over time, however, have revealed a more complex picture than just a "conservative move to the right" with the progression of age. There is considerable evidence that older persons retain many of the political attitudes and orientations they developed earlier in life. Orientations deemed "liberal" by society in an earlier era (which constituted the formative years of political socialization for a contemporary-aged generation) may become socially defined as "conservative" as the person ages. For instance, if little or no change has occurred over the years in the attitude toward social welfare of a woman whose pre-New Deal sentiments were in her own day considered "liberal," are we justified in portraying her as

having "moved to the right" or as having "become more conservative with age" on social welfare issues? Conversely, consider the
man whose "isolationist" stance against American foreign involvements were considered conservative in the 1920s and who remained
isolationist with respect to American involvement in Vietnam
during the 1960s. Did he actually "move to the left" or "become
more liberal?"[6]

Thus at least part of the observed "shift to the right" with age
may be a product of society's definition of a person's political
stance, not merely a shift of perspective within the individual per
se. Whether or not the political orientations of older persons are
conservative is a combined product of both personal and social-
historical factors. Aging citizens become a "conservatizing" force
within the political community relative to the altered value structures of successive political contexts into which they find themselves thrust by the onward march of time. American political
culture in general has experienced an overall shift in a liberal
direction over the past fifty years, and the trend has been somewhat slower and less pronounced among older age groups (Glenn,
1974). This age discrepancy in rate of change has had the effect of
exaggerating the apparent conservatism of older citizens. The
"time lag in attitude change" explanation would predict, for example, that if the current somewhat more conservative trend in the
American political climate were to continue undisturbed over the
next half century, the comparatively "liberal" generation who
experienced their formative years in the social ferment of the
1960s might well come to be regarded as "liberal old fogies" by
(conservative) early twenty-first century youth.[7]

Studies of party identification (from which we can infer underlying attitudes) provide additional evidence that attitude stability,

---

[6]In the period between the two world wars, the dominant approach to American foreign
policy was one of isolation. The United States refused to join the League of Nations and the
World Court, discouraged international trade by raising tariff barriers, and adopted neutrality
legislation. Against this background, "antiwar" stances opposing foreign involvements were
the *prevailing* popular sentiment and constituted an argument to preserve the status quo in foreign affairs. This is in contrast to the situation in the 1960s, in which the reverse became true.

[7]It is also quite conceivable that some views considered liberal in the 1960s will come to be
defined as conservative by the early part of the next century.

rather than "conservatism," may be the key factor that increases with age. These have shown that both the strength and the stability of a person's identification with a political party increase with age. Aged voters are less likely to identify themselves as "independents," and they are less likely to engage in split-ticket voting than is the case for younger age groups. One reason is that party attachments, once formed, act to reduce ambiguity and to provide a sense of security. Voting experience through a series of successive elections is a form of political learning in which reinforcement of an initial party attachment occurs due to the psychological rewards of simplicity and clarity (Butler and Stokes, 1971).

However, caution is called for when interpreting these patterns. Evidence of an increase in stability of political orientations with age might lead one to the conclusion that older people are necessarily less flexible and less willing to change in their political views. Again, conventional stereotypes of the political propensities of the aged can bias our evaluation of the evidence if we are not careful. The "primacy principle" has been considerably overstated in the literature on childhood socialization and ego development, and this has led to the faulty assumption that aged persons will necessarily tend to be highly inflexible in their political views once those views have become established (Kellerman, 1979; Searing et al., 1975). A growing body of evidence casts serious doubt on a "hardening of the attitudes with age" interpretation. Several studies have shown that the aged are both capable and willing to alter their political views when circumstances suggest the need for such a change (Glenn and Hefner, 1972).

The simplistic view of older persons as merely "conservative" or "inflexible" politically becomes further suspect if we break down the concept of conservatism into attitudes toward specific issue domains. While the elderly do tend to be somewhat more conservative than younger people on certain types of issues, on others they maintain liberal views in line with the rest of society, and on some issues clearly hold more liberal views than the rest of society.

A variety of studies conducted since the mid-1950s suggest that on select issues persons may become somewhat more conservative as they age. On issues involving civil liberties and civil rights, the predominant attitudes of older persons have been less favorable toward social change than have younger age groups. They are less supportive of housing integration (Hunt, 1960), of busing to achieve racial integration in schools (Killian and Haer, 1958), and of federal intervention to protect civil rights in general. They have also been found to be comparatively more opposed to the idea of a black or a Catholic as president, women's rights, abortion, and the legalization of marijuana (Erskine, 1965; Cutler and Schmidhauser, 1975).

As the above evidence illustrates, the contemporary generation of older people are in general less sanguine about government intervention and expansion than are their younger counterparts. Older persons are more likely to oppose nationalization of industry (Eysenck, 1954; Riley and Foner, 1968), government involvement in central planning of the national economy (Riley and Foner, 1968), and government controls (Cantril, 1951). They tend to be more opposed to public expenditures on educational issues (Campbell, 1971; Clemente, 1975) and government funding of parochial schools (Riley and Foner, 1968).

On issues of foreign policy, the elderly have been consistently more opposed to foreign involvements (Campbell, 1971). Earlier in the century "isolationist" stances were considered conservative but are now classified alongside "dovish" and "antiwar" sentiments.

On political issues that are perceived by the elderly as directly relevant to their own interests as older persons, however, they tend to hold more "liberal" attitudes, often doing so in blatant contradiction to a generally conservative orientation. For instance, where government intervention in the economy is perceived as potentially beneficial to their interests as aged persons, their general opposition to such intervention is overridden by pragmatic considerations. Older persons are more likely than younger groups to favor government-sponsored, low-cost medical care, and they are more likely to favor Social Security tax increases to support higher pension benefits (Erskine, 1961; Campbell, 1962, 1971). On "law and order" issues, elderly persons are more supportive of active government intervention than are younger groups (Campbell,

1971; Glamser, 1974).[8] They are also more favorable toward public housing and public ownership of electrical power (Riley and Foner, 1968). Here again, many older persons are willing to ignore any general conservative ideological predispositions they may have for the sake of concrete benefits which are in their interests as aged persons. Since the need-oriented public policies that would benefit the elderly are most often associated with liberal political positions, this becomes an especially important qualification.

Apparently attitude change occurs rather easily (and flexibly) on clearly defined "elderly issues." For instance, they are more likely than younger groups to favor federal programs to provide public housing (in their interests as aged persons), and yet they are less likely to favor federal intervention to enforce racial nondiscrimination in housing (not specifically perceived as in their interests). This frequently encountered pattern of specific-issue pragmatism among the elderly could have important implications for the development of a cohesive senior power constituency in the future. Available evidence suggests that any conservative ideological predispositions they might have would be unlikely to constitute major impediments to the development of solidarity around elderly concerns.

While the extent of elderly conservatism is typically overstated, there is some truth to the observation. Certain aspects of many aged persons' attitudes toward politics are best described as conservative and perhaps even as inflexible. However, it is useful to make an attempt to understand the aspirations of older persons, as they relate to what appear to be conservative and inflexible political views. As one's life settles down somewhat following the adjustments of early adulthood, interactions with society become more structured and stable. This typically expresses itself in greater stability of political attitudes and in stronger identification with a political party, interest group, or labor union. Since the elderly have usually developed a deeper sense of personal identification with the existing social order (having been instrumental in its

---

[8]A recent national survey conducted by the National Council on the Aging (Harris, 1975) identified "fear of crime" as the second most serious problem (next to health) the elderly perceive themselves to face.

construction and its maintenance over the years) they may react defensively to proposed revisions by younger groups. Such revisions are often perceived as jeopardizing their stability and implying that their lifelong efforts have been substandard, futile, or meaningless.

When "arrogant" young reformers began hurling disrespectful insults at the existing social order during the 1960s period, advocating replacement of "outmoded social institutions" with new ones, many older people reacted defensively, often with a sense of moral outrage. The following excerpt from an article featured in *The New York Times* in 1966 captures the tone of such defensive responses:

> It is high time for someone . . . to argue against victory by the young in their warfare with the old. . . . The older generation is bad, youth says, and only youth can be relied upon to act with pure motives. From that notion stems the moral arrogance so noticeable in the pronouncements of youth leaders. We must have lost our moral nerve if we cannot say, at least to ourselves, that such accusation comes with poor grace from a generation saved by its parents from Dachau and Belsen; a generation saved from physical destruction in World War II and political destruction in the cold war; a generation in which the diseases that slowly killed Shubert and Keats . . . can be arrested (Brown, 1966:57).

Thus older persons' underlying needs for a sense of stability and security and their identification of self-worth with the social order they helped construct can lead to a defense of the status quo. This conservatism may express itself as a healthy respect for hard-won traditional institutions. But, when in response to social pressures to adopt unfamiliar new values and life-styles, it may also assume the form of political rigidity and fear of change.[9]

"Conservatism" as a political label is misleading to the extent that it implies older persons necessarily shift to the right politically due to changes that occur primarily within the individual with the passage of time. Given existing research findings that show increases in attitude consistency, strength of party identification, and preference for stability, one would expect the aged to

[9]For more discussion of the psychology of elderly attitudes toward society and politics, see Erikson (1950), Bengtson and Kuypers (1971:249–260), Kellerman (1979), Riley and Foner (1968), Rosow (1973; 1974; 1976), Lowenthal (1975), and Neugarten (1964).

appear to move to the left relative to the rest of the population
whenever the wider political culture shifts decisively in a conservative direction. In some societies, and in certain historical periods, the aged have been more liberal or further left politically
than younger age groups. One example from recent history is the
disproportionate support the Nazi movement in Germany received
from younger segments of the population. Older groups were less
enthusiastic about ultra-right-wing fascist practices and beliefs,
having developed many of their "liberal" political orientations
during the Weimar period (Foner, 1974). As illustrated in Figure
5-1, the tendency of youth to be inclined to idealism and extremism and the corresponding tendency of the aged to be more pragmatic and moderate provides us with a better explanation of their
respective political orientations than does a left-right, liberal-
conservative continuum.[10]

There are many other historical examples in which the aged
have been further left politically than their younger cohorts. The
original generation of communist revolutionaries who fought to

---

[10]This two-dimensional approach to modeling elderly political attitudes is based in part on a
related discussion by Lipset (1959:173).

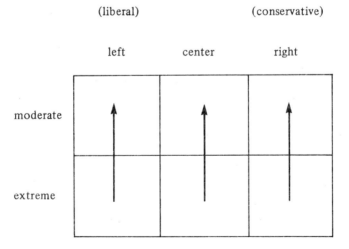

Figure 5-1. Movement of political attitudes during the aging process: a two-
dimensional model.

establish the People's Republic in 1949 has since that time found it increasingly difficult to instill the original revolutionary enthusiasm in successive generations of comparatively more conservative party members and peasants (Pye, 1968, 1972). Similarly, Cuban youth are less supportive of Fidel Castro's revolutionary socialist regime than are their elders who lived through the revolution (Foner, 1974). In Swedish society, today's youth are often indifferent to the social democratic reforms that inspired their grandparents to great heights of passion in the 1930s and 1940s.

Given the negative connotations associated with the idea of elderly conservatism and given the considerably distorted stereotypes of the aged as cranky, inflexible change-resisters, perhaps a better description would be to say that older persons become more pragmatic, stable, and moderate in their views with advancing age, *regardless of whether those views were originally liberal or conservative in emphasis.* With increasing experience in the political realm, persons usually (but not always) become less inclined toward extreme, idealistic views of either the right or the left. Their often-observed tendencies to become less tolerant of nonconformity and change (Campbell et al., 1960; Stouffer, 1955) are better understood as movement toward the attitudinal mean of their culture, due to their extensive socialization in its norms. Any generalization about "the aged" that implicitly assumes a homogeneous population aggregate obscures both the diversity and the complexity of political orientations among older persons. Aging is not necessarily accompanied by more conservative views and behavior. Any number of examples can be given of specific individuals who moved to the left rather than the right as they grew older. Similarly, there are many well-known individuals who have moved to the left or retained a leftist perspective even on issues about which the elderly tend to hold more conservative views.[11]

---

[11]Supreme Court Justice William O. Douglas embraced some of his most controversial causes during his later years. Eighty-five-year-old architect-inventor Buckminster Fuller has recently proposed idealistic scenerios for the future of "spaceship earth," which make even the most ardent liberals blush. Defense attorney William Kunstler has espoused increasingly radical causes as he has grown older, acting as counsel in the "Chicago Seven" and "Wounded Knee" trials, among others.

The Politics of Aging

Mass Media and Political Interest

A common misconception regarding the elderly is that level of interest in political affairs declines with age as part of a general process of gradual "disengagement" from active involvement in social life. Several studies have shown that the percentage of people who answer "no opinion" to questions on political surveys increases with advancing age (Turk et al., 1966; Gergen and Back, 1966). This has been interpreted as indicating that the elderly become disengaged from political involvement. However, if one compares young and old persons with the same level of education (the elderly are consistently less educated as a group), older people are found to be *more likely* to form political opinions than their younger counterparts (Glenn, 1969). This pattern holds true with respect to both national and international affairs. Moreover, older persons exhibit stronger interest in current public figures than do those who are younger; again, if educational level is properly controlled so as to make age groups comparable (Glenn, 1969).

Several studies indicate that there is a more or less linear relationship between degree of political interest and age, although the largest increase occurs during the transition from youth to middle age, rather than from middle age to old age. Perhaps more convincing has been the finding, first established by Glenn and Grimes (1968), that the highest level of political interest is consistently found among persons age 60 and above.[12] Using data from a Gallup poll, Glenn and Grimes report that 35 percent of persons 60 and over say they have a great deal of interest in politics, compared with 23 percent of those between 40 and 59, and 19 percent of those 21 to 39. This pattern holds for both sexes and across most educational levels.[13] While a few studies have indicated a decline in public opinion formation with age, countervailing influences such as level of education apparently more than compensate for this trend if they are properly controlled for.

---

[12]See also Glenn (1969).

[13]Among female high school graduates, for instance, 16 percent of the 21–39 age group report high interest in politics, compared with 26 percent of those age 40–59, and 48 percent of those over age 60 (Glenn and Grimes, 1968).

Political interest is closely intertwined with level of information about politics. Research findings from a variety of sources indicate that older persons follow political events more closely in the media (television, newspapers, radio) than is the case among younger groups. This high level of awareness when considered together with evidence of high interest in political affairs has important implications for the development of senior power. Elderly persons have more available leisure time than other age groups. Several recent surveys indicate that the elderly use television more extensively than do persons at any other point in the life cycle. Comstock et al. (1978) report a positive correlation between age and increased viewing of television. A 1976 Nielson study estimates that women over 50 watch about 5 hours per day, and a Harris (1974) poll showed people over 80 still watching over 2 hours per day. Watching television is the single most time-consuming activity among the aged in the United States, and this has apparently been the case since television first came into widespread use in the 1950s (Meyersohn, 1961; Schramm, 1969; Davis et al., 1976; Comstock et al., 1978).

This high rate of television use is especially significant in light of the programming preferences of the elderly. Older persons, particularly those over 65 years of age, prefer news and public affairs programming to other types (Schramm, 1969; Hwang, 1974; Davis, 1975; Comstock et al., 1978). They are comparatively more attentive to political campaigns than are younger persons (Dimmick et al., 1979). They are more likely to seek "practical" knowledge about political events as opposed to "academic" knowledge. Comstock et al. (1978) report that the elderly use television for information more than for any other purpose. Hwang (1974) found that persons pay comparatively more attention to programs dealing with health, housing, finances, and social security as they grow older. Entertainment becomes less important for them than practical information (Davis, 1971). These findings corroborate the tendency noted earlier for older persons to become more pragmatic and realistic in their politically related tastes as they age.

Thus far, few investigations have made an effort to distinguish between media use by the "young-old" and the "old-old." Typically, they are simply lumped together into an all-inclusive "aged" category, which obscures the considerable differences between the two age groups, particularly in level of physical infirmity. Among the "old-old" (75 and over), available data are especially sketchy. Television viewing apparently reaches a peak at around age 70, then declines somewhat, although it remains higher than during earlier phases in the life cycle (Harris, 1974).[14]

It is particularly relevant to the political potential of the aged that television, as a mass medium, tends to cut across social class, ethnic, and educational differences. Variables such as education and income have little impact on the extent of television use (Comstock et al., 1978; Young, 1979). Thus television, as a homogenizing mass medium to which the elderly turn for information regarding their environment, could in the future act to foster unity among elderly persons who come from different ethnic, social class, and educational backgrounds. Daniel Lerner (1958) has demonstrated convincingly that use of communications media and the development of the capacity for interpersonal empathy are related, and this has been corroborated repeatedly in subsequent mass communication studies. Young (1979), for example, suggests that informational television use among the elderly indicates an expanded sensitivity to their surrounding environment. Also, there is considerable evidence to suggest that many older persons use television in order to combat disengagement (Schramm, 1969; Hess, 1974, Davis et al., 1976). Prolonged societal involvement is likely to be accompanied by continued political involvement.

Unlike television use, newspaper readership declines slightly with advancing age, especially after seventy (Comstock et al., 1978). This may be due to discomfort or inconvenience associated with reading small print, rather than to declining interest per se (Young, 1979). Despite this slight decline, newspapers continue to be important sources of public affairs information for the elderly. As persons age they pay less attention to the comic and sports pages of the newspaper. This is accompanied by an increase in

---

[14]Elderly women, who live longer and are therefore disproportionately represented among the old-old, watch more television per day than do men of the same age (Schramm, 1969; Davis et al., 1976 Comstock et al., 1978).

reading of public affairs news and editorials (Schramm and White, 1954; Young, 1979).

While disengagement theorists may or may not be accurate in portraying old age as a process of gradual withdrawal from societal attachments, the evidence clearly suggests that no appreciable disengagement of interest, opinion, and awareness occurs with respect to the political realm. Both political interest and level of information remain high well into old age and frequently increase in intensity. With higher education levels among the elderly in the future we can expect more interest and awareness, and this could increase the potential for political mobilization around aging issues.

Equally significant in its implications for senior power as patterns of media use by the elderly is media content about the elderly. Negative portrayals of old age abound in the mass media, and their effects can be just as stigmatizing and restrictive to a positive elderly group identity as similar stereotypes have been to blacks, women, and other groups.

Data which presently exist on mass media portrayals of older persons deal mostly with images of the elderly on television. One type of media misrepresentation of the elderly that has implications for their political clout is the consistent underrepresentation of their numbers. In one survey, three out of four television viewers agreed that "on the whole, television programs show young people, not old people" (Harris, 1974). The same study found that only 1.5 percent of a sample of 464 prime time characters were cast as being over 65. Similarly, a study by Francher (1973) revealed that only 2 percent of a random sample of 100 television commercials portrayed older characters.[15]

The number of older reporters and anchorpersons on network news programs is also disproportionately small, due in part to the impact of mandatory retirement policies on network news. Regardless of their level of competence as professional journalists, reporters and anchorpersons tend to suddenly disappear from view when they reach sixty-five. (An example of this was Eric Severeid's

---

[15]This statistic can be compared with 11 percent—the proportion of the United States population that is over age 65 (Harris, 1978).

disappearance from CBS Evening News following his sixty-fifth birthday.)

When older characters do appear on television, their roles are usually negative. A study of prime time dramatic characters by Aronoff (1974) found that older males were much more frequently portrayed as "bad guys" than were younger persons. Similarly, older females were more likely to be portrayed as "failures," whereas younger persons were more often portrayed as successes. Gerbner (1977) found that televised dramas disproportionately portray elderly women as victims. Three older female characters are portrayed as victims to every one portrayed as superior or dominant. Aronoff (1974) concludes that in daytime television drama "aging is associated with increasing evil, failure, and unhappiness." Hemming and Ellis (1976) asked readers of *Retirement Living* magazine to choose three adjectives from a list of twelve words that describe how persons over 60 are depicted on major television programs. The three adjectives most frequently chosen were "ridiculous," "decrepit," and "childish." Of the total choices, 67 percent identified negative attributes.

Images of old age in media advertising can also be highly negative. Commercial advertising frequently plays upon fears of loss of vitality and youthfulness in its attempts to promote products and create markets. Advertisements imply that becoming old is necessarily a disagreeable experience, that aging is ugly, that the elderly are constantly plagued with constipation, denture problems, baldness, unsightly facial wrinkles and spots, and chronic backaches—all of which require a plethora of commerical panaceas in order to restore the look and feel of youth.

The effect of such commercial portrayals, if perhaps not the conscious intention, is to promote ideals of youthful beauty which accentuate existing unfavorable stereotypes. To the extent that media commercialism continues to promote such stereotypic portrayals, the "old is (or can be) beautiful" mentality necessary for the development of a positive elderly group identity will find it difficult to thrive. As is the case for persons of all age groups, the elderly have a strong need for role models. Since the mass media, particularly television, perform an increasingly important function in combatting disengagement and providing surrogate companionship in the later years, the types of role models available through the media take on added significance. If only heavily stereotyped role models are available for elderly consumption, they will tend to become self-fulfilling prophecies to the extent that older persons incorporate them into their identity structures.

The mass media of communication, due to their central role in the dissemination of information and images and to their indisputable overall impact on society, will necessarily be a key battleground in attempts to combat age stereotypes in coming decades. Television, in particular, holds the power either to reinforce or to fracture existing negative images of old age.

That substantial attitude change can be accomplished was demonstrated in a national survey of 1,104 adults conducted to evaluate the impact of "Getting On," a nonfictional television program about the elderly. The study found that "Getting On" succeeded in helping to change the audience's negative images of older persons (U.S. House of Representatives, 1977). Prior to the program, only 15 percent of younger respondents (18–39 years old) perceived older people as "up to date." After watching the program, 40 percent reported that they considered older persons "up to date." Similarly, 27 percent considered the elderly to be "open-minded" before the program, as compared with 46 percent afterwards. The number of people who perceived them as "energetic" climbed from 25 percent to 49 percent as a result of the program. Those who saw them as possessing "keen minds" went from 27 percent to 52 percent, and those who felt older persons were "capable of managing" rose from 50 percent to 66 percent. The researchers concluded that television has the capacity to influence people's perceptions of the elderly, and that this capacity can operate either to reinforce negative stereotypes or to build positive images of older persons.

One impediment which could seriously inhibit the expansion of senior power via the mass media is the profit orientation of the broadcast industry. Commercial advertisers, in conjunction with Nielson ratings, largely determine the style and frequently also the content of most programming. Their assumption (which is only partially accurate today and will become even less so in years ahead) is that the older age group is not a good source of purchasing power.

While commercial advertising has thus far held tenaciously to its promotion of "youthful vigor and beauty" ideals to sell its products, there are signs of change. Some advertisers have begun making concessions to a more positive view of old people and the aging process. The frequency of appearance of older people in commercials in nonstereotyped roles has increased somewhat over the past few years. For instance, they have become members of the "Pepsi® generation," which had previously been the exclusive province of the young. The real significance of such changes may be that they foreshadow the reversal of past advertising assumptions that older persons do not constitute an important consumer market. As the percentage of elderly in the population continues to increase over the next several decades, we can expect advertisers to begin to relax some of their prejudices against the elderly. As the elderly become recognized as more important consumers, greater sensitivity to their media portrayals is likely to follow suit, since to do otherwise would be to risk alienating a potentially profitable market.

Elderly persons have a vital need for age-specific information about their environment. Improved access to such information through the media would help them better control important aspects of their life situation both individually and collectively. The dependency of commercial broadcasting on its marketplace economic base, which tends to discourage age-specific programming in favor of mass appeals, is beginning to be superseded in some respects. The creation of a fourth PBS network, which is intentionally noncommercial and therefore minimally subject to commercial constraints, is a step in the direction of filling this need for programming which is age-specific in content.

Especially promising in its possibilities for specialized programming for the elderly is cable television. This technological advance, which has begun to receive acceptance in major metropolises, has the capacity to open up virtually limitless numbers of additional channels. In so doing it creates opportunities for variety in programming, which could cater to special interest groups such as the elderly. In addition, cable television has much greater potential than large network television for opening up visual communications media to use by non-professionals and therefore it would be a boon to many disadvantaged groups including the aged. These potentials are inherent in cable television as a medium, but thus far they remain largely unrealized.[16]

Other technological trends may also have implications for the ability of the elderly to organize around age-specific causes. For example, the increasingly interactive nature of modern communications opens up the possibility of access to vast stores of information, for either personal use or in political organizing, through home computers and interactive consoles. *The electronics revolution has reduced the importance of physical distance and with it the importance of physical mobility.* If "electronic democracy" is adopted, the ability to get to the polls may become less relevant as a determinant of elderly electoral participation. This is especially important for the old-old, for whom lack of mobility typically presents a greater problem. Thus, the *lower mobility threshold* made possible by the electronics revolution in mass communications could have important electoral consequences, in combination with the steadily increasing percentage of older adults in the total population. Since social disengagement is a result not just of physical infirmity per se but also of reduced mobility, emerging communications possibilities such as teleconferencing will yield new opportunities for the formation of senior interest groups and voluntary associations around age-specific concerns.

If "electronic democracy" were to become widely adopted as a more efficient and convenient means of public input into the policy-making process, the political consequences associated with this transcending of mobility limitations would be particularly relevant for the elderly, as their age-related disadvantage would be minimized. Voting and "instant public opinion polling" on important local or national issues would be reduced to the mere choice of which button to press on an interactive television console. Even

---

[16]Another recent technological breakthrough that could in time help to disseminate more age-specific informational programming is the videocassette playback system. Available for use either at home or in libraries, videocassette programming could provide a substantial informational resource to the elderly for use in their (considerable) leisure time and is devoid of commercial messages. Videocassettes would allow them greater freedom of choice in their media-consumption habits, both in terms of personal time scheduling and in type of content.

the most bedridden of the old-old would be able to manage this effort. (Scenarios of senile patients making unwise choices are largely unfounded, since "truly senile" responses would tend to randomize in their effects on electoral or public opinion poll outcomes.)

Considered together with evidence of high elderly political interest and awareness levels, trends such as these suggest that over the next several decades we can reasonably expect mass media technology to enhance the elderly's potential for effective mobilization around political issues they perceive as important. As a caveat, however, this outcome is contingent on two general developments: (1) a marked reduction in media-reinforced stereotyping of the aged, reflecting an increased sensitivity among both members of the broadcast industry and federal regulatory agencies (FCC, FTC) to the social effects of perpetuating such stereotypes; and (2) an increase in elderly access to age-specific programming, so that they have adequate information regarding resources within their environment with which to gain more control over conditions that affect them. Without these minimal media-related preconditions, significant expansion of senior political activism would be less likely.

The ultimate political ramifications of media-facilitated attitude reversals such as those we have outlined should not be underestimated. Transforming pejorative mass media interpretations of older persons into positive portrayals and replacing assumptions of powerlessness with assumptions of potential power would, if it were to occur, yield substantial increases in age consciousness.

Political Party Identification

Self-identification with a political party provides us with another indicator of the extent of elderly involvement in political affairs. To the extent that meaningful ideological distinctions can be made between political parties, party identification can tell us something about an aged person's ideological preferences. Several studies have indicated that party identification shows no sign of declining with age; in fact, the opposite is usually the case. The classic "American voter" study, conducted by Angus Campbell et al. (1960), was among the first to demonstrate that both strength and stability of party attachment increase with age. Since then, a variety of subsequent studies of American voters have arrived at the same conclusion: aged citizens are the least likely age category to identify as independents and are less prone to "split ticket" voting (Nie et al., 1976).

This pattern appears to hold in other nations as well. A similar investigation conducted in Great Britain by Butler and Stokes (1971) confirms the earlier Campbell findings, indicating that strength of partisan self-image continues to increase with age through the eighties. Of those who were age 20, 47 percent described themselves as being "very" or "fairly strongly" attached to a political party. This increased to 65 percent among those age 31–40, to 73 percent among those aged 41–50, and to 88 percent among those over age 80. In an effort to explain why this steady increase in strength of party identification occurs, Butler and Stokes employed a social learning perspective. They hypothesized that voter participation over a series of elections is a political (social) learning experience in which "reinforcement" of party attachment occurs through "rewards" of simplicity and clarity.

Although recent studies indicate that party identification is twice as strong among persons over sixty-five as among those in their twenties, these findings must be interpreted with caution. Results from cross-sectional studies such as these must be considered within the context of broader historical trends. The past few decades in the United States have been marked by consistent overall declines in party affiliation *within the entire electorate*. This trend has been accompanied by a dramatic rise in "issue voting" and in the proportion of the electorate who are independent voters. Americans have begun voting more on the basis of isolated issues of personal interest to them and on the basis of the perceived leadership qualities and abilities of individual candidates, rather than relying on the former practice of using parties as a guide. These overall declines in party identification have been most pronounced among recent generations entering the electorate and have developed more slowly among older generations (Nie et al., 1976). This has had the effect of creating an exaggerated impression of *age* differences in strength of party identification which are at least partially attributable to *generational* differences.

This steady, pronounced decline in party identification has taken place more slowly among the aged. Their generation was socialized politically in an era when parties were more accepted as effective channels for political action and expression. Voters were more likely to follow their party line and to vote a straight party ticket. If present trends continue with respect to declines in party identification, we can expect to see considerably lower rates of party attachment among the elderly when today's youth reach retirement age. We can also expect this trend to narrow the gap between young and old voters in strength of party identification.

Considering the proportion of elderly voters who identify with each of the two major parties in the United States, one finds that approximately as many of today's elderly identify with the Republican party as with the Democratic party (Campbell et al., 1960; Riley and Foner, 1968). Since the proportion of Democrats is higher among younger segments of the electorate, this might lead one to conclude that as people age, a shift takes place toward Republican party affiliation. Upon closer scrutiny, however, it becomes apparent that this pattern resembles the illusory "movement toward the right with age" phenomenon mentioned earlier in the discussion of conservatism. Recent electoral research has shown that people do not appear to change their party affiliation from Democratic to Republican as they age (Cutler, 1969). Moreover, a number of analysts maintain that a majority of Democrats should emerge among the aged now that those who entered the electorate during or after the New Deal are reaching old age (Riley and Foner, 1968; Abramson, 1974). Also, past studies have often failed to properly control for socioeconomic status. Republicans survive longer due to their higher socioeconomic position and are therefore disproportionately represented among those at the older end of the age spectrum.

Continuing declines in political party identification, accompanied by increases in issue voting and independent voting, suggest that traditional party loyalties may be less of a divisive factor among future generations of older people. This trend is particularly important with respect to party-based splits along socioeconomic lines, which have heretofore created considerable diversity among older voters. The reduction of these partisan divisions could open up new possibilities for organization of elderly coalitions around age-specific issues.

Political Alienation

Investigations of the relationship between age and political alienation have focused largely on alienation among youth. This youth emphasis was especially popular in research conducted during the turbulent decade of the 1960s (Kenniston, 1965; Whittaker and Watts, 1969; Friedenberg, 1969). Until recently, patterns of political alienation among the elderly have received less attention.

There is still much disagreement as to the definition, appropriate measurement, and conceptual usefulness of "alienation" as a theoretical construct. The most widely used formulation of the concept, proposed by Seeman (1972, 1975), distinguishes six dimensions of the experience of alienation: powerlessness, self-estrangement, cultural estrangement, social isolation, normlessness, and meaninglessness.[17]

As older persons become progressively more isolated and "disengaged" from mainstream social and political activities, they may begin to experience a sense of estrangement from the culture, which in some respects resembles symptoms encountered by younger generations attempting to initially integrate into it. Feelings of meaningless and normlessness may accompany this process of cultural estrangement. Erik Erikson (1950) popularized the idea that adolescents may undergo an "identity crisis" in attempting to define themselves in relation to existing social arrangements. Proponents of "activity theory" suggest that a similar identity crisis can occur late in life if a person withdraws (voluntarily or involuntarily) from longstanding political and social involvements. This withdrawal, whether gradual or abrupt, may trigger a sense of estrangement from society, estrangement from oneself, or both. This estrangement often has consequences for political attitudes and behaviors of older persons.

An intriguing theory developed by Martin et al. (1974) suggests that middle-aged citizens constitute the "command generation."

---

[17]For precise definitions of these dimensions, see Seeman (1959, 1972, 1975) or Martin et al. (1974:267).

Modern industrialized societies such as the United States, West Germany, and Great Britain tend to evaluate a person's social worth more on the basis of performance than on the basis of needs. The "command generation" in modern societies controls a large portion of the total societal resources and participates extensively in the activities of the system. Hence they tend to monopolize or "command" it. This may create problems of integration into the system for youth and the elderly, resulting in alienation, since both groups have been relegated to a marginal status by the dominant, middle-aged group. Both are assumed by the command generation to have lower productivity potential—youth due to lack of skills, the elderly due to lack of vigor.

Martin examined several of Seeman's dimensions of alienation across the age spectrum. He theorized that alienation would vary inversely with the degree of a person's engagement in the political structure. Consequently, he expected that alienation would be lowest in middle age, highest in youth, and intermediate among the elderly. The hypothesis was, in general, confirmed. However, unanticipated patterns emerged on specific dimensions of alienation. The elderly scored the lowest of the age groups on measures of self-estrangement and social isolation and highest (even higher than youth) on powerlessness and meaninglessness. Interestingly, the aged were most alienated from *political* life and less so from *family* relations.

Probably the most politically relevant of Seeman's dimensions of alienation is "powerlessness." Powerlessness is the belief or expectancy held by a person that his behavior cannot effectively determine the outcomes he seeks. It has been variously conceptualized as "external control expectancy" (Rotter, 1966; Lefcourt, 1976), "learned helplessness" (Seligman, 1975), and lack of a sense of "personal control" (Renshon, 1974). In a cohort analysis of three nationwide surveys, Agnello (1973) found that both the young and the old experience high levels of powerlessness. He attributes this to both age groups being effectively denied equal access to societal power and resources by the dominant middle-age group. But this is where the similarities between the two age groups end. Whereas the process of aging increases feelings of powerlessness for the old, it decreases such feelings for the young. As they move toward middle-age, young cohorts acquire greater access to the means of political power in society. Hence their sense of effective control over political outcomes increases and experienced powerlessness decreases. The opposite holds for the old. As middle-age cohorts approach old age, they begin to lose effective control over resources, and so their sense of efficacy declines. This sense of efficacy reaches its lowest ebb among the old-old (age 75 and over), since they often occupy a virtually powerless position vis-à-vis their environment, particularly if they are no longer physically mobile. Agnello's most important overall finding was that the subjective sense of powerlessness is consistently higher among the old than among either the young or middle-aged persons.

What are the implications of these high levels of powerlessness for future attempts to mobilize elderly political activity? Most studies have found an inverse relationship between political alienation and degree of political activity; the more alienated tend to show lower rates of political participation.[18] Seligman's (1975) research on "learned helplessness" suggests that the experience of powerlessness is likely to produce political inactivity among the elderly. His investigations with a variety of organisms, from laboratory rats to humans, indicate that the experience of "uncontrollability" over relevant outcomes in one's surrounding environment saps the motivation to respond toward that environment. One "learns" that one is "helpless," and therefore, the frequency of attempts to alter the environment declines accordingly, eventually culminating in "extinction" of responses. As applied to the elderly, this theory predicts that if society effectively denies them equal access to important resources, the resultant sense of powerlessness will produce diminished levels of political activity. Conversely, those among the elderly who expect that their personal efforts can have an effect on political outcomes will be inclined to participate actively. A study by Campbell et al. (1960), for instance, found that voting turnout increased uniformly with the extent of an individual's "sense of political efficacy." Of those

---

[18]However, some studies suggest that powerlessness can also lead to increased political activity. Boderman (1964) found that feelings of political powerlessness were positively correlated with involvement in extremist political activity. Similarly, Silvern and Nakamura (1971) found a positive correlation between powerlessness and activism.

The Politics of Aging

with the highest sense of political efficacy, 91 percent voted, whereas only 52 percent of those with low efficacy voted (a difference of approximately 40%).[19] Similarly, Rosen and Salling (1971) found that level of political activity was negatively correlated with the experience of powerlessness.

While some of this tendency toward alienation among the aged can be traced to other influences, such as social class, race, ethnicity, and gender, it is nevertheless apparent that lack of meaningful involvement in political and social life for older, as well as younger, segments of the population can be largely attributed to their marginal status in the political system relative to the "command" generation. This is particularly likely to be the case in societies that evaluate social worth primarily on the basis of performance criteria. The "command generation" theory can be used to argue that societies which are more need-oriented (less productivity-oriented) will generate comparatively lower levels of alienation among the youngest and eldest group. Since their worth to society as persons is not judged primarily on their ability to produce, young and old people in more need-oriented cultures are likely to be better integrated into the overall social fabric and hence to occupy a less-marginal status. Consequently, they are likely to be less susceptible to feelings of alienation. Kuypers and Bengtson (1973:195) suggest that the development of freedom from a "social-worth ethic" is crucial to the maintenance of self-esteem for the elderly.

PARTICIPATORY BEHAVIORS OF OLDER PERSONS

Political Participation

Attitudes and opinions are at best indirect inputs into the policymaking processes of government and, hence, are likely to be limited in their impact. The fact that the elderly strongly favor an

---

[19]In a study based on a sample of between 520 and 716 factory workers in each of six countries (India, Bangladesh, Israel, Nigeria, Chile, and Argentina), Williamson (1969) found a positive relationship between a sense of efficacy and various forms of political participation. Inkeles and Smith (1974) come to a similar conclusion based on their analysis of the same data.

increase in Social Security benefits does not ensure the enactment by Congress of a bill proposing such an increase. Politicians can easily ignore public opinion and go on about their business unimpeded unless they are made to feel electoral pressures from elderly voters or to witness political demonstrations staged by (or on behalf of) them. Active participation in the political process by older citizens whether in the form of voting, membership in political parties and community organizations, protest activity, or officeholding can exert a much more direct influence on public policy than does public opinion alone. The various types of participation engaged in by older persons can be thought of as concrete, tangible *behaviors*, as distinguished from the less concrete *attitudes and orientations* that have been emphasized to this point. As such, they indicate a more intense involvement by the elderly in the political affairs of society.

Voting is the most common form of popular participation in the political process by elderly citizens. Age patterns in voting behavior follow a consistent and well-documented path across the life span. A repeatedly observed pattern (*see* Fig. 5-2) found in nearly a half century of voting studies conducted in a variety of cultural contexts is that voter participation increases with age, reaches a peak in the forties and fifties, then gradually declines somewhat after sixty (Milbrath and Goel, 1977; Wolfinger and Rosenstone, 1980). A pioneering cross-national study by Herbert Tingsten (1937) identified this general pattern in five different countries. Later analyses by Campbell et al. (1960), based on United States data, and by Almond and Verba (1963), based on data from five nations, yielded the same distribution in voter turnout.

Several of the more recent investigations have indicated that the relationship between age and voting is considerably more complex than was once thought. These later studies demonstrate that when selected controls are introduced for the effects of variables such as gender, level of education, marital status, and socioeconomic status, the frequently observed "gradual voting decline" among the aged almost entirely disappears. That is, most of the dropoff in voter turnout attributed to older persons apparently results not from the effects of aging per se but from the fact that the aged as a group are less educated, disproportionately widows

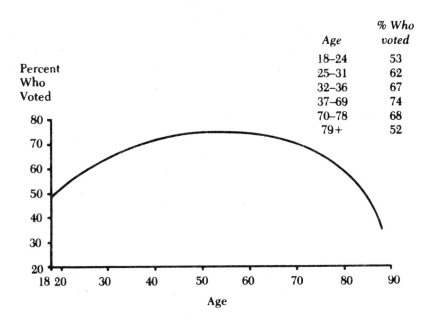

Figure 5-2. Turnout by age in the 1972 United States national election. From Wolfinger, Raymond E., and Steven J. Rosenstone: *Who Votes?* 1980. Courtesy of Yale University Press.

(women live longer), and lower in socioeconomic status compared with the rest of the population. In fact, Wolfinger and Rosenstone (1980) report that once education, marital status, sex, income, occupation, and labor force participation are controlled, aging produces not a decline, but an increase in turnout (*see* Fig. 5-3). Verba and Nie (1972) come to a similar conclusion, controlling socioeconomic level alone. Wolfinger and Rosenstone (1980) give particular emphasis to the role of education, marital status, and sex in their analysis. Married people are more likely to vote than those who are not married, and women are less likely to vote than men; thus turnout tends to be lower for widows, who make up an increasing proportion of older age groups.

    Voting is a relatively weak form of involvement in the political process when compared with other more active participatory roles. Elections are infrequent political events. They offer the aged

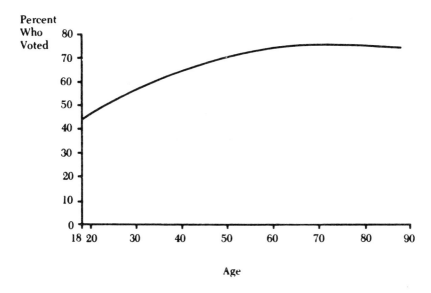

Figure 5-3. Turnout by age in the 1972 United States national election controlling for income, occupation, labor force participation, education, marital status, and sex. From Wolfinger, Raymond E., and Steven J. Rosenstone: *Who Votes?* 1980. Courtesy of Yale University Press.

person at best a rather narrow choice among limited alternatives—usually two preselected candidates, one Democrat, one Republican. At least from the standpoint of the individual, a single vote among millions of others cannot realistically be expected to have a very meaningful impact on political outcomes. It is not surprising, therefore, that the majority of American citizens simply do not bother to vote. The elderly are, of course, no exception.[20]

In most respects the pattern of participation by the elderly in nonelectoral activities (such as party campaign work, contributing money, writing letters to public officials, or demonstrating) roughly parallels that for voting. There is, however, a minor difference worth noting. The gradual decline that begins after sixty is more pronounced for other participatory behaviors than for voting.

---

[20]For a discussion of the social psychology of nonvoting in the American context, see Hadley (1978). Renshon (1974) links these nonvoting trends to the frustration of a hypothesized "need for personal control."

This is because voting is an easier act to engage in and is more likely to become a habit (Nie et al., 1974; Smith et al., 1980). The most thorough investigation of the relationship between age and political participation to date was conducted by Nie et al. (1974). They constructed an "index of participation" based on a variety of different behaviors. Their index emphasized participatory behaviors other than voting, including attending rallies, working for a political candidate or party, persuading others, joining community organizations, and writing letters to public officials. This participatory index was applied to data collected in Austria, India, Nigeria, Japan, and the United States. The authors intentionally singled out for analysis five nations whose cultures, histories, and stages of political development were dissimilar. This approach was adopted in hopes of isolating a common life cycle pattern of political participation that would hold across different political contexts. They reasoned that any deviations from this observed cross-national uniformity in the age-participation relationship would reflect patterns peculiar to each nation, i.e. each country's unique historical, cultural, or generational circumstances. Nie et al. conclude that in many respects the patterns in the various countries are "remarkably similar." For instance, in each of the five nations studied: (1) both the youngest and the oldest age strata participate less than the middle group, and this pattern holds for both sexes;[21] (2) overall participation rates in all five nations are lower for women than for men, throughout the life cycle; and (3) the shape of the life cycle curve is approximately the same for both sexes in all five nations.

In the course of their investigation of cross-cultural similarities, Nie et al. managed to unearth some equally intriguing cultural differences in the age-participation relationship. Their data show that:

1. There is considerably less age variation in India compared with the other four nations studied. For Indian women there is almost no appreciable variation over the life span. This contrasts sharply with the patterns for Nigerian, Japanese, and American women.

---

[21]Note the consistency here with Martin et al.'s (1974) theory of social dominance by the middle-aged "command generation."

2. There were also interesting cross-cultural variations in the location of the peak years of participation within the life cycle. In Austria the peak comes early (in the thirties) and then gradually declines with the progression of age. One can compare this pattern with Nigeria and the United States, where the peak comes nearly ten years later, and Japan, which peaks even later in the life span.

3. The sex differential in participatory levels is considerably less in the United States than in the other four nations across the entire life span, virtually disappearing in the 30–40 year age range.

Probably the most dramatic finding of the Nie et al., five-nation study was that when the influence of selected variables (length of residence, education, sex, socioeconomic status) is controlled for, the gradual decline in elderly participation that had been noted in earlier studies almost entirely disappears.[22] Since aggregate education levels among the elderly are expected to continue to increase over the next several decades, the implication of these controls is that elderly participation will be substantially higher than is observed today, particularly when combined with the effect of their expanded numbers.[23]

Nie et al. (1974) suggest an explanation for the relatively lower old age and youth participation rates (vis-à-vis the middle age group), which in some respects resembles the notion of "disengagement." Both youthful and elderly persons experience a kind of participatory inertia, although for quite different reasons. Youth have not yet developed a stable basis for involvement in politics, so they experience problems of "start-up." Old age presumably brings a gradual withdrawal from societal attachments, accompanied by physical infirmities in the latter stages, so the elderly experience problems of "slowdown." While Nie et al. do not attempt to provide any rigorous proof for this explanation,

[22]Note the parallel here with the evidence cited earlier for the United States (*see* Fig. 5-3). See also Wolfinger and Rosenstone (1980), as well as Verba and Nie (1972).

[23]When sex and length of residence are controlled in addition to educational level, elderly participation declines are reduced even further and in most cases can no longer be discerned. Similar studies have shown that controlling for differences in socioeconomic status can also reduce this participation decline among the elderly (Verba and Nie, 1972).

some support is to be found in their observation that aged citizens who continue in the work force also remain more active politically than do those who simply retire. Continued involvement in society in general is apparently accompanied by continued involvement in political affairs.

Research on political participation indicates that people tend to maintain high levels of participation well into old age. Expected increases in elderly educational levels suggest that in the near future older persons will engage in higher rates of voting and other forms of mass participation than they do at present. In addition, the impact of this increase in rate of political participation will be magnified by their increasing proportion of the voting-age population (Binstock, 1976).

Elite Participation: Leadership and Officeholding

Thus far we have discussed several instances in which popular assumptions about the political attitudes and activity levels of aged persons are inaccurate. One common belief about the political behavior of the elderly that is essentially correct is that they are likely to be disproportionately represented in positions of political leadership. For most advanced industrialized countries there is an impressive body of research that points to a distinct relationship between advancing age and the occupation of major positions of political authority. Abundant evidence also exists for the predominance of this pattern among primitive tribes as well as among societies that are in transitional stages of political development between traditional and modern forms (Simmons, 1945). In general, it holds true in a wide variety of cultural contexts that *the older a political incumbent becomes, the higher the office he or she is likely to occupy.*

Incumbency in political office differs from the other types of political participation we have discussed both in form and in intensity. Elderly persons who occupy major positions of political authority (city council or mayor, judge, ambassador, senator, president, Supreme Court justice, prime minister) are participating in the political process from within the policymaking structure itself, rather than making demands on the system from the outside, as would be the case in voting for president, signing a petition, or taking part in a sit-in against nuclear power plants. This means that elderly political incumbents are in a position to exercise more extensive power, authority, and control over policy outcomes than is possible for older persons through lesser channels of participation. Elderly statesmen have greater access to political resources to get things done, as they are closer to the roots of power and therefore exert more influence.

Throughout history, in almost every cultural context, political leadership positions have consistently been occupied by older persons. If one arbitrarily chooses any point in history one finds the vast majority of the world's people under the political jurisdiction of relatively aged persons, and the present era is no exception. Deng Xiao-ping, who is in his mid-seventies, as present leader of the People's Republic of China, presides over no less than a quarter of humanity. Soviet leader Leonid Brezhnev, also in his mid-seventies, presides over another substantial portion of the human race, and over half the full members of the Soviet Politburo are at least sixty-eight (Kellerman, 1979). In communist and noncommunist countries alike, most high-ranking positions of political authority are acquired and then maintained roughly between the ages of fifty and seventy-five.

Focusing on noncommunist regimes, early pioneering research on this question by Lehman (1953) established that the tendency for aged persons to occupy highly influential, prestigious, and authoritative positions in society holds true in a number of modern Western political contexts. Lehman found the same general pattern among British chief ministers (920–1720) and prime ministers (since 1721), and among American presidential candidates, Supreme Court justices, cabinet members, and ambassadors. Presidents, ambassadors, and prime ministers are most likely to serve in public office between the ages of fifty-five and fifty-nine. Thereafter, frequency of officeholding gradually declines, but substantial numbers of aged officeholders continue to serve into their seventies and eighties, with those seventy-five years old still serving at a higher rate than those in their early forties.

Joseph Schlesinger (1966) carried this line of inquiry one step further by demonstrating that, at least in the American context, *the age at which a political office is first attained corresponds with the*

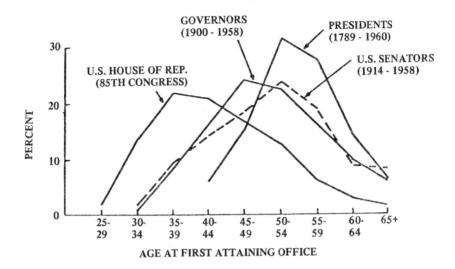

Figure 5-4. Age and achievement of major office in the United States. From Schlesinger, Joseph A.: *Ambition and Politics: Political Careers in the United States,* 1966. Courtesy of Rand McNally.

socially defined importance of that office. Election to the House of Representatives is likely to occur earlier in life than election as governor, which occurs earlier than senatorial election, with the presidency occurring latest in the life cycle (*see* Fig. 5-4). In a 1967 extension of his United States research, Schlesinger tested similar hypotheses by using data on five different countries and discovered that this same relationship between age and level of incumbency applied in all five.

In the United States Senate and House of Representatives, elderly statesmen have traditionally wielded substantially greater power over the fate of legislation than their younger peers. The primary reason for this has been the longstanding seniority system in Congress. Older experienced members who have served for many years are granted special privileges, such as chairmanships on the most prestigious and influential legislative committees. Similar rewards for senior status exist in European parliaments and in most legislative bodies. The average age of members of the

United States House of Representatives usually hovers around 50, with 19 percent of the Senate over age 65 in 1977. Since elected officials are not subject to mandatory retirement laws, members of Congress may remain in these powerful positions well into their seventies or even eighties if they are not unseated in elections by younger challengers. In a study of candidates for the House of Representatives in the 1958 election, Fishel (1969) concluded that (1) opposition to incumbents came primarily from younger challengers, (2) in general, there was no discernible tendency for younger challenging candidates to be more liberal than older ones, and (3) among those under 40 who had been nominated for the first time, both Democratic and Republican candidates were more conservative than older candidates. As is true of elderly persons in the general public, legislative officeholders do not necessarily become more conservative as they age.

The Supreme Court, as a repository of social justice and presumed wisdom based on years of experience, is in some respects a modern vestige of the "council of elders" found in primitive societies. Supreme Court justices, typically appointed in their late fifties, are the least susceptible of all American officeholders to pressures for retirement and are very likely to continue their service well beyond age 65. The average age of Supreme Court justices as of 1978 was just over 65, with five of the nine justices age 70 or over. The youngest justice, Justice Renquist, was 54.[24] Since retirement is contingent on personal desire, some justices have continued to serve beyond age 90. Despite the relatively older age of its members, the Supreme Court, far from being especially conservative, has sometimes taken fundamentally progressive stands that have led the rest of society in initiating major social changes. The Warren court was particularly noteworthy for this role, initiating such controversial decisions as Brown vs. Board of Education of Topeka in 1954, and Miranda vs. State of Arizona in 1966.

While election to the presidency usually occurs later in life than incumbency as a senator, member of the House, governor, or mayor, prior to Reagan's election in 1980 only one President,

---

[24]These figures are based on statistics in the Congressional Directory of the 95th Congress (U.S. House of Representatives, 1977).

William Henry Harrison, had ever been elected to the American presidency who was over 65 at the time he assumed office (Harrison was 68 at the time of his inauguration). Many have attained that age, however, *while* they were in office.

In a youth-oriented cultural climate, which places a premium on vitality in its leaders, older candidates may find it necessary to combat popular ageist stereotypes in order to get elected. Ronald Reagan was faced with this age hurdle in his 1980 campaign. Since Reagan was, at 69, older than any previous American president, his fitness for office came into question. The perception that Reagan might be "too old" to perform effectively unquestionably cost him some votes despite the substantial margin of his victory. Media coverage of the campaign was at times biased. This bias was difficult to counteract since ageist messages in the media were largely implicit and subliminal. Newquist and DiMento (1980:A21) give the following description of the portrayal Reagan received in the print and broadcast media:

> Splicing footage (or inches) from hours of observation, the news media have caught him in moments when his public presence has been less than optimal. Television shows him asking his wife what message was just given over the public-address system, it intimates that he is hard-of-hearing or not focusing rather than simply preoccupied with the remarks he is about to deliver. At other times, quiet and deliberate tones are interpreted as weaknesses in the candidate—signs of aging by a man once forceful and charismatic . . . they emerge as innuendos and vague references.

Popular fears concerning Reagan's suitability for office reflected assumptions about the effects of aging on leadership capacity. Could a sixty-nine-year-old man possibly possess sufficient stamina, responsiveness, and mental alertness to be equal to the demanding tasks of the presidency? Would he become disabled by illness or die in office? Popular sentiment tended to take the form of a concern that he was "too old" chronologically, rather than an appraisal of whether he had any potentially debilitating health disorders that might seriously impair his capacity to perform.

Much research has been done on the relationship between aging and performance capacities, and some of it has implications for the suitability of elderly candidates for public office. For example, studies show that average life expectancy for men who reach the age of sixty-five is seventy-nine, an additional fourteen years. Thus, a sixty-five-year-old presidential candidate could expect to live out a two-term presidency, plus an additional six years. Contrary to popular assumptions, aging is not inevitably associated with poor health, and when people do become incapacited in their later years, it is often the result of specific diseases, not old age per se. Reasoning along these lines, arguments were made during the 1980 presidential campaign that in evaluating the potential performance of a political leader the decisive variable should be functional age, rather than chronological age (Newquist and DiMento, 1980).

How well an individual performs is more important than year of birth. Konrad Adenauer, for example, initiated the most productive period of his political career while in his seventies and continued as a vigorous leader of Germany well into his eighties (Kellerman, 1979). Mental alertness and intelligence do not necessarily decline appreciably with advancing age. In fact, some components of intelligence and problem solving may actually increase with age in select individuals. This is particularly true of persons, such as public servants, whose career-demands keep them continuously exposed to a stimulating environment (Baltes and Schaie, 1974; Labouvie-Vief, 1976; Wang et al., 1970; Eisdorfer and Wilkie, 1973).

Whereas the problem in Reagan's case was to overcome popular assumptions of incompetence in order to gain access to a leadership position, the Chinese have recently been faced with precisely the opposite dilemma. Elderly officials in the top echelons of the Communist party have become firmly entrenched and are reluctant to retire, despite mounting evidence that they are now in fact too old to perform competently. The problem for the Chinese consists of finding means to convince an entrenched gerontocratic elite to relinquish their leadership positions. The dilemma is exacerbated by the persistence of the traditional Chinese veneration for age. Persons in their sixties are considered middle-aged in China, while those in their thirties and forties are considered young. Another reason for the reluctance of elderly Chinese officials to give up their positions is loss of status. In the Communist system all prestige, power, and privileges flow from political position (Butterfield, 1979).

This aging, brittle leadership constitutes a genuine and serious problem for Peking. Deputy Prime Minister Deng Xiao-ping, who wields substantial power, is seventy-five. In the National People's Congress, the nominal legislature, the average age is seventy-nine. In the principal decision-making body, the Communist party Politburo, the average age is now sixty-nine (Butterfield, 1979). At a November 1979 meeting of leading artists, musicians, and writers, the average age of the nine men selected as heads of the cultural associations was seventy-three. Most of China's prominent scientists and doctors are now in their sixties and seventies.

In a speech to the National People's Congress on the thirtieth anniversary of the People's Republic, eighty-one-year-old Chairman Marshal Yeh Jianying strongly urged that, "We must make up our minds to promote to leading posts within a given period of time a large number of fine officials in the prime of life." A nurse accompanied Yeh to the rostrum, and he read only the first ten minutes and the final paragraphs of the two-hour speech; the rest of which was delivered for him by a radio announcer. In a 1979 pronouncement, the state council ordered government offices to explore various means of persuading high-ranking elders to retire. Peking has recently shown considerable interest in the Yugoslav system, in which aging officials are appointed to a token body known as the Council of the Federation in order to make room for younger men (Butterfield, 1979).

The average age of political officials can reflect the age of an entire political regime. In the early revolutionary stages of a new regime (e.g. the newly established American republic, or Russia, China, or Cuba immediately following their respective revolutions) the age of influential political leaders tends to be lower. Fidel Castro, for instance, was only 33 when he came to power in 1959. Increases over time in the average age of political leaders can reflect a progression from early revolutionary stages through more stable and entrenched periods in the evolution of a national political culture. With respect to American experience, Lehman (1953) found that among both senators and representatives a consistent increase occurred in the average age of political incumbents between 1799 and 1925. In 1799, the mean age of members of the House of Representatives was 43; by 1875 it had increased to 48; and by 1925 it had risen again to 53. Similarly, among senators the mean age was 45 in 1799; it had risen to 53 by 1875; and by 1925 it was 57.[25] As the infant post-colonial United States moved further and further away from its initial revolutionary legacy, it became a more stable and entrenched political order, and the solidification of its political functions into permanent institutions was reflected in the relatively greater ages of its leaders.

A study of the relationship between age of political incumbents and macropolitical change by North and Pool (1966) argues that only during periods of revolutionary change is it possible to find elites with an average age as low as thirty or forty. North and Pool explored age patterns of Chinese communist and Koumintang elites beginning with the 1920s and found that a gradual rise in average age of elites occupying major positions had taken place for both groups. A similar process has been well-documented for the average ages of Soviet Politburo members. Since the 1917 Russian Revolution there has been a consistent increase in average age, accompanying the progressive consolidation of the regime over time (Rigby, 1972; Blackwell, 1974).

Further support for this relationship between age of regime and age of leaders was found in an investigation by Lerner et al. (1966). They observed that within the German Nazi elite leadership, *younger leaders had occupied more central revolutionary roles.* Compared to the average age of all members of the Nazi party, Nazi administrators tended to be younger, and the "propagandists," who played key party roles, were the youngest of all officials.

Given the premium our society places on youthful vigor, many elderly politicians prefer to think of themselves as still middle-aged rather than identify with negatively valued old age, which could become a political liability.[26] If the number of elderly voters

---

[25]A credible alternative explanation for this phenomenon deserves mention here. Much of this increase in average age of congressmen could be explainable as a function of overall increases in life expectancy within the entire United States population.

[26]There are also a number of other important factors to take into consideration in any assessment of why it is that elderly elected officials do not necessarily side with the elderly. For example, such persons depend on support from a variety of special interest groups to finance their campaigns. The need to be responsive to these special interests may outweigh the advantages of taking a pro-elderly position on a particular piece of legislation.

increases substantially and if negative stereotypes of old age relax, elderly political leaders may become more willing to openly identify themselves with the elderly. To the extent that this does occur it will further increase the political power and influence of the elderly.

FUTURE PROSPECTS

We began by asking how much power the elderly are capable of wielding as an organized political force, i.e. whether the expected rise in numbers of the aged is likely to translate into an increase in political influence. Having briefly discussed the empirical evidence with respect to a variety of attitudinal and behavioral predispositions during recent years, we are now in a better position to assess the potential influence of the aged in the years ahead.

Taking all of the evidence discussed to this point into consideration, it would seem that we have underestimated the future potential of the elderly to mobilize effectively around political issues they perceive as important. This tendency to underestimate their political potential is due in part to a number of stereotypes concerning the political behavior of older persons which are not borne out by the evidence. These stereotypes, many of which are held by the elderly themselves, often act as self-fulfilling prophecies, inhibiting the introduction of policy changes that could improve the quality of life for older citizens. If elected officials view the elderly as physically incapacitated, disinterested in politics, disinclined to vote, uninformed on public affairs, and resistant to change, they will have little incentive to take elderly interests seriously.[27] If, on the other hand, consciousness of the political potential of older persons were to develop among both the elderly themselves and among governmental officials, a substantial increase in the political influence of the aged could result. A pivotal issue in the near future, then, will be one of age con-

---

[27]A recent study by Riemer and Binstock (1978) indicates that American politicians are beginning to pay at least limited attention to older voters as a potentially influential voting bloc. But thus far candidates are apparently still reluctant to make major commitments of campaign money, staff, publicity, and time to swaying the elderly vote at the expense of other electoral constituencies.

sciousness, i.e. whether an "old is beautiful" orientation will emerge among the elderly with sufficient momentum to counteract the effects of existing stereotypes of old age within a predominantly youth-oriented American culture.

Given what we know about their attitudes and behaviors, the development of a sense of in-group solidarity among the aged would be most likely to arise in response to a combination of a discernible political opposition and a sense of relative deprivation as a group.[28] The expected increase in the size of the elderly population in coming decades is likely to produce a substantial gap between public willingness to supply services and increasing elderly needs and demands for those services (Binstock, 1974). This is likely to provide the first major arena of conflict between elderly and nonelderly coalitions. The resultant polarization could lead to the emergence of a stronger age-based consciousness. An identifiable political foe would provide a concrete focus for the development of solidarity among elderly persons who might otherwise have little in common with each other. Such an aged-based focus could conceivably cut across social class, ethnic, and educational backgrounds which at present tend to restrict the formation of coalitions among the aged.

The *potential* for elderly political influence is clearly increasing. Whether that potential will in fact translate itself into concrete political gains for older persons within the next several decades is much more difficult to predict; it could easily go either way. In coming years the elderly may remain the relatively weak political force that they are now. On the other hand, there are compelling reasons to expect that they could develop considerably expanded power and influence. As we have seen, there are a variety of social, economic, technological, and political changes that may take place over the next fifty years that could greatly increase the probability of the latter outcome, although they in no way ensure its occurrence. These include substantial alterations in the age structure of the electorate, technical innovations in mass communications

---

[28]For an elaboration of some of the social and psychological functions performed by "in-group solidarity supported by displacement of aggression against out-groups," see Etheredge (1976:12–13); see also Levine and Campbell (1972).

making possible interactive and diversified programming, continuing declines in party identification, a corresponding upsurge in issue voting and independent voting, an increase in the educational level of the elderly, medical advances leading to increased longevity, and possible adoption of "electronic democracy" as an electoral and public opinion polling vehicle.

Binstock (1974) and Campbell (1971) have tended to either downplay or to exclude altogether from their forecasts the conceivable impact of trends such as these on prospects for elderly political power over the next fifty years. Their forecasts are largely based on "if present trends continue" assessments. In particular, Binstock's assessment that future gains in elderly clout are highly unlikely relies heavily on the assumption that major political activity in the United States will continue to express itself primarily through the traditional channels of party-oriented voting in current-style elections and current-style pluralistic interest group competition. A narrowly defined "if present trends continue" predictive base of this sort tends to preclude an adequate consideration of the cumulative impact of qualitative changes and innovations of the sort we have outlined.

Fifteen years ago, Arnold Rose (1965a, b) first advanced the idea that there is a growing subculture of the elderly. He saw an emerging age consciousness and assumed that forces of homogeneity among the aged would eventually outweigh forces of heterogeneity of interests. In recent years, however, Campbell (1971) and Binstock (1974) have disputed this possibility, pointing out that there is a substantially greater heterogeneity of interests among the old than among younger groups, which works against any potential for effective mobilization. Elderly persons at different economic levels, for example, would not benefit from the same types of pension, taxation, and welfare legislation and would therefore be unlikely to develop a common age consciousness as their primary political identity.

In contrast to this position, Carroll Estes (1978, 1979) predicts the dramatic expansion of the "aging network" beginning in the 1980s, which will be a powerful network of numerous agencies and organizations specifically devoted to the delivery of health and social services for the aged. This network would comprise a powerful coalition of the elderly, professional practitioners, and academicians who together could exercise substantial influence over policy, particularly through interest group activities.

Bernice Neugarten (1974) emphasizes the importance of distinguishing between the "young-old" (55 to 75-year age group) and the "old-old" (over 75 years old) in speculating about the future political role of the aged. The young-old are more likely to become politically influential than are the old-old and could conceivably decide against political identification with them. The "frail elderly" would find it difficult to become an effective political force if their interests were to become separated from the young-old. Finally, as Neal Cutler (1976) points out, it is not necessary to assume a high degree of unanimity among the elderly in order to predict that age could be a salient political referent in the future. Senior power, even if characterized by a wide diversity of interests, could nevertheless become highly influential politically in the form of a multifaceted, multi-issue, loose coalition of interests that converge on some issues while diverging on others. The black and women's movements did not require such unanimity in order to be politically influential, and the same may hold true for senior power.

Chapter 6

THE POLITICS OF GOVERNMENT
PROGRAMS AND POLICIES

The decade of the 1970s signaled the end of an era of abundant resources earmarked for the solution of the nation's social problems and the beginning of an era of increasing fiscal stringency in budgetary policy. The seemingly inexhaustible supply of resources available for the solution of old age, disability, poverty, and unemployment problems, which had produced rapidly escalating budget allocations for social programs since shortly after World War II, began to look annoyingly finite. Growing concerns over depletion of nonrenewable resources, soaring inflation rates, and deficits in the balance of trade led to debates about the "limits to growth," "the new problem of scarcity," and "no-growth economics." By the end of the 1970s a growing chorus of observers were predicting a period of substantially reduced economic productivity in the United States (Thurow, 1980; Barnet, 1980; Cook, 1979; Ophuls, 1975; Meadows et al., 1972). Some observers were suggesting curtailments in the rate of expansion of social programs. Others went much further, advocating substantial reductions in funding of existing programs.

In proposing his 1981 budget, President Carter recommended that expenditures for social services be kept austere and lean. Less than a decade earlier, Republican President Richard Nixon had agreed to such progressive measures as the Family Assistance Plan with its guaranteed annual income; now a Democratic president was suggesting reductions in social services. Clearly the political climate had changed dramatically in the interim, with needy groups suddenly facing the prospect of vying with each other for access to a shrinking share of the social services "pie." Budget cuts in social programs initiated during the Carter administration, designed primarily to control runaway inflation, did not meet with cries of

146

moral outrage from the American public. In fact, in the 1980 presidential election the electorate turned to Ronald Reagan, who promised even more extensive budget cuts. The public was for the most part content to join the experts (and in many cases to lead them) in its enthusiasm for discovering new and better ways to exercise restraint in government spending. By the late 1970s this public demand for fiscal restraint and taxpayer relief was evident in such developments as California's Proposition 13 and similar property-tax-reduction measures in other states. By the end of the decade, fully 71 percent of Americans were in favor of social program cutbacks as a method of controlling inflation (*New York Times*, 1979).

In an altered political atmosphere of this sort, the previously sacrosanct status of social programs for the elderly can no longer be taken for granted. In a political climate of economic stagnation and perceived resource scarcity, the public costs of social programs, if not their very *raison d'etre*, are being seriously scrutinized. Further expansion of old-age programs is, at least for the time being, an unlikely prospect. For advocates of social services for the elderly, consolidation and entrenchment are the order of the day.

These recent trends underscore the importance of understanding the historical and cultural setting in which social policies for the elderly are forged, maintained, and revised. Many planners, researchers, and program administrators, having become somewhat complacent about generous levels of program funding and having largely ignored the significance of the changing economic, political, and ideological context within which such programs operate, have found themselves caught off guard by these developments.

Differences in political culture can produce substantial variations in the public response to changing economic and historical circumstances. In Sweden, for instance, similar economic pressures and perceptions of scarcity have recently produced a conservative mood in politics, leading in 1976 to the ousting by Swedish voters of the Social Democratic party and its ally the Communists, after 44 consecutive years of Social Democratic rule. As has been the case in the United States, portions of the Swedish electorate

have begun to clamor for tax relief (Childs, 1980).[1] But in the
Swedish political context these burdensome economic pressures
have not resulted in retrenchments in social program commitments. During the last four years, conservative non-socialist governments have increased spending on social programs for the aged
and other groups at approximately the same generous rate that
the Social Democrats had maintained since 1960 (Vinocur, 1979).
They have done little to alter policies previously instituted by the
Social Democrats in support of full employment and the welfare
state. Similarly, the Mitterand government in France has responded
to economic pressures by substantially *expanding* social benefits to
the elderly. Subjected to similar conditions of economic constraint,
political elites and mass publics within the context of the Swedish
and French political cultures have responded differently.[2]

The unique American political culture, both through the nature
of its political institutions and through its dominant political
belief system of individualism, has produced a distinctive brand of
old-age policies that differs significantly from those which have
developed in other modern industrial nations such as Great Britain, Belgium, the Netherlands, Denmark, Sweden, and West
Germany. Cross-cultural comparisons with other modern states
make it easier to differentiate between those aspects of American
social policy which are inherent in the development of all modern
societies and those which are peculiar to the distinctive set of
American historical and political circumstances. Through such
cross-cultural contrasts we can better isolate and understand the
specific impact that American political culture has exercised on
the development of present-day programs for the elderly.

There are considerable similarities in the old-age policies of all
modern societies, and this trend toward convergence should by no
means be overlooked (Williamson and Weiss, 1979; Williamson
and Fleming, 1977). All advanced industrialized countries have

---

[1]Among non-socialists, 66 percent now favor a tax cut. Among socialists, 23 percent favor a
tax cut. Overall, those favoring tax reductions remain slightly in the minority at 42 percent
(Zetterberg, 1979).

[2]Despite taxes that are almost twice those paid by Americans, a 1978 survey by the Swedish
Institute for Opinion Research (SIFO) showed that those favoring social program cutbacks
because they are too expensive remained a minority at 39 percent (Zetterberg, 1979).

initiated some form of basic provision for old-age, survivors, and disability insurance; unemployment insurance; and workers' compensation. But within this modern trend American policies and programs have remained distinctive and in some respects underdeveloped. The comparative examination of old-age policy provisions that we present in this chapter bears out this American exceptionalism. When contrasts are made with the policies of other western nations, one consistently finds significant differences in the quality and extensiveness of programs designed to meet the needs of elderly citizens. In addition to those benefits provided to the elderly in the United States, most other advanced countries also offer more generous national health insurance coverage, cash sickness benefits, housing supplements, and more by way of home health services.

Divergent phenomena such as the late passage of the American Social Security legislation (1935), low expenditures on Social Security as a percent of GNP, higher elderly poverty rates, large income discrepancies between rich and poor aged, and failure to initiate comprehensive health insurance suggests the extraordinary tenacity of the ideology of nineteenth century liberal-individualism in the United States. We will see that these persistent differences between American social policies and those of European countries stem in large part from peculiarities of historical development and policy rationales which reflect deeply ingrained cultural attitudes toward relief for nonproductive members of society.

HISTORICAL DEVELOPMENT OF OLD-AGE POLICY IN THE UNITED STATES

The historical evolution of social policy affecting the welfare of the elderly in the United States can be divided into three general phases, on the basis of the predominant social principles which served to justify existing practices and policies during each period. These three phases roughly correspond to the stages through which other western nations have passed in developing modern social policies, although timing and completeness of transition from one phase to the next have often differed from country to country.

In the preindustrial period, which extended from colonial days through roughly the early nineteenth century in the American context, social policy toward the aged was characterized by protectionist practices imported from Western Europe. Throughout the nineteenth century, accelerating forces of industrial change began to usher in a new set of social attitudes toward marginal, dependent groups, such as the elderly. During this period the political ideology of liberal-individualism, with its emphasis on self-reliance and fear of state interference, reached its purest form as a dominant belief formula, justifying free enterprise practices and discouraging public expenditures on needy groups. In the third and most recent phase, the transition from the individualism associated with nineteenth century industrial capitalism to a stronger sense of social responsibility for the welfare of marginal dependent groups has led to the adoption of state-administered social security and pension programs associated with what has come to be known as the *welfare state*. Whereas most European countries entered this last phase around the turn of the century, the United States did not begin to demonstrably experience this transition until the era of the Great Depression.[3]

As we shall see, differences between American social programs and those of West European and Scandinavian democracies, which became most pronounced in this last phase, can be traced in large part to the persistence of the liberal-individualist tradition in the American context. The conflict between the liberalist heritage and the ideal of social security has retained a strong individualist flavor in the United States, reflecting at best only partial (and hence conceivably reversible) concessions to the principle of the inherent desirability of state intervention to ensure social protection for the elderly and other marginal groups. Elsewhere, in Scandinavia and most of Western Europe, the transcendence of the individualist stage has been much more complete. In this sense, the United States remains somewhat of a historical anomaly in its social security and welfare policies. This American exceptionalism becomes apparent when we compare the rate and extent of devel-

---

[3]This tripartite classification of phases through which western nations have passed in developing social policies is similar to that proposed by Rimlinger (1971:11).

opment of American old-age policies with those that have arisen in Scandinavian and West European contexts.

Preindustrial Protectionism

Similarities between the United States and other developing western nations in patterns of social care of the aged were perhaps greatest in the preindustrial phase, which extended from colonial days through the early decades of the nineteenth century. The political orientations and institutions of the American republic in its early years were those of a "fragment" political culture, reflecting a congeries of political ideas and practices that had been transplanted from the European context, but minus any experience of the prior stages of social evolution which had led up to them historically (Hartz, 1955, 1964).

Traditional, preindustrial notions of social protection for the aged, handicapped, and indigent had been evolving in Europe since medieval times. Care of disadvantaged societal groups in medieval Europe was left to private charity. Relief efforts for the elderly were administered by the clergy, through local parishes and monasteries. By the sixteenth century, political elites in England, France, and other emerging nation-states began to pay serious attention to the alarming presence of large numbers of indigent persons. Since the unfortunate were in fact the majority and since this posed a potential threat to regime maintenance, it became necessary to make at least token efforts to ameliorate their harsh lot. Thus the need was recognized for some minimal form of publicly administered social protection for the masses.

Old regime traditions of protectionism involved a sense of social provision for the aged and other dependent groups, not so much for their own sake as for that of society. Charity was *given* to the old, the handicapped, and the poor. It was not to be regarded as a *right*. The assumption prevailed that if sources of support were kept minimal, uncertain, and unreliable, this would discourage idle dependency (Rimlinger, 1971).

When adventuresome Europeans began establishing colonies in the New World, they brought with them many of the Old World protectionist ideas and practices that had accompanied the late mercantilist period in Europe. In addition, some settlers brought emerging liberalist notions of limited government. Early American patterns of social care of the aged therefore reflected a hybrid of these influences—the preindustrial protectionism associated with the mercantilist era, mixed with emerging liberal-democratic notions of limited state sovereignty.

The American nation has from its inception been a highly pluralistic, heterogeneous society with an adamant preference for responding to the needs of the citizenry through private, voluntary associations. Throughout his travels in the United States during the early nineteenth century French social commentator Alexis de Tocqueville (1954) had been impressed by the tendency of Americans to join a wide variety of social clubs, professional associations, and other voluntary associations. These voluntary associations were able to accomplish collective ends and to mediate between individual and society without the necessity of delegating responsibilities to the "coercive" powers of centralized governmental authority. Early cultural assumptions about the importance of voluntarism[4] and self-sufficiency were therefore closely intertwined with political notions of limited government, intentional diffusion of power, and anti-statism.

Substantial numbers of early settlers in colonial America were indigent and of necessity dependent on some form of public assistance; of these, a disproportionate number were elderly. The social burden of supporting nonproductive elderly persons was heavily borne by the family and religious organizations. This usually took the form of "charitable assistance." Christian charity was a double-edged sword in that it also served the societal function of maintaining social control over the aged. Older persons in the community who could not obtain adequate support either through familial or church-related sources were forced to rely on whatever crude public provisions existed on the local level (Trattner, 1974; Coll, 1969).

British dominance of the American colonies in the seventeenth century had led to the adoption of English poor laws as an initial social policy blueprint. Early American poor relief imitated essen-

---

[4]*Voluntarism* is used here according to Lubove's (1968) definition as "organized action by nonstatutory institutions" (*see also* Smith et al., 1980).

tial features of the English Elizabethan statute of 1601 and the English Law of Settlement and Renewal of 1662. These laws maintained an exaggerated distinction between the *able* poor and those categorized as the "lame, impotent, old, blinde, and such other among them being poore and not able to work."[5] Popular belief among early Americans consistently held that the majority of those dependent on public relief were "able-bodied" and were in fact capable of performing work to support themselves. At the same time, popular sentiment consistently underestimated the proportion who were aged and disabled. The end result of this distortion was low levels of public funding and, hence, poor-quality care for all dependent groups, including the elderly. Their crime was guilt by association (Coll, 1972).

In fact, able-bodied persons typically comprised only a small minority of recipients of public aid. Calculations made by economist and pamphleteer Matthew Carey in 1833 showed that out of a sample of 549 persons on relief in Philadelphia, 390 persons (71%) were over 60 years of age.[6] A similar classification of inmates in the Blockley almshouse in Philadelphia also bears out the substantial discrepancy between public assumptions of ability to work among the poor, and the reality. Out of a total of 1509 persons only 13 percent were actually capable of working. In contrast, combined elderly and infirm inmates comprised 77 percent of the total (Klebaner, 1952).

The assumption of actual ability to work on the part of the majority of inmates (accompanied by presumed laziness or character deficiency) was deeply embedded in the almshouse approach. The distortion apparently provided a convenient rationale for minimizing public expenditures in support of society's least productive members, a rationale that was consistent with emerging political-cultural values of individual self-reliance, the Protestant work ethic, and fear of unwarranted government intervention in private affairs.

These prejudicial popular attitudes toward relief and the resultant low levels of funding produced conditions for elderly inmates

---

[5]See Coll (1972:133).

[6]These figures are cited in Coll (1972:147–148).

in city and county almshouses marked by severe overcrowding, insufficient provisions, and frequent physical abuse of inmates by staff. Elderly persons whose personal and familial resources had been exhausted often had no recourse but to cohabitate with the most unsavory characters in the community. Since the fate of almshouse residents was popularly assumed to result from deficiencies in moral character, personal indiscretion, and lack of motivation, the general public was largely indifferent to their plight (Trattner, 1974).

Emergence of Social Darwinism

The emergence of individualism out of preindustrial protectionism as the dominant social rationale affecting social policy toward the aged continued to develop in roughly parallel fashion in American and European contexts throughout the nineteenth century. The impact of "liberal" individualism was somewhat stronger in the United States, however, and social policies in the two contexts began to noticeably diverge toward the end of this phase in the early decades of the twentieth century.

In nineteenth century America the rapid expansion of industrial capitalism, accompanied by territorial expansion into the frontier regions, produced a social ideology of "rugged individualism." It was during this period that the American variant of the political ideology of Lockean individualism reached its purest form as a dominant belief formula justifying capitalist free enterprise practices (Hartz, 1955; Fine, 1967; Lodge, 1976). In particular, two value assumptions associated with the Lockean liberalist ideology had direct implications for the conduct of social policy toward the aged and other needy groups: (1) the idea that the individual was responsible for his own welfare (and hence should rely on his own resources); and (2) the idea that the distribution of societal benefits should be on the basis of performance or productivity, rather than need.

In the decades following the Civil War, America found in social Darwinism an intellectual formula which justified existing practices of unrestrained laissez faire while simultaneously discouraging public expenditures on disadvantaged groups. Similar justificatory functions were performed by Malthusian theories of population during industrialization in England. That social Darwinism "took" so well in the American context compared to other nations in the years following the Civil War is significant. Herbert Spencer's philosophy was adamantly opposed to notions of societal responsibility for the aged, infirm, and indigent, and to any form of collective intervention whatsoever on their behalf, as being contrary to human evolutionary progress. Within this ideological framework, charitable aid to the unfit, whether provided by the state or by advocates of the poor, was regarded as not only *un*productive but clearly *counter*productive, due to its interference with processes of natural selection:

> It seems hard that widows and orphans should be left to struggle for life or death. Nevertheless, when regarded not separately, but in connection with the interests of universal humanity, these harsh fatalities are seen to be full of the highest beneficence—the same beneficence which brings to early graves the children of diseased parents, and singles out the low-spirited, the intemperate, and the debilitated as the victims of an epidemic. . . . That rigorous necessity . . . these paupers' friends would repeal, because of the wailings it here and there produces (Spencer, 1969:323–324).

In a letter to Spencer in 1866, Henry Ward Beecher had written that, "The peculiar condition of American society has made your writing far more fruitful here than in Europe" (Hofstadter, 1945:18). During this same period, Spencer's foremost American disciple, William Graham Sumner, became a vocal exponent of social Darwinism. Sumner's ideas reflected the essential compatibility of American individualism and social Darwinist philosophy, particularly in advocating the minimization of the protective role of the state. Sumner maintained that the social structure of modern societies like the United States was based on contract, and that in such a state composed of free, independent men "sentiment" was a matter of private relations, to be regarded as independent of the public sphere or of considerations of social class. It followed that free individuals could not legitimately claim the right to receive help from others, nor were they to be expected to provide help to others out of private resources (Sumner, 1963).

The necessity for some form of social legislation to provide security in old age grew more urgent as a function of rapid industrialization, urbanization, and modernization from the period following the Civil War on into the early twentieth century. By 1913, Germany, Denmark, Belgium, New Zealand, Australia, France, Britain, and Sweden had all enacted progressive old-age pension schemes. America, however, was not yet in a mood to do this. This reluctance became clear in a premature "Quest for Social Justice" in the presidential campaign of 1912. Three competing factions emerged, each with its own proposed revision of the relationship between the individual and the state. Inspired by European efforts, American socialists insisted that it was the responsibility of the state to assure the economic security of the individual at social expense. Representing a more influential faction, the platform of Theodore Roosevelt and his Progressive party advocated the protection of home life against the hazards of sickness, irregular employment, and old age through the adoption of a system of social insurance adapted to American use. But in 1912 the country was not yet willing to accept the principles of either the socialists or Theodore Roosevelt. Americans favored Woodrow Wilson's "New Freedom" based on faith in the inherent virtues of the competitive system. They preferred Wilson's "program of liberty" to Roosevelt's "program of regulation." Wilson's electoral triumph over Roosevelt demonstrated the country's unwillingness to venture beyond a minor compromise with the liberalist tradition (Rimlinger, 1971).

The Welfare State

Historical differences between the United States and other modern democratic nations have been most pronounced with respect to the completeness of the transition from the liberal-individualism associated with nineteenth century poor relief to the welfare state of the twentieth century. This third and most recent phase witnesses the United States beginning to conspicuously lag behind European and Scandinavian governments in the provision of state-administered social protection, despite the availability of abundant resources for the purpose. By the time the United States had enacted its Social Security Act in 1935, twenty-seven other nations had already passed legislation establishing national retirement systems. The failure of the United States to clear the third hurdle without stumbling suggests that, unlike European states, the transcendence of nineteenth century liberalism and its associated rationales of self-reliance and rugged individualism has never really been convincingly accomplished in the American context. Rather, the hegemonic ideology of individualism has persisted, with only those concessions to the principle of social insurance being accepted as legitimate policy revisions which have proven necessary to insure the continued functioning of the social order.

Events that led up to the Social Security Act during the first two decades of the twentieth century are instructive. As will be recalled from our discussion in Chapter 4, three distinct groups took it upon themselves to address important old-age policy questions during this period, competing for the attention of elected officials and the general public (Pratt, 1976). The first group, whose most prominent spokesperson was Jane Addams and whose organizational vehicle was the National Conference of Charities and Corrections, consisted of social workers and managers of established voluntary charity arrangements. Clinging to nineteenth century liberal ideas of individualism, they continued to discuss the problems of the elderly within the vocabulary of "poor relief" and continued to advocate social policies involving voluntary charity as the solution.

The ideas of the second group were more corporatist than individualist. Espoused primarily by economists and other social scientists acting through the American Association of Labor Legislation, the corporatist recipe for old-age policy reform entailed the creation of industrial pensions through a process of collective bargaining between employers and labor, subject to regulation by the government. Richard Ely, Henry Farnum, and John Commons were among the proponents of this approach.

A third group comprised of reformers inspired by European social insurance systems was socialistic in its approach to old-age policy reform. The group proposed the adoption of compulsory social insurance on a nationwide basis and saw this as inextricably linked to larger purposes of expanding the public sector and redistributing private income. Despite the efforts of all three groups—individualist, corporatist, and socialist—American politicians remained adamantly opposed to the idea of publicly administered old-age pensions (Pratt, 1976).

Private pensions did not fare much better in the American context during this period; by 1900, only twelve American corporations were providing any form of pension plan for their workers. Overall, by 1914 old-age pension coverage was still a luxury possessed by less than 1 percent of American workers (Achenbaum, 1978a; Fischer, 1979).

It took unprecedented widespread unemployment, misery, and social dislocation on the magnitude of the Great Depression of the 1930s to force significant readjustments in American attitudes and social policies. Cumulative pressures generated by the Fraternal Order of the Eagles, the Ham and Eggs group, the Townsend Movement and other such reform organizations finally succeeded in creating an environment in which politicians had to take notice. In 1934, President Franklin Roosevelt appointed a cabinet committee, led by Secretary of Labor Frances Perkins, to draft a system of social insurance. A bill based on the committee's recommendations reached Congress within six months and was passed into law in 1935. Even this policy compromise involved at best only partial concessions to the alien principles of societal responsibility and distribution according to need. In the forging of the 1935 Social Security package, fundamental American individualistic beliefs were merely reformulated to the minimal extent necessary to reestablish normal social functioning. Established political tradition prevailed (1) in the continued emphasis on the equity principle of private insurance, (2) in the conscious downplaying of government contributions, and (3) in the insistence on contributory, work-related criteria for eligibility and benefit distribution (Lubove, 1968).

Hastily conceived in an atmosphere of crisis, the Social Security Act was as much an attempt by worried politicians to appease threatening constituent anger as it was an effort to draft effective social reform aimed at elderly needs. While promising a sweeping alleviation of the economic plight of the elderly, the provisions of the legislation were much less spectacular than the accompanying rhetoric. It was consciously designed to avoid redistribution of wealth. If anything, its regressive tax system exacerbated economic inequalities. Under the formal guise of improving the economic situation of aged workers, it provided a convenient means of reducing unemployment among young workers by encouraging earlier retirement (Schulz, 1980). Its major success was political, rather than social, in that it effectively quelled the recurrent complaints of the old-age movement of the day.

In this political-cultural environment dominated by a recalcitrant individualism, post-Depression era social policies, while propelled in the direction of assumption of societal responsibility for elderly well-being, have been inhibited by a continual gravitational pull back toward the fundamental liberal-capitalist tenets; those tenets have resurfaced most conspicuously during periods of perceived scarcity, inflation, or recession. The consequences of these trends have included the necessity of repeatedly couching old-age policy reforms in terms consistent with the basic political-cultural values and with their social policy-specific derivatives: individual responsibility and distribution of benefits according to performance (rather than need) criteria.

After years of relative quiescence, unsolved problems of the aged resurfaced in the 1960s in the form of what has come to be called the "gray lobby," which confronted taxpayer groups over Social Security issues, the American Medical Association over Medicare, and major corporations over mandatory retirement issues. Again, politicians reacted to mounting pressures in a spirit of political crisis. Congress enacted Medicare and the Older Americans Act in 1965 and created the Medicaid program for the elderly poor. In the early 1970s additional gains were won as a result of pressures and recommendations by the White House Conference on Aging.[7]

Hastily conceived in response to threatening periods of political crisis and constructed in piecemeal fashion, the American network of social programs and policies for the aged abounds with gaps in services and coverage and leaves much to be desired in terms of the extensiveness of its provisions. The limitations of the original Social Security legislation and in the various amendments enacted over the years reflect a deeply embedded cultural attitude of reluctance to allow the public sector to assume "undue" responsibility for the welfare of the aged, a reluctance which has

---

[7]These gains of the 1970s are discussed in Chapter 4.

in general been less pronounced in West European and Scandinavian contexts.

The incompleteness of the move beyond liberalism, anti-statism, and individualistic self-help principles toward post-industrial notions of comprehensive social insurance has led to important old-age policy differences vis-à-vis European democracies. These cultural differences become more apparent if we compare the American pattern with the evolution of old-age policy in a political context such as that of Sweden, which in many respects typifies the European pattern of development.

EVOLUTION OF OLD-AGE POLICIES IN THE SWEDISH CONTEXT

Patterns of social care of the elderly that have evolved over the past three centuries in Sweden provide an instructive contrast with the American experience. Both countries are modern industrial democracies, and both have passed through preindustrial protectionist, nineteenth century liberal-individualist, and modern social security phases in forging their current social policies toward the aged. Yet, in the Swedish context, the transcendence of nineteenth century liberalism has been much more complete, and this has resulted in qualitative differences between its social security policies and those of the United States. These differences have expressed themselves both in the timing of old-age policy innovations and in the quality and extensiveness of coverage provided. The Swedish pattern is, in general, exemplary of the pattern of old-age policy development in the other Scandinavian countries and most of Western Europe (Koblik, 1975; Board, 1970; Zetterberg, 1979).

The Swedish context differs historically from the American in several respects. Swedish society has been characterized by a much greater demographic homogeneity, and this has created a stronger social fabric; hence, a sense that all Swedes are in the same boat (Board, 1970). Traditional cultural predispositions such as a lack of resistance to government activity, preference for compromise and consensus in policy formulation (Anton, 1969; Heisler and Kvavik, 1974), strong community bonds, and an emphasis on systemic outputs (Anton, 1969) comprise the underlying political culture that has contributed to the character and rate of evolution of Swedish social programs. As the Swedish economy has moved from one of scarcity to one of relative affluence, approaches to the maintenance of citizen welfare in old age have changed over time from minimal, largely voluntary, social protection to comprehensive societal guarantees of a satisfactory standard of living—so-called "cradle to grave" security.

The evolution of social programs in Sweden through the mid-nineteenth century roughly parallels that in the United States—consisting of preindustrial protectionist and liberal-individualist stages. But beginning with the 1907 parliamentary discussions about the insufficiency of existing old-age support arrangements, the idea of substantial societal responsibility for citizen welfare began seriously to be advanced.

What emerged during the first three decades of this century in Sweden was a growing social consensus around the goal of economic democracy. The nineteenth century liberal notion of freedom from state interference in the life of the individual was foregone in favor of a quite different set of freedoms: freedom from economic insecurity, from poverty, and from the social effects of underproduction. As Leif Lewin (1975:286) has pointed out, the Swedish conception of freedom "included a freedom for the state." There was considerably less resistance to the concept of long-range state economic planning than was the case in the United States during the same period. The idea was accepted as quite natural by Swedes that state activity would increase an individual's personal freedom by providing social protection against economic misfortune. This was felt to be especially true with regard to the hardships of old age, around which many of the early parliamentary debates centered.

The old-age insurance committee's report of 1907 in the Riksdag declared that existing forms of old-age assistance were financially insufficient, as well as humiliating to the personal integrity of the elderly. The committee further suggested that economic security in old age be socially and legally regarded as a "right," justified by a life-time of contributions to Swedish society:

> It does not satisfy the present consciousness of justice that, for example, a man who has worked throughout a long life to support himself and his

family and thereby at the same time contributed in his degree to society's progress shall perhaps see no other way out than to turn to poor relief or to accept the dole from his relatives when his working strength ebbs. Rather, even the most modest career must be regarded as giving the right to support, which may not be extended in humiliating forms (Samuelsson, 1975:338).

If one compares this 1907 statement to the 1935 rationale that accompanied the American Social Security Act (see previous section), it becomes apparent that the Swedes were making much more rapid progress in transcending nineteenth century liberal-individualistic doctrines in the direction of modern forms of social care for the aged than were their American counterparts. The recognition of the elderly's earned *right* to social care arrived earlier and was more extensive in the Scandinavian context. From 1907 on, the principle of social security as a right, to be provided by society as a buffer against circumstances that the individual could not control, took hold among a remarkably widespread array of political groups in Sweden. The passage in 1913 of the *folkpension* (usually translated into English as the "basic pension," but literally means "people's pension") established a social right to economic relief against misfortune and thereby established the principle of national insurance. The state was to function as a sort of colossal insurance company against the misfortunes of old age. This precedent rapidly spread to encompass the related hardships of involuntary unemployment, poverty, and accident, becoming the prototype for the modern Swedish welfare state.

The electoral vehicle for these newly emerging social security rationales was the Social Democratic party. During the 44 years of continuous Social Democratic dominance between 1932 and 1976, the degree of political consensus and cooperation that was achieved with other parties (Conservative, Liberal, Center, Communist) in building the Swedish social welfare edifice was nothing short of remarkable, at least if one compares it to the highly pluralistic, competitive political bargaining atmosphere that prevailed in the United States.

What has emerged from these years of consensual bargaining within an atmosphere of solidarity is a system of "comprehensive social care" in which no Swede need fear personal economic ruin brought on by old age, illness, unemployment or similar contingencies. Poverty has been all but eliminated. Pensions, health care, hospitalization, education, housing subsidies, maternity benefits, day care, dental care, and even annual five-week vacations are guaranteed to all citizens irrespective of personal income. Working-class tenants, for instance, are ensured that the proportion of their monthly income devoted to rent payment will be no greater than that of middle-class tenants. Even parking fines are graduated according to personal ability to pay.

It would be naive to simply attribute these sweeping developments in social policy over the past half century to the predominance of socialistic philosophies as against capitalism. The Swedish Social Democrats have utilized the ideas of Keynes as a policy blueprint to a much greater extent than those of Marx. The Swedish economy remains highly capitalistic in orientation. Unlike their American counterparts, most Swedes have come to regard the development of socialistic state welfare policies alongside capitalistic private enterprise as a natural partnership, with public and private sectors performing their respective functions in a symbiotic fashion. Production of goods and services is left largely to the private market, whereas the state handles their allocation and distribution.

SOCIAL PROGRAMS AFFECTING THE ELDERLY

Due to the prevalence of similar economic and social circumstances in advanced industrialized countries, the United States shares with Europe certain universal characteristics of modern social insurance systems. These include basic provision of old-age, survivors, and disability insurance, unemployment insurance, and workers' compensation. But, in addition, most advanced industrial countries offer their citizens generous national health insurance coverage, sickness and maternity benefits, cash allowances for families with children, housing supplements, and home health services. While the United States has designed programs to provide some of these benefits, it has usually done so in a more restrictive and selective manner. Most West European nations have chosen to administer their programs through the public

sector at the national level, and the benefits offered are usually
more comprehensive. American programs, in contrast, have been
an uneven patchwork of private and public provisions administered
and regulated at different levels of government. A brief examination of the major programs that presently exist in the United
States bears out this American exceptionalism. When contrasts are
made with the policy outputs of other industrial nations, one
consistently finds significant differences in the quality and extensiveness of programs.

Indicators of Societal Commitment to Social Security

One means of judging a nation's commitment to the health and
welfare of its elderly citizens is to look at when old-age pension
schemes were first adopted. The first modern-style "welfare state"
social programs designed to provide economic relief for older
persons came with the enactment of health, accident, and old-age
legislation in Germany in the 1880s. Thereafter, similar pension
schemes followed in rapid succession in Denmark in 1891, Belgium
in 1894, New Zealand in 1898, the Australian states in 1901, France
in 1903, the Australian federation in 1908, Britain in 1908, and
Sweden in 1913. The United States did not enact such a pension
system until 1935.

Another indicator of concern for the health and welfare of the
aged is the proportion of a nation's gross national product that is
devoted to the provision of social security. The percentage of the
GNP devoted to spending on social security programs has remained
substantially lower in the United States than in any major Western
European or Scandinavian country (*see* Table 6-I).[8] Of the major
industrial nations only Japan ranks lower than the United States
in social security expenditures as a percentage of GNP. Most
European countries spend at least twice the percentage for the

[8]Discussions of Social Security in the American media often shy away from cross-cultural
comparisons of *relative* GNP figures with those of other advanced countries, preferring to
emphasize the *absolute* size of overall American expenditures (which is a superficially
impressive figure) and the fact that such expenditures have expanded in recent years. This
emphasis on absolute expenditure levels rather than relative ones gives the misleading and
self-congratulatory impression that (1) Social Security benefits are generous in the United
States, and (2) that public expenditures in support of them are excessive and burdensome.
Relative GNP figures, however, reveal a very different picture.

United States. For example, during the mid-1970s in Sweden the figure was 24 percent, in contrast to 12 percent for the United States.[9]

Opponents of further expansion of Social Security often argue that if the United States were to increase its Social Security expenditures, this would necessarily have to be accomplished at substantial sacrifice to the overall economy in terms of growth, inflation, and productivity rates. This argument has become especially popular as perceptions of economic scarcity have increased over the past several years. Yet, if one compares the United States with European countries that maintain high levels of social security spending, this assumption does not appear to be borne out (see Table 6-II). If we look at West Germany and Sweden—two of the countries with the highest expenditures on social security as a percentage of GNP—we find that major economic indicators continue to be equal to or even stronger than those in the United States, despite a greater national commitment to financing social services for the aged and other dependent groups. Levels of economic growth (percent rise in GNP annually), productivity (percent rise in output per hour worked), and industrial production (percent rise annually) remain somewhat higher in these countries than in the United States. Since it is often argued that the extensive social programs provided by European welfare states have undermined individual initiative and work incentives, it is of note that in 1979 productivity increased by 3.5 percent in Sweden and 3.6 percent in West Germany, compared with 0.5 percent in the United States (see Table 6-II). Nor does the argument appear to be valid that generous social security expenditures

---

[9]Trends in social security spending for the most part correspond with overall national trends in government spending. For instance, as of 1978, overall government spending as a percentage of GNP in the United States was 32 percent. In Japan and Australia, where social security expenditures are also comparatively low, one finds a similar trend, with 25 percent and 26 percent respectively of total GNP devoted to government-sector spending. In countries where social security spending is more extensive, this is usually reflective of a societal tolerance of higher levels of public-sector spending. In West Germany, Sweden, France, Netherlands, Belgium, and Denmark, all of which maintain comparatively high social security expenditures, overall government spending as a percentage of GNP is also rather high: 47 percent, 62 percent, 42 percent, 54 percent, 42 percent, and 48 percent respectively (United Nations, 1979a; Organization for Economic Cooperation and Development, 1980:81).

The Politics of Aging

TABLE 6-I

SOCIAL SECURITY SPENDING* AS A PERCENT OF GROSS NATIONAL
PRODUCT FOR EIGHTEEN COUNTRIES IN 1949, 1966, AND 1974

Country	1949	1966	1974
Netherlands	8.1	18.3	25.2
Sweden	9.1	17.5	24.5
Germany (Federal Republic of)	13.7	19.6	22.3
France	11.0	18.3	21.7
Italy	8.2	17.5	21.4
Denmark	7.8	13.9	21.0
Belgium	11.8	18.5	20.6
Austria	11.6	17.6[†]	18.2
Norway	6.5	12.6	17.8
Czechoslovakia	-----	17.2	17.5
Luxembourg	-----	15.6[†]	17.2
Ireland	7.2	11.1	15.8
Finland	6.2	13.1	15.4
United Kingdom	10.6	14.4	14.6
Canada	6.1	10.1	13.9
Switzerland	5.8	9.5	13.9
United States	4.4	7.9	11.9
Japan	-----	6.2	6.3

Source for 1949, 1966: Table 2, Wilensky (1975:30-31).
Source for Austria, Luxembourg 1965: Table 2, International Labour Office (1979:58).
Source for Belgium, France, Germany (FR), Japan, Netherlands, Sweden, United States 1974: Table 1, Ross (1979:4).
Source for Austria, Canada, Czechoslovakia, Denmark, Finland, Ireland, Italy, Luxembourg, Norway, Switzerland, United Kingdom 1974: Table 2, International Labour Office (1979:56-59).

*Defined broadly to encompass related expenditures under public medical care services and cash payments under public welfare programs.

†1965 data.

necessarily result in high rates of inflation. Both Germany and Sweden are presently maintaining slightly lower inflation rates than the United States, despite social security expenditures that are twice as extensive.[10] The West Germans and Swedes have somehow managed to maintain large expenditures devoted to social security for the elderly and other dependent groups without impairing overall economic well-being.[11]

Still another indicator of societal commitment to the provision of social security is the willingness to pay for it through taxation:

[10]The comparison here is based on relative percent GNP figures.

[11]See Taber (1980:54).

TABLE 6-II

SOCIAL SECURITY EXPENDITURES AND ECONOMIC INDICATORS FOR
WEST GERMANY, SWEDEN, AND UNITED STATES

	West Germany	Sweden	United States
PER CAPITA GNP IN U.S. DOLLARS (1978)	$10,419	$10,543	$9,687
Social Expenditures			
Public-sector expenditures as a percent of GNP (1978) ...	46.7	61.6	32.1
Social security* as a percent of GNP (1974)	22.3	24.5	11.9
OASDI as a percent of GNP (1974)	7.9	7.2	4.0
Social security medical benefit expenditures as a percent of GNP (1974)	5.7	7.3	2.6
Percent annual increase in medical care expenditures (1960-1976)	14.5	14.4	10.9
Economic Indicators			
Productivity (percent annual increase in output per hour worked) (1979)	3.6	3.5	0.5
Growth (percent annual increase in GNP) (1979)	4.5	4.0	2.0
Industrial production (percent annual increase) (1979) .	4.5	6.5	2.5
Inflation (percent annual increase in C.P.I.) (1979)	5.7	8.4	12.2
Unemployment as a percent of the labor force (1979) ..	3.8	2.1	5.8

Source for Social Security and OASDI Data (most recent available comparable statistics 1974): Ross (1979:4)
Source for Medical Expenditure Data (most recent available comparable statistics 1974, 1976): Simanis and Coleman (1980: 6,7)
Source for Per Capita GNP (1978): United Nations (1979B:5,8)
Other Economic Indicators (1979) derived from the following sources:
Ministry of Economic Affairs (1980A:19,24; 1980B:6,42,47), Quarterly Economic Review (1980A:5-7; 1980B:5-7; and 1980C:5-7), Organization for Economic Cooperation and Development (1980:12,81), U.S. Department of Commerce (1980: 64), Federal Reserve Bank of St. Louis (1980:24,26,52,54,67,69), United Nations (1979A:437-440,1280-1285,1461-1464).

*Defined broadly to encompass related expenditures under public medical care services and cash payments under public welfare programs.

Swedes pay approximately half of their total earnings to the government each year in taxes to maintain their elaborate system of social welfare programs; West Germans pay about 37 percent of their total in income taxes; and, although per capita income in the United States is comparable with both countries, Americans pay only 29 percent of their total earnings to government (Zetterberg, 1979). Yet Americans find even this substantially lower tax rate to be excessively burdensome, and in recent years this sentiment has produced a minor "tax revolt" in the American context, expressing itself in the form of "Proposition 13"-style referenda designed to lower, or repeal, existing tax measures. As we noted previously, a 1979 poll showed 71 percent of Americans in favor of using cuts in social programs as a method of combatting inflation. By contrast, despite tax rates that are almost double those in the United States, those favoring social program cutbacks remain a minority in Sweden at 39 percent (Zetterberg, 1979).

Health and Medical Care

If one takes a closer look at the provisions of specific old-age programs, differences in extent of societal commitment to adequate services for the elderly become more apparent. Health and medical care provisions are the mainstay of any old-age policy package, since health problems increase in frequency and intensity with advancing age. West European and Scandinavian old-age health care systems are generally described as being at once more comprehensive, more progressive, and more innovative than those in the United States. In addition, they have usually done a better job of integrating the various types of services provided (Miller, 1968; Board, 1970; Townsend, 1968*a,b;* Aging, 1975; Marmor, 1969; Ross, 1979; Simanis and Coleman, 1980).

The United States is the only remaining modern industrial nation that lacks a unified national health insurance plan (U.S. Dept. of H.H.S., 1980). In recent years, attempts to stimulate serious legislative consideration of such a plan in the United States Senate, spearheaded by Senator Edward Kennedy of Massachusetts, have thus far failed to attract sufficient support to produce passage of any program of national health insurance. Many observers expect that when a national health plan does eventually make its way through Congress, it will be a scaled-down version that minimizes the extent of public sector involvement in the process.

In keeping with the central value tenets of individual liberty, self-reliance, and limited government, medical care in the United States continues to be administered primarily through private arrangements, and patients are expected to arrange their own medical insurance through commercial insurance companies.[12] The government now provides limited programs, such as Medicare and Medicaid for the elderly, but only rarely do these programs actually cover the full range of medical expenses an older person incurs during the declining years of life. The usual combination of private insurance coverage and limited government insurance (Medicare), which applies to most Americans, covers some types of expenses, but not others. The following expenses are not presently covered: drugs and medicines (either with or without a prescription from a physician), hearing devices and hearing examinations, eyeglasses and eye examinations, immunizations, dental care, self-administered injections (e.g. insulin), full-time nursing care in the home, and routine foot care. There are also limitations on the number of days of hospital or nursing home care Medicare will cover. Since health expenditures for drugs, prosthetic devices, home-health services, and dental services frequently must be paid by the aged out of private resources, the elderly (especially those who are poor) tend to delay medical care as long as possible. This works against long-range preventive and rehabilitative approaches to health care (Hammerman, 1974).

Existing American health-care practice is based on a medical model of acute illness. Medical care is oriented toward the isolation and treatment of specific ailments and toward dealing with medical emergencies. This emphasis on acute illness means that chronic ailments marked by nonspecific or multiple causation may go unattended for years. By the time such long-term condi-

---

[12]In response to the gap left by governmental reluctance to step in and provide a national health insurance plan, health maintenance organizations (HMO) have begun to emerge in the United States on a limited basis. Health Maintenance Organizations provide comprehensive health services to subscribing members who pay a fixed premium in order to receive coverage of both long-range preventive and acute treatment services.

tions manifest themselves in specific symptoms, it may be too late to reverse the process.

Federal funds available for Medicare have increased in recent years, and the percentage of total health care covered by the program has also increased, but inflation has largely absorbed these gains. Since Medicare was enacted in 1965, the proportion of medical expenses the aged are themselves forced to pay has actually increased. The cost of health care has skyrocketed, and a recent estimate indicates that Medicare covers only 38 percent of the total medical expenses of the elderly (Cohn, 1980).[13] Through its funding priorities, the Medicare program has also tended to emphasize institutional care at the expense of home-health care. Since professional home-health services for the elderly must come largely out of their own pockets, there is a built-in disincentive attached to this option, except for those with high personal incomes.

By contrast with the situation in the United States, in most European countries the costs of health care are more thoroughly subsidized by the government. The American system is based on a "residual" health-care model, in that it is intended to provide help in times of acute need. The general European trend has been toward adoption of an "institutional redistribution of wealth" model (Zetterberg, 1979). Physicians are employed primarily by the government, rather than through the private sector, and costs of medical treatment are financed through collective taxation.

The Scandinavian countries are the world leaders in life expectancy and in the proportion of the citizenry over sixty-five. Their old-age policies are therefore of special import. Contrary to what many Americans believe, the gradual conversion to "socialized medicine" in Scandinavia has not produced corresponding declines in either the overall quality of health care or the attractiveness of the medical profession to prospective doctors. A comparative study of health care in Denmark and the United States conducted by Townsend (1968c) found the quality of health care for the elderly to be generally comparable in the two countries. Physicians in Sweden continue under the "income redistributive" model to com-

---

[13]Counting such other programs as Medicaid for the poor, the government was paying 54 percent of the total health bill at the end of the 1970s (Cohn, 1980).

mand very large incomes by Swedish standards. They are highly regarded as a profession and are supportive of Sweden's National Health Insurance program (Board, 1970).

In Denmark, a country typical of Scandinavia and much of Western Europe, a comprehensive system of medical care is provided to the elderly (and other age groups) through local and state-administered health insurance societies. Ninety-five percent of the Danish citizenry receives its health care in this manner. For elderly persons living on pensions, membership in these societies is free.[14] Medical treatment, hospitalization, and all vital medicines are provided without charge. In addition, the aged are eligible for dental care, physiotherapy, eye care, and pedicures at no cost. Health care is comprehensive in scope, with even funeral expenses being borne by the government (U.S. Dept. of H.H.S., 1980).

The Swedish National Health Insurance program is compulsory and is available to all citizens, foreign nationals, and resident aliens. The program is financed by contributions from the government, employers, and employees. As in Denmark, the scope of health care provided to the elderly is comprehensive, and most services are provided either free of charge or at token cost to the insured. This includes not only the cost of hospital stays and vital medicines, but extends as well to the provision of hearing aids, dental care, wheelchairs, artificial limbs, and eye care (Board, 1970; U.S. Dept. of H.H.S., 1980). Pensioners are even reimbursed for transportation costs to and from medical facilities (Aging, 1975).

In addition to these purely medical functions, the Swedish plan attempts to offset loss of earnings caused by sickness. This is done by providing a sickness benefit that is directly related to the recipient's previous income level. The benefit commences one day after the onset of the illness and continues thereafter until it is replaced by a pension. Given the extensive range of these provisions, it is not surprising that Swedish hospitals are sometimes

---

[14]Pension eligibility usually commences at age sixty-seven for men and age sixty-two for women. In extenuating circumstances persons may be eligible at sixty, and disability pensions are payable to citizens between fifteen and sixty-seven whose earning capabilities have been substantially reduced.

referred to as "medical supermarkets" for the elderly. The extensiveness of these provisions can be attributed to "community minded" cultural traditions that have long prevailed in the Swedish context (Board, 1970).

Combating disengagement by encouraging the continuation of an active, productive life among the elderly is a major Swedish old-age policy objective. In the area of health care this includes (1) ample, easy availability of health services at minimal cost, so that early detection of chronic ailments will not be impeded by fear of undue personal expense, (2) emphasis on home care so as to prolong active, independent functioning whenever possible, and (3) a long-range, preventive-rehabilitative approach to health care (McRae, 1975; Kahn and Kamerman, 1975).

An important feature of Danish, Swedish, and Norwegian health insurance schemes is their emphasis on provision of home-health services. Allowing the elderly to retain independence and self-supervision as long as possible is a high-priority policy objective (Townsend, 1968a; McRae, 1975; Kahn and Kamerman, 1975). This differs from the present American policy, in which Medicare typically covers hospital or nursing home services, but is restrictive in its provision for home-health services.[15] In Scandinavian countries, home helpers and home nurses visit free of charge on a daily basis (if necessary) to help with personal services such as bathing, dressing, shopping, cooking, cleaning, and correspondence. In Sweden, over one percent of the work force are employed as "home-helps," and there is also a program whereby the government will pay relatives for caring for older family members under certain circumstances (Kahn and Kamerman, 1975; Califano, 1981). The home-health emphasis in Scandinavia was adopted not only for humanitarian reasons but also for reasons of efficiency (McRae, 1975). Studies have shown that it costs a municipality less to provide a pensioner with twenty hours per week in home-health services than it would to pay expenses for care in a nursing home (Faramond, 1973).

---

[15]Medicare does not include a provision for full-time nursing care in the home, although it does pay for a limited number of "visits" per year by skilled persons from any agency that participates in Medicare. It does not pay for meals that are delivered to the home nor for services such as cooking, bathing, dressing, or cleaning. For the lowest income category, however, Medicaid often pays for services that would not otherwise be covered by Medicare.

A recent cross-national study of home-health services ranked advanced countries on the basis of the number of home-helps per 100,000 persons in the population. In the first group, with 100 or more home-helps per 100,000 population, were Sweden, Norway, the Netherlands, and Great Britain. In the second group, with 19–99 home-helps per 100,000 were Finland, Belgium, Switzerland, Canada, and West Germany. The third group, with 2–18 home-helps per 100,000, included the United States, France, Israel, Japan, and Austria. In the fourth group, with less than one home-help per 100,000, were Australia and Italy (Beattie, 1976).

Pensions and Income Maintenance

For retired persons the continued maintenance of a standard of living comparable to that which prevailed during the most productive years of employment is an important need. Equally important is the need to make the transition from work to retirement as gracefully as possible, since abrupt changes may adversely affect income level, life-style, and self-concept. Different societies respond to these needs in somewhat different ways, and the response often reflects cultural attitudes toward productivity and the proper role of work.

Official retirement age varies among modern developed countries, but in most cases these differences are of limited significance, and one should avoid reading too much into them. Retirement age in the United States is sixty-five, or sixty-two if the recipient wishes to accept a reduction in benefit amount. West Germans are eligible for pension benefits at age sixty-five. Danish men and married women are eligible for social security at age sixty-seven, and single women become eligible at age sixty-two. In Sweden, all citizens who have been registered for census purposes for at least six years are eligible for a pension at age sixty-seven. There is an additional provision for commencing at age sixty-three, accompanied by a slight reduction in benefit amount. Norway has the highest retirement age of the Scandinavian countries at seventy.

In Japan, the pattern is noticeably different than in Europe and the United States. Most Japanese workers retire at age fifty-five and are often encouraged to retire even earlier—sometimes as early as forty-five (The Economist, 1977). Women usually retire at age fifty. Retirement benefits do not commence, however, until sixty or sixty-five, which tends to place the burden of support heavily on the family during the intervening years. This trend probably reflects a mixture of the Japanese cultural tradition of filial piety and the modern industrial productivity ethic (which attempts to get less productive workers out of the work force as quickly and efficiently as possible).

Several indicators of pension quality can usefully be compared across cultural contexts in order to gain a sense of the relative adequacy of pension systems. These include the level at which pensions maintain the income status of the elderly relative to younger age groups, whether standard payments are issued contingent upon extent of previous earnings, the extent to which the government contributes to social security through general tax revenues, and the extent to which the choice to continue working beyond usual retirement age is recognized and respected by society.

With regard to the first criterion, it is important to note that Social Security in the United States is designed primarily to be a minimum-needs program. Older persons who are forced to rely on it as their only source of income typically find themselves below the poverty line (Schulz, 1980). Thus for some persons retirement can bring almost overnight poverty. When it was enacted in 1935, the Social Security program was not intended by itself to provide an adequate retirement income. Rather, it was intended to supplement private pensions or personal retirement savings. Social Security is also designed to function as a life insurance policy, with the surviving spouse or children receiving the benefits in monthly payments upon death.

For those not adequately covered under Social Security (OASDI) provisions, an ancillary program, the Supplemental Security Income (SSI) has been developed in recent years. Since 1974, SSI has provided a very low guaranteed annual income for the aged, blind, and disabled (Pratt, 1981; U.S. Dept. of H.E.W., 1973). Social Security benefits are supplemented until they reach the minimum level stipulated by SSI.[16]

---

[16]In 1978, this amounted to $208 per month for an individual living in his own household without other income, $139 for an adult living in another's household, and $312 for a married couple (Grundmann, 1979:44).

Considerable improvements have been made in Social Security provisions since 1935, but aged Americans nevertheless remain, by any interpretation of U.S. Census Bureau poverty figures, some of the poorest Americans (Williamson, 1979; Girshick and Williamson, 1982). They are disproportionately represented among the lowest income groups. Whereas they comprise only 11 percent of the population, persons over 65 account for 23 percent of Americans with incomes below $5,000 (Pepper, 1980).

This American pattern compares somewhat unfavorably with the income maintenance records of many West European countries. One investigation comparing pension systems and financial status of the elderly in the United States, Denmark, and Britain concluded that the situation of the aged in the United States is exceptional in the extent of its economic and social inequality and in the heterogeneity of circumstances among older persons (Wedderburn, 1968a,b). As compared with the American pattern, income of the elderly in Denmark tends to be more evenly distributed with less of an income disparity between elderly and nonelderly as well as between rich and poor elderly. The relatively better financial status of the elderly in Denmark can be attributed to a variety of factors: historical traditions of egalitarianism, cultural and social homogeneity, the comprehensive and noncontributory nature of the Danish full pension, the high level (relative to other incomes) at which the pension is set, and direct linking of the full pension to cost of living increases.

Comparing income adequacy in the three countries, Wedderburn (1968b) found that among elderly men in the United States, 36 percent were more than 20 percent below the median income level. This compared with 18 percent in Denmark and 29 percent in Britain. Among elderly women, 32 percent of Americans were more than 20 percent below median income, compared with 12 percent in Denmark, and 23 percent in Britain. In addition, economic inequality is substantially greater among the aged in the United States than in either Denmark or Britain.

A recent study of value concerns among Danish and Norwegian elderly found both Scandinavian groups to be preoccupied with personal issues rather than with economic security (Monk et al., 1976). On a Cantril Scale of perceived economic well-being, economic fears and aspirations were "infrequent and lacking in saliency" in both Danish and Norwegian samples. Since the Danish and Norwegian old-age pension schemes are two of the most comprehensive such systems presently in existence, it is reasonable to hypothesize that this observed lack of concern with economic well-being is attributable to the fact that these pensions influence the attitudes, concerns, and general outlook of the elderly. The evidence suggests that Danes and Norwegians have achieved a sense of psychological freedom that comes with societal assurances of a reasonable degree of economic security, and as a result most people are not particularly concerned about financial problems when old.

There are a number of reasons for making comparisons between the social programs in the United States and those in some of the most progressive Western European nations. One of the most important is to broaden our conception of what might be possible. It is more difficult to dismiss an alternative approach as being impractical or unfeasible if such a program has been working unproblematically for years in another advanced industrial nation. Not only would more ambitious social programs for the elderly be possible, it would appear that they would be possible without necessarily producing an overly negative impact on the economy. Such programs as Medicare, Medicaid, Social Security, and SSI have contributed to an increase in independence and autonomy for older Americans. But comparisons with various European nations suggest that elderly Americans do not achieve much by way of economic independence and autonomy as do their European counterparts.

Income maintenance and health care programs are of particular importance to the elderly. But there are other social programs that are also very important such as those relating to housing and transportation, which we have as yet not considered. Before doing so we will briefly consider the Older Americans Act. Over the years it has evolved into a major source of funding for service programs for older Americans. A major objective of these programs and related legislation is to increase the independence and autonomy of elderly Americans.

Older Americans Act and Other Social Service Legislation

The Older Americans Act (OAA) was enacted in 1965. Originally it was so minimally funded that it had little impact on the lives of the elderly, but with the amendments to the act that have been made over the years, it has evolved into a major source of funding for old-age service programs and a major lobby on behalf of such efforts. Title II established a federal administrative structure, the Administration on Aging, to oversee the various programs mandated by the act. Title IV funded centers for training and research in the area of gerontology. Title III B (originally Title V) funds multipurpose senior centers. Title III C (originally Title VII) funds nutrition programs for the aged. This includes both congregate meals at various nutrition sites and the meals-on-wheels program. Title III A funds regional Area Agencies on Aging for the coordination of social service programs for the elderly in the regional area. Among the services emphasized are transportation, home repairs, and legal counseling. The most important accomplishment of Title III to date is the establishment of this network of approximately 600 Area Agencies on Aging across the country. It constitutes an infrastructure for the coordination of comprehensive services for the elderly, and it also has come to be an active lobby on behalf of services for the aged.

While funding for the various programs established by the Older Americans Act has increased a great deal over the years, it is still far short of what would be required to achieve the very ambitious goals as specified in the original legislation. When the achievements of the program are compared with its stated goals, it is clear that the program has failed to accomplish most of its objectives. In fact, a case can be made that the goals as originally stated were for the most part political rhetoric. Most of the goals are not even dealt with by the various programs established by the act. The goals as specified in Title I of the act are to assure all older Americans:

- an adequate income in retirement in accordance with the American standard of living
- the best possible physical and mental health that science can

make available without regard to economic status

- suitable housing, independently selected, designed and located with reference to special needs and available at costs that older citizens can afford
- full restorative services for those who require institutional care
- opportunity for employment without discriminatory personnel practices because of age
- retirement in health, honor, dignity—after years of contribution to the economy
- pursuit of meaningful activity within the widest range of civic, cultural, and recreational opportunities
- efficient community services that provide social assistance in a coordinated manner and which are readily available when needed
- immediate benefit from proven research knowledge that can sustain and improve health and happiness
- freedom, independence, and the free exercise of individual initiative in planning and managing their own lives

Based on an examination of more than eighty federal programs related to the Older Americans Act, as well as the efforts of various state and local agencies to implement them, Estes (1979) concludes that the programs do not meet the goals defined in the Older American Act and that the status of the aged relative to other age groups has been altered very little by these federal programs. Estes attributes this conspicuous policy failure to such factors as (1) the lack of a coherent, comprehensive American old-age policy, (2) inability or unwillingness to alter the dominance of public policy decisions by powerful special interests, (3) failure to substantially alter existing patterns of resource allocation, (4) lack of accountability in implementation of programs by local and state agencies under "revenue sharing" and the "New Federalism," (5) inadequate feedback as to the outcomes and actual effectiveness of programs, and (6) restrictive levels of funding for OAA provisions, so that it is only possible to provide assistance to the elderly at token levels.

We have already discussed some of the deficiencies of American old-age policy in the vital areas of medical care and income maintenance. Another basic need of the elderly is for adequate housing. For aged persons living on fixed incomes, constantly rising rent and housing costs can be a serious financial burden. Overall, housing accounts for 29 percent of the total expenditures of the elderly (Brotman, 1978). Among renters, the problem is particularly acute. Renters with annual incomes below $5000 typically pay out 35 percent of their income in rent. Those who are 75 or older pay nearly 50 percent of their income (Estes, 1979).

Since the early 1970s periodic recessions, high inflation, and escalating energy costs have all accentuated the difficulty for the aged of affording adequate housing. Heating and utilities costs have increased at unprecedented rates. In many dwellings occupied by elderly persons physical conditions are substandard. Based on census data, Estes estimates that at least 30 percent of the American aged live in dwellings that are deteriorating, dilapidated, or scarcely inhabitable.[17]

The shortage of housing that has developed over the past fifteen years has been especially troublesome for older persons. The supply of adequate, low-cost housing has lagged behind demand, driving up prices of most rental units beyond levels affordable by elderly persons dependent on Social Security or SSI. The final report of the 1971 White House Conference on Aging (1971) described the supply of adequate housing available to the elderly as "woefully short."[18] Responses by the federal government to the impact of such shortages on the aged have included special programs offering low rent public housing and direct loans. Also, some states offer property tax relief to the elderly after they reach

---

[17]Based on data from the Department of Housing and Urban Development's Annual Housing Survey, Struyk and Soldo (1980:42–49) found that 6.2 percent of renters 65–75 years of age and 7.1 percent of renters 75 and over live in dwellings with deficient plumbing. Among single elderly below the poverty line, 11.9 percent live in such dwellings. Among elderly blacks the figure climbs to 13.6 of renters, in addition to which 11.2 of this same group have inadequate kitchen facilities, and 13.6 percent live in buildings in which two or more of these indicators of inadequate structural maintenance exist: leaking roof; substantial holes in walls, ceilings, or floors; peeling paint or broken plaster in excess of one square foot.

[18]According to one report there are some 99,000 aged persons in need of housing units in the Los Angeles area alone with an average of 5 applicants per available unit (Estes, 1979).

a specified age. Although this falls short of a full-scale solution to elderly housing dilemmas, it has at least helped to alleviate the shortage on a temporary basis in some areas.

During the past two decades the elderly poor living in inner-city areas have with increasing frequency found themselves displaced by urban renewal and condominium conversion projects. Relocation in housing that would be at once affordable and livable is difficult. Displaced elderly persons may find themselves with no financially feasible choice than to move into grossly inadequate quarters elsewhere. The final report of the White House Conference on Aging (1971) states that over 200,000 persons per year are forced to relocate, and about 20 percent of those households are headed by persons over 60. The 1970 Housing Act took an important first step toward improving this situation with its provision for an advisor service to counsel individuals forced to relocate. A large share of this displacement problem can be traced back to an earlier federal housing program. The Housing Act of 1949 initiated the urban renewal programs that replaced existing central city dwellings with housing, but was often affordable only to middle and upper-income groups. The net result was that those groups tended to benefit from the program at the expense of the poor, elderly, and minorities—who were displaced in the process (Butler, 1975; Anderson, 1965; Gans, 1966).

Elderly home owners, while usually not as disadvantaged as their apartment-dwelling counterparts, have nevertheless experienced their own set of problems in recent years. The prices of home heating oil, insulation, maintenance, and repairs have risen sharply in conjunction with inflation and energy costs.[19] In 1977, the Carter administration initiated an ongoing program designed to aid low-income elderly and handicapped persons in insulating and weatherizing their homes. But the meager initial appropriation of $27 million was indicative of the intentionally restrictive

---

[19]For example, the Community Services Administration found it necessary to appropriate $200 million to assist the elderly in the crisis resulting from the severe winter of 1976–1977 and to do the same again for the winter of 1977–1978. Funds were allocated to the states for emergency assistance in weatherization and to prevent utility cutoffs due to inability to pay the large bills. This government crisis response did not, however, carry any extensive or long-term commitment to the elderly (Estes, 1979).

scope of the program, limiting its effectiveness from the outset and proving to be little more than a token political gesture (Estes, 1979).

The problem of the *limited* nature of American housing programs for the elderly has been a recurrent one. Beginning in the New Deal era, federal legislation aimed at improving the housing situation of the American elderly has included such measures as the Housing Acts of 1937, 1949, 1959, and 1961, the Housing and Urban Development Act of 1964, the Model Cities programs of 1966, and the Housing and Community Development Act of 1974. Despite repeated enactment of housing legislation of this sort, less than 2 percent of all American families have been affected by these programs.

Given the reduced physical mobility of many of the aged and particularly the very old, the availability of transportation facilities assumes exaggerated importance. Health care and social services cannot be utilized if they cannot be reached. Transportation is also necessary to get to shopping areas, senior centers, and to visit friends.

For a variety of reasons, a large percentage of the aged do not drive. Costs of maintaining a car or health problems (e.g. vision, hearing, reaction time) often preclude use of an automobile. One study found that 30 percent of aged persons in the United States do not drive. This figure is substantially higher among the poor, women, and minorities. Another study reports that among elderly poor whites, 62 percent do not drive (Andrus Gerontology Center, 1978). In the absence of easy access to an automobile, many older persons must rely on public transit. Subways and buses are available in urban areas, and many cities offer reduced fares for the elderly and disabled. But millions of nonmetropolitan aged in the United States are without such transportation alternatives. For the urban elderly, elevated ramps and long, steep flights of stairs in subway entrances often create problems of access for aged and handicapped persons.

The Department of Health, Education, and Welfare (now Health and Human Services) and the Department of Transportation have initiated several programs designed to improve the transportation situation of aged persons. Amendments to the Urban Mass Transit

Act of 1964 have granted public transit corporations funds to incorporate features into buses and trains that will improve accessibility for the aged and handicapped. Also, small grants have been awarded to transportation companies to provide transportation in vans and mini-buses on a call basis.

Unfortunately, as with other types of federal aging programs, underfunding has been a chronic source of failure to achieve transportation program objectives. For instance, a program designed to pay volunteers for transporting elderly persons in their private cars has attracted few takers. Offering a federal stipend of seven cents per mile, the incentive proved too weak to attract significant numbers of volunteers (U.S. House of Representatives, 1976).

In the half century since the Social Security program was first enacted, the United States has slowly moved in the direction of a national aging policy. But the patchwork of partial federal programs that has evolved in the American context does not yet constitute a unified national approach. Typically, federal programs of restricted scope have arisen in response to the inability of private sector institutions to provide meaningful solutions to specific dilemmas posed by old age. As Heidenheimer et al. (1975) have pointed out, Americans remain reluctant to invoke public solutions if there is any possibility of private solutions.

It is not easy to admit that we in the United States are not the world leaders in the provision of adequate social services for the aged. To acknowledge that this situation may derive in part from some of our most cherished beliefs is even more difficult. Another barrier to adequate social services is cost, accompanied by an elaborate web of rationalizations as to why we can't, or shouldn't, or don't need to pay the price. If Americans wished to provide elderly citizens with social security coverage more on a par with that of many European nations, it would be possible to find economically viable ways to accomplish that goal. But those ways would require higher taxes — most likely of an income-redistributive sort. At present, Americans are unwilling to forego other advantages in order to pay that price, and this apparently constitutes the strongest source of popular resistance to further policy innovations. In fact, recent surveys indicate that many Americans are becoming increasingly reluctant to continue to provide even *pres-*

ent levels of funding—at least if doing so requires taxation extracted through the public sector (*New York Times,* 1979). In the last analysis it is today, just as it was two centuries ago, a question of societal priorities and how we choose to rationalize them.

The proliferation of programs, difficulties in implementation, problems of accountability, and the powerful influence of entrenched special interests have often impeded efforts to improve the circumstances of older Americans. To cite a prominent example, according to some analysts Medicare and Medicaid have proven more successful in aggrandizing physicians, hospitals, and the drug and health service industries than they have in assuring access to quality medical care for the elderly at an affordable price (Marmor, 1973; Hammerman, 1974). Rapid inflation in the costs of old-age medical care occurred in the wake of legislative enactment of the Medicare and Medicaid programs. High levels of fraud and abuse by old-age health service providers prompted Claude Pepper (1978), chairman of the House Select Committee on Aging, to describe the situation as a full-scale national scandal amounting to a billion-dollar "rip-off" of taxpayer dollars targeted for the elderly.

One factor contributing to the ineffectiveness of most social programs lies in the minimal level at which they have been funded relative to the ambitious objectives they have set out to accomplish and relative to the actual needs of aged Americans. In many cases restrictive funding has made it possible to provide assistance at only token levels or has limited distribution of services to a fraction of those persons actually in need of help. Total dollar amounts spent on elderly services can look superficially impressive, and sensationalistic media features dealing with "the high cost of Social Security" often seize on this tactic to drive home their point. But the reality of the problem of chronic underfunding becomes readily apparent if one calculates the amount of assistance received per elderly person. Cohen (1977) determined that Title III of the Older Americans Act, which provides a range of social services to the elderly (including home help, legal help, transportation, and housing renovation) receives funding at a level that makes possible a provision of less than fifty cents per month per elderly American.

ALTERNATIVE FUTURE SCENARIOS

Given these realities of the American policymaking environment, what sorts of developments can reasonably be expected in
old-age policy over the next few decades? Two alternative scenarios are discussed next.[20]
    In the United States the combination of a rapidly increasing old
age dependency ratio (ratio of elderly population to working-age
population) and declining economic growth could trigger a backlash against old-age programs. Indeed, there are indications that
we may already be in the early stages of such a development. The
historical reluctance of the United States to move beyond a political ideology of liberal-individualism suggests that in times of
perceived economic scarcity a reversion to earlier "self-reliance"
rationales may take place in order to justify cutbacks in social
programs that have become unnecessarily burdensome to the economy. This argument has been convincingly documented by Piven
and Cloward (1971) with respect to cycles of unemployment. They
argue that relief policies are determined in a market economy by
the needs of dominant political and economic interests. Expansive
welfare policies are initiated as a crisis response in order to mute
potential political disorder. Restrictive relief policies, designed to
reinforce work norms, are likely to reemerge when political pressures to maintain social programs are low relative to other resource
demands in the society. This same pattern is likely to apply with
minor modifications to old-age policy. Thus, the persistence of the
Lockean political formula could, under conditions of perceived
scarcity, provide the social rationale for a backlash against old-age
legislation, although the "undeserving poor" (e.g. AFDC, General Relief) would be the most likely *initial* targets of such a
retrenchment (Cook, 1979; Powell, 1980).
    There is another quite different scenario that is also possible. It

---

[20]There is a third and somewhat less plausible alternative that we should at least briefly
mention. Some have argued that as a result of the expected competition for federal funds, the
aged may become an increasingly cohesive political constituency (Weaver, 1981). What starts
out as an anti-aging backlash could end up having the unintended consequence of unifying
the aging and their advocates into a strong coalition that comes away from the conflict with
increased rather than decreased influence.

has been argued that a continuation of the weak economy of the 1970s may produce a change in the consumption habits, attitudes, and life-styles of Americans in the direction of a "post-industrial" value system such as that which has already begun to take hold in parts of Western Europe and Scandinavia (Lodge, 1976). According to this perspective, the pressures of the energy crisis, a no-growth economy, and the necessity of more frugal life-styles could be expected to gradually usher in a post-industrial deemphasis on productivity as a paramount social value. With the declining emphasis on industrial productivity and economic growth as primary indices of human progress, "quality of life" and "need satisfaction" might ascend to higher positions as social priorities. In such an environment, the provision of adequate social services to elderly persons could be expected to become a higher-priority economic demand than it is presently (Bell, 1974; Habermas, 1975; Ophuls, 1975; Green, 1975; Daly, 1975).

Unfortunately, of these two alternative scenarios the more optimistic one is not the most likely. For the United States, as well as most of Western Europe, the economic expansion phase that produced existing social programs is apparently over for the near term. Modern societies are entering a new era of caution and restraint, which foreign officials have begun to refer to as a "plateau" in the provision of social services (Ross, 1979). Erosion of earlier policy gains could be greatest in the United States, where existing programs are somewhat at variance with indigenous cultural values of individual self-reliance and limited government.

In advanced societies, different cultural reactions to this common economic stimulus of resource shrinkage will hinge on the existence of "zero sum" versus "non-zero sum" bargaining environments.[21] The highly competitive, heterogeneous, "zero sum" policy environment in the United States will most likely be characterized by various interest groups competing for scarce economic resources. In such a political context, the winning of policy gains

---

[21] In a "zero sum" environment a gain for one group implies a corresponding loss for others competing for the same portion of the policy pie, and action is based on self-interest rather than on the larger societal interest. In a "non-zero sum" environment, compromises are seen as possible in which several or all involved parties may gain without anyone necessarily losing.

by the most powerful interest groups at the expense of other groups (e.g. the aging coalition) is likely to be viewed as a normal, just, and legitimate outcome of competitive interest group bargaining.[22]

A dialectical model is useful for the analysis of competition in a zero-sum environment of this sort. The stronger one coalition becomes and the greater any increase in its share of societal resources, the greater the incentive for opposing coalitions to organize in an effort to regain that portion of resources that has been given up. The stronger the aging coalition gets, the stronger the anti-aging coalitions can be expected to become. Similarly, the stronger any aging backlash, the more likely the elderly will be to organize in self-defense.

In contrast, the policy atmosphere of social homogeneity, economic egalitarianism, and political compromise that has prevailed in countries like Denmark and Sweden is likely to view resource scarcity from a more consensual, non-zero sum perspective. The sense of community and shared destiny is likely to produce a long-range governmental response that does not entail significant cuts in social programs (Anton, 1969; Heisler and Kvavik, 1974; Kvavik, 1974). Zetterberg (1979) outlines three likely alternative responses of the Swedish welfare state to these emerging pressures: (1) continued evolution toward a social service system in which government assumes total responsibility for providing services free to all citizens; (2) replacement of the present "institutional redistribution of wealth" welfare model with a cheaper "residual" model resembling that of the United States (which provides help only in times of considerable need); and (3) renovation of the present social service system away from "free services" toward offering more services on a "fixed, small charge" basis. Zetterberg concludes that the third-policy alternative is the most likely adjust-

---

[22]In an article dealing with the future of American social programs for the aged, Hudson (1978a) predicts that the cost burdens of meeting elderly needs will produce heated debates over the distribution of scarce social service dollars. New cost-based and competitive political pressures will increasingly place agencies servicing the elderly under new and harder scrutiny. Since their "political legitimacy" is likely to erode as a bargaining resource, they may be left with only their "political utility." Within this zero-sum political context, the more the elderly seem to be enjoying themselves and the healthier they are, the more young workers may resent the economic burden of providing for them (Samuelson, 1978).

ment in the Swedish context, since the legitimacy and popularity of existing programs make dismembering the welfare establishment unthinkable to most Swedes. Guaranteed health care, housing, income maintenance, and education have become culturally established *rights*.

As Wilensky (1975) and others point out, there are substantial differences among advanced industrial nations with respect to "social security effort" (social security expenditures as a percent of GNP). How are we to account for these differences? To this point our emphasis has been on differences in political culture. An alternative perspective is to emphasize structural differences, particularly differences in the strength of those segments of the population that stand to benefit most from such programs, i.e. lower and middle-income groups. Here the argument is that differences in social welfare policy (of which programs for the aged are a major component) are due to differences in the ability of those in the "working class" (defined so as to include most of those in lower and middle-income categories) to impose their will on the state (Myles, 1981; Stephens, 1979). Thus, differences in social welfare policies between Sweden and the United States reflect differences in the outcome of "class struggle" (Gough, 1979).

Even class theorists must account for differences between nations in the strength of the working class. In this context, differences in historical experience are crucial. Historical factors help explain differences in the extent of cultural heterogeneity in the working class and differences in political culture. One important reason for the relatively underdeveloped state of social welfare programs for the aged in the United States is the relative weakness of the working class compared with a country such as Sweden. This weakness can be historically linked to the cultural diversity of the working class, which has tended to reduce class cohesiveness and political influence. It can also be historically linked to the American political culture with its emphasis on rugged individualism.

To this point in the book our emphasis has been on the macropolitics of aging. We have considered such issues as social policy, political culture, modernization, voter turnout rates, and historical trends. But we have given relatively little attention to issues of power and influence as they are reflected in the everyday lives of elderly people, particularly in their social interaction with others. The analysis of family relationships provides an appropriate forum for the study of this micropolitics of aging. One goal of the next chapter is to analyze the micropolitics of family relationships; another is to illustrate the link between the micro- and the macropolitics of aging by taking into consideration broader structural and cultural factors.

PART III:
POWER AND CONTROL
IN EVERYDAY LIVING

Chapter 7

POWER IN FAMILIES

$\mathbf{F}$amily life is very much a matter of give and take. But who gives, and who takes? Such issues are resolved by a process of negotiating and bargaining, and power is inextricably bound up in this process. Indeed, the concept of power is a key to understanding family relationships. Aging has complex effects on the power structure of the family, since the passage of time affects the members differently. For example, adult children generally gain in power relative to their aging parents; children may even attain dominance. The shifting balance of power between the spouses is complicated by the differential effects that aging has upon the personal power of men and women.

We begin our discussion by outlining "resource theory"—a theoretical framework useful for the study of family power. This framework is then used to analyze changes in the balance of power between elderly parents and their middle-aged children.[1] With respect to intergenerational power relationships, we argue that in recent years the autonomy of elderly parents has increased, but their power and influence over adult children has decreased, and this trend is likely to continue in coming decades. Resource theory can also be used to analyze changes in marital power relationships as couples age. Most studies of power relationships between elderly spouses have an important limitation: they tend to reflect yesterday's definitions of male and female roles. Recent changes in these roles may significantly alter the social meanings of aging for both men and women in coming years.

RESOURCE THEORY

A widely recognized theoretical framework for studying family

---

[1]For discussions of children in relation to family power, see Broderick (1975), Elder (1963), Scanzoni (1979), and Sprey (1972).

power is "resource theory," first formulated by Wolfe (1959) and subsequently elaborated by Blood and Wolfe (1960). The theory is strongly influenced by the earlier work on marital inequality by Herbst (1952). It is a variant of exchange theory (Blau, 1964; Homans, 1961; Dowd, 1980).[2] Resources are defined as anything one individual family member can offer another to help that person satisfy needs or attain goals. According to resource theory, the balance of power in decision-making is on the side of the individual who can offer the greater resources (Blood and Wolfe, 1960). Thus, the family member who has the greatest number of resources with which to meet other family members needs and goals is perceived to have the greater power within the family unit. The person desiring resources is assumed to be willing to relinquish power over his or her own conduct in exchange for access to those resources (Cromwell and Olson, 1975b). Resources are the currency in negotiations and are used to bargain for desired goals within the family (Scanzoni, 1979).

The idea that individuals have preferences, interests, and objectives that they desire or want to implement is central to resource theory. Marriage and family life provide a means of attaining specific goals, and these relationships persist as long as the ratio of costs to rewards is experienced by both parties as favorable (Scanzoni, 1978; Rubin and Brown, 1975).

The kinds of resources generally considered by those who have used this theory are income, education, and occupational status—the traditional determinants of status in social stratification. But these are not the only resources at the command of family members. Physical attractiveness, love, affection, and attention (Heer, 1963; Waller, 1937) can be used to bargain within the family unit. Physical strength is also a power resource, including the ability to

---

[2]The term *resource theory* is most closely associated with the work of Blood and Wolfe (1963) and those who have attempted to replicate it more recently (Cromwell and Olson, 1975a). Also, it is entirely consistent with the exchange theory perspective of Homans (1961) and Blau (1964). Resource theory is more focused on the issue of resources and has not been as fully elaborated as has exchange theory. Resource theory has been primarily used in the analysis of marital relationships and in this context it owes a debt to an earlier work by Herbst (1952) on marital inequality. In his use of exchange theory in the analysis of power and dependency among the aged, Dowd (1980) discusses "power resources"—a concept very close to the use of the term *resources* in the present context.

physically abuse another person, as in the case of the abuse of the elderly by their children (Steinmetz, 1978).

The exchange value of a given resource within a relationship is dependent on several factors: (1) whether one's exchange partner has resources at hand with which to bargain so that there is a balance in the relationship with this exchange partner; (2) whether or not a resource is readily available elsewhere, so that one partner is not totally dependent on the other for that resource; and (3) the ability of the partner to do without the resource if need be (Emerson, 1962; Blau, 1964).[3]

It is also important to recognize cultural limits on the use of resources to gain power. For example, children, despite their lack of socioeconomic resources, are protected from parental power by norms concerning their care. Men's greater physical strength and women's sexual favors typically have been considered resources. However, such resources are not relevant to power distribution in cultural contexts that forbid husbands' physical dominance of their wives or in which women take it for granted that they are to submit to their husbands' sexual desires (Rodman, 1972). The law in many societies limits the marital contract in ways that preclude full exercise of power, regardless of resources; thus, financially dependent wives are entitled to minimal food, clothing, and shelter.

Finally, the distribution of family power is dictated by social factors other than resources. In some families, husbands can demand more deference simply by virtue of being men and therefore "head of the family" (Rodman, 1967). Regardless of their other resources, such men have power derived from a traditional orientation that ascribes status to men on the basis of male authority

---

[3]Several theoretical and methodological criticisms have also appeared concerning resource theory (*see* Safilios Rothschild, 1970, 1976; Olson, 1969; Olson and Rabunsky, 1972; Turk and Bell, 1972; Sprey, 1972; Cromwell and Olson, 1975a; Price-Bonham, 1976). What is often criticized is the nature of the resources themselves. Safilios-Rothschild (1976:356), for example, argues that resource theorists typically do not discuss the full range of resources exchanged between spouses. These theorists are criticized for giving so much attention to a relatively small number of resources, particularly income, occupational prestige, and education. Safilios-Rothschild provides a detailed description of the variety of resources that may be exchanged between spouses. For a discussion of personality traits in relation to family power, see Centers et al. (1971). For a discussion of cultural differences in power relationships within families, see Rodman (1967).

and dominance (Scanzoni, 1970). Komarovsky (1962) found more of this "rule by authority" in lower blue-collar marriages than in high blue-collar families. A lower blue-collar wife feels her husband "has a right" to power because of his position as husband and that it is her "moral duty" to accept male dominance. There are, of course, variations of this pattern. Working-class families in which both husband and wife are employed often share the decision-making power more equally than do middle-class families in which both partners are employed. The typical middle-class working wife's contribution to the family income is small in proportion to her husband's. For the typical working-class family, the disparity between husband's and wife's income is not so great, and the disparity in power is correspondingly less.

The continued presence of a patriarchal ideology prevails among some ethnic groups (Spiegel, 1971). Among Spanish-speaking Americans the concept of "machismo" is perhaps the best-known example of the ideal of patriarchal authority: husbands must conceal their emotions from their wives, avoiding exposure of personal weaknesses and needs. Instead they must play a dominant, powerful, "macho," role.

THE BALANCE OF POWER BETWEEN PARENT AND CHILD

Demographic trends indicate that today's middle-aged adult is more likely to have a living parent than his or her counterpart in the last century (Treas, 1977). When we compare parents' and offsprings' resources, a difference is found. The parents' resources tend to decline steadily with advancing age while their offsprings' resources are increasing. This growing inequality in resources tends to produce an increasing dependency of parents on their children.

There tends to be a curvilinear relationship between power resources and age: the possession of resources is limited during the younger years, increases during the middle years, and declines with advancing age (Dowd, 1975). This relationship remains even for individuals at the upper socioeconomic levels, except in cases of extreme wealth.

Several researchers have noted that as the elderly's income diminishes with retirement and their social circle of friends and relatives begins to grow smaller through death and illness, children become socially and economically more important to them (Shanas and Streib, 1965; Carp, 1968). The loss of a spouse, a common occurrence at this point in the life cycle, further heightens the elderly's dependence (Adams 1970; Rosow, 1967). Elderly parents have a greater investment in maintaining a good relationship with their offspring, for their children may be the only alternative source of acceptance, approval, and aid (Matthews, 1978). When they are unable to offer their children resources of equal value in exchange for their help (and when they lack the opportunity to obtain these resources elsewhere), the elderly are often left with the sole option of placing themselves in a dependent and powerless role in relation to their adult children.

The diminution of the elderly's resources and their subsequent heightened dependency on offspring have led some researchers to claim that there is a reversal in the power relationship. In effect, parents are said to reverse roles with their children (Glasser and Glasser, 1962). Children may assume a greater role in the day-to-day decision-making for their dependent parents, and such role reversals can lead to personal problems and conflict within the parent-child relationship. Matthews (1978) notes that compliance with the child's definition of the situation is not uncommon. However, many parents react to their position of dependency by feeling angry and uncomfortable. There is some evidence that elderly men and women respond differently to the dependency role. Men want to be able to advise their children and are less likely to transfer authority over to them. Women, on the other hand, are more likely to accept the advice of their offspring and are more willing to transfer the authority and judgment of the husband to their own children (Clark and Anderson, 1967).

There are cultural limits on the extent to which children can exert total power over their parents, and there are powerful norms of filial responsibility that dictate certain respect toward and care for one's aged parents. Seelbach (1978) notes the importance of this norm and states that children are influenced by it. Shanas and Streib (1965), for example, found that a majority of those over sixty-five, as well as a majority under that age believed that support of older parents was an offspring's duty. Parents are aware of

this norm and may use it to gain leverage in an unbalanced
situation by evoking guilt in their offspring for not living up to it
(Matthews, 1978). Yet, there are limits to guilt as a mechanism of
control. Other cultural norms limit the responsibility that children have to their parents. For example, when sons and daughters
marry, loyalties are expected to shift.

Middle-aged adults with aged parents often have increased their
earnings, but at the same time they find that they are caught up in
a life cycle squeeze: their incomes are peaking, yet their expenses
continue to rise as their children go off to college or get married
(Oppenheimer, 1974; Hess and Waring, 1978). These life cycle
events place demands upon middle-aged parents. Recent demographic changes have compounded the problem, as population
shifts have created a situation in which there are fewer siblings to
share the burden of physical, financial, and emotional support of
elderly parents (Treas, 1977).

Women, who have traditionally been the "kin-keepers" (Shanas,
1965; Treas, 1977; Hess and Waring, 1978; Ward, 1978) are more
reluctant to be involved in "parent caring." Many find that it is
economically necessary to work, and that there is little time left over
to care for the needs of their elderly parents. Many of these women
feel caught between the needs of adolescent children, husbands,
and aging parents (Neugarten and Brown-Renzanka, 1978).

There are important class differences in the responses of adult
children toward their parents' dependency. Lieberman (1978) notes
that working-class children are more willing to tell it like they see
it to their parents. Middle-class children, on the other hand, are
more reluctant to intrude into their parent's affairs and are likely
to view such intrusions as an invasion of privacy. This delayed
reaction on the part of middle-class children may postpone the
recognition of important changes taking place with one's parents
and may also mean a greater reluctance among middle-class children to assume personal responsibility for their parents.[4]

---

[4]There are ethnic distinctions in children's willingness to take on responsibility for their
parents. Schorr (1960) notes that among blacks, there is more willingness to feel that aged
parents should be helped than among whites. Clark and Anderson (1967) note that among
immigrant families where kinship bonds are the major source of support in old age, the
continuation of the family line is of great importance; consequently, being a grandparent is
the equivalent of being the head of a dynasty.

In recent decades there has been an increase in the proportion of the elderly living in independent households and a corresponding decrease in the proportion living with children (Kobrin, 1976). As a result, there has been a decrease in economic dependence on their middle-aged children. The Social Security program has made a significant contribution to this trend (Johnson and Williamson, 1980). While it is the single most important factor, there are a number of others that have also contributed to the trend, including: the general rise in the standard of living; increases in the prevalence of private pension benefits, Medicare and Medicaid, and the Supplementary Security Income program; and the decline in the prevalence of poverty among the elderly (Williamson, 1979). The economic position of the elderly is much better today than it was twenty years ago (Schulz, 1980), and this trend has increased the autonomy of the aged. The reduction in economic dependence on middle-aged children has reduced the extent of the power middle-aged children have over elderly parents. However, the trend toward independent households for the elderly has also contributed to a decrease in the control these older parents have over the lives of their middle-aged children. Elderly parents are in a better position to influence and in various ways control the lives of their middle-aged children when living with them (Johnson and Williamson, 1980). Looking to the future, it seems likely that this trend will continue. The autonomy and financial independence of the elderly should continue to increase, and the extent of control over their middle-aged children should continue to decrease.

THE BALANCE OF POWER BETWEEN SPOUSES

In order to understand the power changes that take place between spouses as they age, it is necessary to analyze the roles and resources of men and women through their lives. Social roles not only affect marital power directly, they also have an indirect impact by limiting access to the resources on which power is based.

Sex differences in power and access to valued resources have consequences for many aspects of everyday life. This leads Karp and Yoels (1979) to conclude that there are differing life-curves for men and women in our society that can be accounted for in terms of the power differential that "ages" women faster than it does

men. A number of studies have presented empirical evidence
suggesting that persons who are more powerful are less sensitive
to the evaluations of others. One form this takes is their being less
able to view themselves from the perspective of others; that is,
they are less able to role-take or put themselves in the place of
others. One study reports that fathers are less accurate role-takers
than mothers, who in turn are less accurate than their children
(Thomas et al., 1972). This finding is entirely consistent with a
ranking of these actions with respect to power and resources.
Similarly, it can be argued that the general tendency for women to
be better able to pick up nonverbal cues (Rosenthal et al., 1974) is
linked to their having less power than men (Karp and Yoels, 1979).

The factors frequently considered important and those emphasized in resource theory are money, education, and occupational
status. Traditionally, access to these highly valued resources was
influenced by norms that defined a woman's place at home and a
man's at work (Gillespie, 1975; Rodman, 1967), and the resulting
economic inequality contributed to an imbalance of power within
marriage.

The traditional female role of housewife is nonpaying and, as
such, is devalued in the culture and in family negotiations, even
though studies have shown that housewives spend enormous
amounts of time at their occupations (about 100 hours per week)
according to a recent Chase Manhattan Study (Walum, 1977). The
Dictionary of Occupational Titles even rates animal caretaking
higher than homemaking.

When women are employed outside the home, their power
within the family is still not equal to that of their husbands,
because women do not typically gain the positions that can provide them with resources equal to men. They earn less and have
jobs of relatively low status.

However, according to western cultural tradition, women are
not without resources. They possess physical beauty, charm,
nurturance, and supportive attributes. But these resources not
only have little exchange value, some are also short-lived. Beauty,
for example, is a resource that women are taught to emphasize
(Bart, 1975). However, cultural definitions of female beauty tie it
firmly to a youthful appearance, dooming women to the loss of

this significant resource as they age (Sontag, 1972). A woman's worth is also determined by the resources she offers as wife and mother; these are tied to her supposed affective and nurturing attributes. Yet these roles also decrease in importance over time (Bell, 1976). The role of wife may be lost at any time through separation, divorce, or widowhood (Howe, 1977). Even if a wife remains married, her children will inevitably grow up and leave home, leaving her without an appropriate "market" for her resources.

In this century for the first time in history, substantial numbers of people have come to experience a stage in the family life cycle that begins when the last child leaves home. Primarily because of increased longevity, this post-parental stage has increased considerably. The resources of the wife improve during this post-parental stage, because she now has the option of expanding her resource base outside the family unit in the world of work, and she need no longer define her status and sense of worth entirely in terms of her role within the family. Even women who have worked through all or part of their childrearing years have more time and energy to devote to development of personal resources. This is said to be an important developmental phase for women, with its freedom to develop a personal identity (Aldous, 1978; Deutscher, 1964; Rubin, 1979; Williams, 1979).

Yet women may also experience a crisis of purposelessness or meaning when their days of active mothering are behind them, when their primary role has therefore been lost (Bart, 1971; Bernard, 1971; Karp and Yoels, 1979). Depression is common and is most prevalent among women who have made the deepest commitment to motherhood and domesticity.

Some argue that the problem facing a middle-aged woman is not so much that her children have left home, per se, but that they have left her powerless. What further exacerbates the middle-aged women's sense of powerlessness is that men at this same stage of life continue to direct much of their energies toward job and career. The middle years represent the peak of a man's influence and earning power. If we consider the occupational role one of the primary resources, the middle-aged woman is relatively powerless compared to her male contemporary. The power differential between

men and women can only add to a woman's dismay at reaching
middle age (Butler, 1978).

Even if women go to work, they have difficulty gaining access to
the higher paying jobs, since women of this age are often ill-
equipped for the work force. Many lack work experience outside
the home and formal education or training to compete for well-
paying jobs (Butler, 1978).

Other research provides a somewhat more optimistic view for
women: several researchers report that menopause is not perceived as a central or even a distressing event by women in or past
that stage (Neugarten et al., 1960; McKinlay and Jeffreys, 1974).
Campbell (1976), on the basis of his recent survey, concluded that
the empty nest has a reputation that is not deserved. Other studies
confirm that women whose children have left home have a lower
incidence of depression and a higher level of well-being than
women living with young children (Barnett and Baruch, 1979).[5]

The resources a husband brings to a marriage are relatively
strong throughout his working life. It has been argued that for
many men power and status tend to increase during the middle
years and in so doing increase the resource inequality between
husband and wife (Sontag, 1972; Bell, 1976). The difference in
median income between men and women tends to be at a maxi-
mum during the ages of forty and sixty (U.S. Bureau of the
Census, 1978). This trend is particularly true for middle class as
opposed to working-class males. For example, Kreps (1976a) points
out that the age at which people's incomes are maximized tends to
be later for those with more education. Recently, however, Rosenbaum (1980, 1981) has come up with some evidence that suggests a
somewhat different conclusion. He finds that promotion rates
drop off very rapidly after age forty, with rates peaking for both
managers and workers at about the same age in the middle thirties.
This would suggest that it is the rare rather than the typical man
who continues to be promoted. For most men, increases in status
and income during the middle years are quite modest. During the

---

[5]The divergence in the findings on women in mid-life may partly be due to the fact that the
studies were done in different years. The social meaning of aging is changing for women as
sex roles change. We would expect that women in different birth cohorts will have different
experiences at mid-life.

years up to about age forty, the resource gap between husband and wife tends to widen, but from that point through retirement there is typically little by way of an increase in the resource advantage for the husband. With retirement, the resource gap begins to close.

Retirement may mean a substantial loss of income (pension and Social Security checks replace salary and wages), and the overall standard of living generally declines.[6] More importantly retirement means the loss of occupational status and withdrawal from the many resources associated with participation in the work world. Retirement generally results in the husband spending large blocks of time at home—a setting that for most men is devoid of roles associated with a sense of accomplishment or meaningful expenditure of effort (Aldous, 1978).

The impact of retirement varies, though there appear to be class differences in reactions to the loss of work roles. Aldous reported that only 20 percent of lower status men and 46 percent of their wives mentioned some unpleasant aspect of retirement, as compared with 81 percent of the higher status husbands and 93 percent of their wives (Aldous, 1978). Middle-class men appear to have a greater stake in work roles than working-class men and thus have a more difficult time adjusting to retirement (Crawford, 1971). Their careers tend to be more satisfying in terms of intrinsic interest, employment conditions, and prestige. In addition, they more often find personal identity in their careers and occupations; thus, they have more to lose in retirement. Working-class men are more likely to feel relieved to be finished with the dull routine of the same old job, although they may miss the companionship of their workmates (Aldous, 1978).

Maleness itself may become more of a resource in the later years, because men are in scarcer supply. Also, the fact that men have more potential partners than women do (since they not only have women of their own age but can also select younger partners) enhances their value. A wife might see her husband as more valuable, warts and all, when her friends become widows.

---

[6]Aldous (1978:198) reports that there is a 15 percent drop in income between the ages of 55–64 and 65–74. Poverty rates are also higher for those over age 65 than for persons in their middle years (U.S. Bureau of the Census, 1980c).

The family life cycle begins with the marriage of the young couple and continues through the reproductive years until children are raised and launched, leaving the couple alone together again, finally ending with the inevitable death of one spouse (Glick, 1977: Schram, 1979). At different stages in the cycle there are shifts in the distribution of power within the family (as one would expect from the previous discussion of resource changes over this period), but the husband maintains power through *most* of the life cycle.

The first major study of marital power, done by Blood and Wolfe (1960), measured family power by asking, "Who usually makes the final decision?" in eight significant areas of family life. They found that husbands control most of the decision making. It is noteworthy that not all areas are of equal importance. Husbands not only make more decisions, they are also more powerful regarding more significant issues. Safilios-Rothschild (1976) makes a distinction between "orchestration" and "implementation" power. The more powerful spouse, in resource theory terms, has "orchestration" power; that is, he (for it is usually the husband) makes the "big" but infrequent decision that provide a context within which the many dozens of smaller "implementation" decisions are relegated to the less powerful spouse.

Results from a study of 776 husbands and wives in the Los Angeles area (Centers et al., 1971)—a study that closely follows Blood and Wolfe's (1960) procedure—essentially confirms their picture of marital power. Blood and Wolfe's index of decision-making power has been used in studies in Western Europe as well, with the consistent finding that husbands have greater power than wives (Scanzoni, 1979). Results indicated that husbands also have more power than their wives when it comes to resolving conflicts. Nearly half the husbands, but less than one third of the wives prevailed in the area considered most significant. The remaining couples claimed to compromise or to never disagree (Scanzoni, 1972).

The greater the resources (income, occupational status, and social class), the greater the power (Gillespie, 1975). We can thus expect that husbands of higher social standing have more power within the family (Blood and Wolfe, 1960). Middle-class husbands make more of the family decisions than do working-class husbands, who in turn make more such decisions than lower-class husbands (Scanzoni, 1972).[7]

The balance of power between husband and wife changes through the life cycle. The husband's power relative to that of the wife has been found to increase with the birth of the first child and with the birth of each additional child (Blood and Wolfe, 1960; Heer, 1958). During the period in which there are small children at home it is common for the wife to stop working or at least reduce her commitment to work. She thus loses valued resources by withdrawing from the work world and at the same time becomes more dependent upon her husband to meet her economic as well as social and emotional needs. The husband's situation during this same period of time can be quite different. His resources, which are typically based outside the home and in the work place, are maturing. The wife's power has been found to pick up again as each child enters school and as the children leave home and she returns to work or devotes more attention to it. At this stage, the husband's career may be leveling off, and he may be moving toward retirement.

After the last child leaves home, the husband and wife find that they are alone together again for the first time in many years. The couple must now renegotiate their relationship, since their stock of resources has also changed. The wife is no longer responsible for the children on a daily basis, while her husband's investment in work roles is declining. During this life cycle stage there is the tendency for both spouses to be more flexible in their social roles (Aldous, 1978). In their sample of elderly couples, Clark and Anderson (1967) noted that those couples who reported happy marriages tended to characterize their relationship as more egalitarian. Husbands and wives become social equals, dividing up household tasks, and in the process blending masculine and feminine roles. Retirement generally contributes to a more egalitarian home situation with an increasing emphasis on a more com-

---

[7]Other research indicates that husbands report less power for themselves than their wives claim for them, and that wives similarly view themselves as less powerful than their husbands perceive them (Heer, 1963). But both husbands and wives attribute more power to husbands than to wives.

panionate marriage.[8]

As people grow old their marriages tend to become more egalitarian, but the balance of power continues to favor the male. While the husband's decision-making power does decline, there are still strong cultural norms and structural factors that tend to perpetuate the power inequalities that have evolved over the years. This is especially true within working-class families, where strong norms of male authority persist.

Looking to the future we anticipate a continuation of present trends. Marriages will continue to become more egalitarian, and the extent of role blurring will increase. But there are a number of structural constraints that are likely to preclude complete equality of power in the foreseeable future. One such factor is the tendency for women to live approximately eight years longer than men (Harris, 1978). Even if more women select partners their own age as opposed to older partners, there will continue to be far more elderly women than elderly men. There is no evidence that the sex difference in life expectancy is decreasing. The relative abundance of elderly women relative to elderly men will continue to provide men with a bargaining chip in the marital relationship.

A second structural advantage favoring men is their greater earning power during the preretirement years. There is no evidence that this difference is going to be eliminated in the foreseeable future.[9] While the male advantage does decline at retirement (Schulz, 1980), the consequences of having earned more will tend

---

[8]Not all marriages in old age move in the direction of more compatibility. Clark and Anderson (1967) report a number of unhappy marriages where there is great deal of hostility between couples. Moreover, there are social-class differences that affect the extent to which the husband's involvement in the home and sharing of household tasks are seen as desirable. There is more of a tendency for working-class couples to experience conflicts based on the husband's guilt and the wife's irritation at having had their role spheres invaded (Kerchoff, 1966).

[9]Rosenbaum (1980, 1981) has made some interesting observations as to structural factors that contribute to the continued inequality in earnings between men and women. He presents data that are consistent with a "tournament model" of job advancement within a large organization. He finds that the chance of advancement is greatest for the 25–35 year age group, and that the chance of significant promotion after age 35 is greatly reduced. Women who are simultaneously involved in childrearing are at a disadvantage in this competition and risk being passed over for advancement. Once this occurs the chance of future advancement is reduced.

to persist. A substantial minority of elderly males (some 20%) remain in the labor force (U.S. Bureau of the Census, 1976). Others will have pension benefits that a wife would be ineligible for in the event of divorce.[10]

CHANGES IN SEX ROLES AND FAMILY POWER

Traditional sex role expectations limit women's access to a range of economic and social resources by defining her place to be at home, raising children. What happens as sex roles, especially women's roles, change? Of all the changes that are taking place in women's roles, increased employment is perhaps the most important with regard to power. In addition, the trend towards rationalization of childbearing and the increased availability of birth control increase women's access to resources and power. More women are deciding not to have children or to have small families, and they are able to act upon these decisions. As these changes take place, they are enhanced by altered expectations and norms concerning women's proper role and power within marriage.[11]

Child-free wives have relatively more power during the first two decades of marriage than do wives with children. Many more of these wives are likely to continue working and have independent access to valued resources. Blood and Wolfe's (1960) study included a comparison of the power distribution for couples with children and those without, which Leslie (1973) presents in graph form (*see* Fig. 7-1).

According to resource theory, the wife who works makes a valuable contribution to the household. She gains a valuable

---

[10]Recently, Social Security regulations were modified, making it possible for a woman who was married for more than ten years to collect benefits based on her husband's work history in the event of divorce, but such a provision is not found in many private pension plans.

[11]These findings are not without controversy. Corrales (1975), for example, found no evidence that the coming of children decreased the wife's power by creating needs that lead her to become more dependent on her husband. Sprey (1975) pointed out that the situation for the husband of having a wife and small children at home creates additional needs for the husband, some of which likely increase his dependence on the wife.

resource — money — with which to bargain within the marital unit.[12]
Empirical data confirm that employed wives have greater power
in the family than nonemployed wives (Bird, 1979; Heer, 1963).
Heer (1963) found that wives who provided between 25 percent
and 40 percent of the family income had more power as decision
makers. Other research has reported that the longer the wife's
participation in the labor force, the greater her power (Gillespie,
1975; Blood and Hamblin, 1958; Blood and Wolfe, 1960). The

[12]This description of shifts in marital power derives from a resource theory approach and
applies to the "typical" white, middle-class family. Many families do not follow such a cycle,
but end in separation, divorce, or the death of one spouse. Some individuals may repeat
these stages through remarriage.

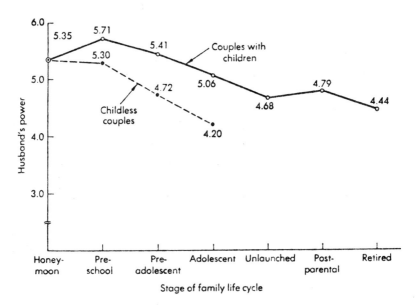

Figure 7-1. Husband's power by stage in family life cycle, Detroit area couples.
(Data for childless couples were tabulated separately by equivalent length of marriage through twenty-two years of marriage. After twenty-two years, data on the
childless couples are merged with those on the childbearing couples for the
remaining stages of the family life cycle.) From *The Family in Social Context* by
Gerald R. Leslie. Copyright © 1967, 1973, 1976, 1979 by Oxford University Press,
Inc. Reprinted by permission.

increase in power occurs primarily in those external decisions regarding finances and the provider role. Employed wives, compared to nonemployed wives, have more influence on the major economic decisions, such as what car to buy, what house to choose, whether to buy insurance, and strangely enough, whether the wife should work (Blood, 1963). Her employment seems to have little effect on her power with respect to internal decisions, such as those concerning child care, family recreation, and housekeeping (Bahr, 1974).

Although working wives have more power than nonworking wives, they still have less power than their husbands. In most cases, the working wife is a junior partner to her husband (Scanzoni, 1972). The husband typically, although not always, earns more money; the wife's income is thus sometimes perceived as unimportant (Walum, 1977). However, the amount she earns generally does influence the power balance (Bird, 1979).

Cultural definitions of a woman's place (in the home) still serve to devalue women's resources, even among those women who work. Heer (1963) observes that women may not use their power because of traditional beliefs that the husband is the authority figure. Traditional attitudes do not die easily, even when the wife earns as much or more than her husband, as about a quarter of the husbands in Bird's study claimed for themselves the right to decide whether the wife may work (Bird, 1979).

While more women are sharing provider responsibilities with their husbands, change in the traditional allocation of housework and child care occurs slowly. Women who are employed outside the home spend less time on these traditionally female tasks, but more time than their husbands, although husbands are gradually accepting the idea that they need to "help their wives" (Davidson and Gordon, 1979). It seems unlikely that wives consider their housekeeping and child-care activities as "helping their husbands."

There are distinct differences in the power situation of minority working women as compared with the nonminority working woman. Minority women face both sex and racial discrimination; thus they have less access to the resources working can provide.

Despite these economic disadvantages, black women have relatively greater power within the family than do white women.

Black males also lack access to the important economic resources that would enable them to gain power equivalent to white males. The black woman earns less than the white woman, but her husband also earns less than the white husband. The disparity between the earnings of the black wife and husband is smaller (U.S. Bureau of the Census, 1978); thus her contribution to the family income is proportionately higher. Blood and Wolfe (1960) noted that, in their sample, more than twice the proportion of black families were dominated by women, 44 percent, compared to 19 percent of white families. Although they attributed this to the concentration of black men in the lower class, they also found that this disparity persisted when the social class was controlled. Even among stable middle-class black families there is greater female power (Scanzoni, 1972).

Changing sex roles have already begun to affect the aging process for women, as shown by comparisons of women born in different eras. Neugarten and Brown-Renzanka (1978) compared the social characteristics of three age groups of women:

1. GROUP A—women who had lived during the Depression now aged 60–65 and exiting mid-life;
2. GROUP B—women who had lived during World War II, now aged 40–45, and entering mid-life; and
3. GROUP C—women who were part of the baby boom now aged 25–30 who will enter mid-life in the late 1980s.

The women in Groups A and B, the oldest age groups, are least well prepared to cope with mid-life. Their access to the valued resources of income, education, and occupational status are minimal. Group A, for example, is the least educated. Many were born into large families, to foreign-born parents; they entered adulthood during the Great Depression. These women were older at the time of marriage and, as a result, had fewer children. The women in Group B have more education, although few finished college. These women were reared in small families and entered adulthood during a period of economic expansion; they tended to marry early and have large families. These women spent a large span of time in the bearing and rearing of children, a period in the life cycle during which women's power in the family is said to be at its lowest level (Blood and Wolfe, 1960). Many of these women grew up during that period of time characterized by what Betty Friedan (1963) calls the "feminine mystique," a time in which it was not considered proper for women, especially mothers, to work.

The women in Group C have the highest education and occupational level, and one-fourth are already in professional and technical jobs. These women will spend the most time in the postparental stage (their longevity is greatest, and they show signs of having smaller families). It appears that these women are better prepared to cope with the problems of mid-life. Their resource base is increased by their continued work experience over the life cycle and by their higher level of education and occupational skills. Neugarten and Brown-Rezanka (1978) suggest that with this group the total distribution of women workers will become comparable to that of men workers.

Considering all mid-life women as one homogenous group ignores the heterogeneous life experiences of these women. While mid-life may be a problem for some women, it is not necessarily such for others. Some researchers predict that as the group of more highly skilled and educated women reach mid-life in the 1980s, they will press for more egalitarian family relationships.

THE POWER STRUCTURE OF THE FAMILY IN THE FUTURE

Some argue that the power relationship in the family closely resembles the position of men and women in the existing stratification system of society (Gillespie, 1975; Lipman-Blumen, 1975). The present stratification system excludes women from attaining equal access to valued positions in the economic, educational, political, and legal institutions of society. Unless this changes, inequality in the family will also persist, despite egalitarian efforts on the part of individual couples.

Although women's resources are increasing, women still hold a secondary status in the labor market and educational system. By 1974, the proportion of females aged 18–19 going to college equalled the proportion of young males (Cahn, 1977); yet fewer women go on to earn higher professional degrees. In the labor market, women continue to be concentrated in what have been called "female ghetto" jobs — secretarial, retail trade, saleswork, bookkeeping, private household work, elementary school teaching, waitressing, typing, cashiering, and nursing. These jobs are relatively low-paying and remain at the lower rungs of the job ladder. Many such jobs provide no chance for advancement. Women continue to earn far less than men; they earn less than 60 percent of men's earnings (Cahn, 1977).

Among women who do not work there is a movement to place a "market value" on the homemaker's work. Given the prevailing attitude that unpaid work is not work, the conversion of housework into a marketable resource would permit women to bargain for increased power in the family. Some economists are now trying to determine the monetary value of housework. Estimates range from $4,705 (1972) to over $13,000 per year (1973), depending on whether the work of the homemaker is considered equivalent to an unskilled, skilled, or a professional worker. For example, is child care comparable to babysitting at seventy-five cents an hour, to care by a nursery school aide at three dollars an hour, or to care by a child psychologist at thirty dollars an hour (Glazer et al., 1977)?

It may be that with the recent increases in women's resources, they will have greater influence within the family, especially in terms of the allocation of financial resources. The implications for husbands are uncertain and need further exploration. It has been suggested that the husband in the future may take on more responsibility for intrafamilial decisions as his wife's influence on extrafamilial decisions increases. Will men come to turn down overtime, reject transfers, and refuse travel because of the work commitments of their wives or the needs of their children? Moore and Sawhill (1976) suggest that maybe they will.

As we move into the 1980s there is evidence that wider structural changes in the educational and economic institutions are occurring. Given these changes at the macro level, we should see some shift in the family power arrangement toward a more egalitarian situation as more and more wives continue to work outside the home. Perhaps women's greatest resource increase has been through their substantial rise in labor force participation and the increased continuity of this participation. By 1976, the proportion of women between the ages of 18 and 64 who were in the labor force reached 56 percent, and in every age group the proportion of women who were working was steadily increasing (Cahn, 1978). Women will also gain power in the future as more and more women opt to remain childless. In resource theory terms, the child-free wife is able to develop her "human capital," in terms of education and work experience and her access to more responsible and higher-paying jobs. The emergence over the past ten years among contemporary women of a preference for a "child-free" style of living, especially among the well-educated women, has been documented (Scanzoni, 1979; Veevers, 1974).

But even the group of women who have been traditionally the most powerless (i.e. women with children) will gain substantially. Their employment in recent years has accounted for the most significant labor force increases. The labor force participation rate for married women with husbands present and with children under the age of 18 more than doubled between 1950 and 1975, while for those with children under the age of 6, the rate more than tripled (Cahn, 1978).

Some researchers predict that more and more bargaining will be built into the marital structure as women gain access to outside opportunity structures and men no longer control all the resources (Scanzoni, 1979). While the contemporary woman reaching her middle years can look forward to more opportunities than in the past, new problems may develop. As more women enter the labor force, more aging working women may face the same retirement difficulties as their male counterparts. The more resources her job has given her, the more she may feel she stands to lose as she ages and leaves the economic market place. Also, because of the increased longevity of the American population, mid-life women will also find the future filled with the filial responsibilities of "parent caring" (Neugarten and Brown-Renzanka, 1978). Although most older people want to and do remain independent of their families as long as possible (Troll et al., 1979), the mid-life woman is the one who is primarily responsible for caring for the major and minor needs of her parents and, perhaps, grandparents.

There is also evidence that the nature of the relationship between the aged parent and the adult-child will change in the future. The bonds between parents and children will be based more on "mutual respect" and less on economic dependency (Hess and Waring, 1978). This conclusion is based in part on the changes in social roles mentioned earlier. In addition, the new cohorts of the elderly will have increased resources with which to live compared to earlier cohorts. There is evidence that the status of the aged is improving in terms of their health, education, and finances (Palmore, 1976).[13] For instance, the elderly's financial support has become less tied to the family as more and more of the economic burden of caring for the aged is given over to the federal government. The elderly receive Social Security, Medicare, and other services, which tend to free the parent from total economic and social dependence on their offspring (Treas, 1977).[14] Women, in particular, will increase their resources as they enter the ranks of the aged, and more are obtaining a higher education and are entering and remaining in the labor force. There is also evidence that men are beginning to gain in social resources. They are starting to take a larger share of the parenting responsibility for their children; in older age, perhaps they will have alternative sources of gratification from their families to turn to after retirement. This may lead to more companionate relations with their wives and children (Hess and Waring, 1978). However, despite the increase in equality and despite the increase in the relative power of women, it is highly likely that the balance of power is going to continue to favor men for quite some time.

It appears that future parent-child relations could well be less conflictful. Children may not need to make choices between the needs of their own children and those of their parents. In coming

---

[13]If we look at trends in median income adjusted for inflation, we find that the economic status of the elderly has been improving during the past several decades. But when we look at the median income of the elderly relative to other age groups, we get a different picture. There has been no long-term improvement in the relative income of the elderly since 1947, when the median income for elderly families was 60 percent of that for all families. In 1975 it was actually a bit lower (54%) (Williamson, 1979).

[14]Some argue that Social Security and also social services still make the aged dependent on their children, as they must help them fill out forms, etc. This tends to create a new role for children as the mediators between institutional bureaucracies and the elderly (Sussman, 1976).

years the autonomy of elderly parents will tend to increase as they become less economically dependent on their middle-aged children. If the bonds between aged parent and child are not based so heavily on economic dependency, they may develop more on a basis of mutual respect and affection.

In this chapter we have viewed Social Security primarily as a resource increasing the autonomy of the elderly. More generally, a case can be made that various government income maintenance, health insurance, and social service programs associated with the expansion of the welfare state, particularly since the end of the World War II, have tended to increase the resources of the elderly. But at the same time these programs have made the elderly increasingly dependent upon the state. Freedom from dependence on one's children has often come at the price of dependence on the state and the state's impersonal bureaucratic functionaries. This has made many of the elderly vulnerable to new forms of social control, about which we will have more to say in the next chapter.

Chapter 8

SOCIAL CONTROL OF THE ELDERLY

For centuries philosophers and social theorists have been concerned with the relationship between the individual and society. They have asked questions about how social order came to exist, why it persists, and whom it most benefits. Such theorists have been particularly attentive to the tension that exists between the desire for freedom and autonomy on the one hand and the desire for order and security on the other. Some philosophers such as Jean Jacques Rousseau (1712–1778) and John Locke (1632–1704) emphasized freedom; others such as Thomas Hobbes (1588–1679) emphasized social order.[1]

The work of Herbert Spencer (1820–1903) and other social Darwinists drew a Hobbesian picture of humankind as naturally animalistic and competitive. In this context, nineteenth century social theorists became interested in the study of specific mechanisms of social control whereby the group (society) constrains individual behavior.[2] These controls range from the use of police

---

[1]In *Leviathan* (originally published in 1598), Hobbes (1958) argues that in the so-called "state of nature" (that time prior to the establishment of any government or civil order), life was "solitary, poor, nasty, brutish, and short." Thus he saw the "social contract" and with it the establishment of a strong government to preserve law and order as highly desirable. By contrast, in *The Social Contract* (originally published in 1762), Rousseau (1950) emphasizes the oppressive aspects of governments: they tend to best serve the interests of the wealthy. Locke was yet another social contract theorist; he argued that people created government for the purpose of guaranteeing their freedom. If the government ceased to do so, the contract had been broken and the people had the right to rebel.

[2]The positivist school of thought underwent a major change with the application of Darwinism in its "social" form. In the eighteenth century, positivists assumed that the problems of humankind could be solved through rational thought. Once heredity and environment replaced free will and choice as the bases of action (per Darwinism), a Hobbesian description of nature resulted. Now a "struggle for existence" characterized relations between individuals, not a shared concept of social order (Hughes, 1958). For some of the early work dealing with the issue of social control as such, see the following: Cooley (1956); Durkheim (1947); Ross (1928); and Sumner (1911).

214

force, to the subtle transmission of values and norms through socialization. In all instances the question lurks: "Whose interests are best served by a society's organizational arrangements and how do those not well-served come to accept boundaries or controls on their options?"

The evidence suggests that the community whose interests are best represented and served by existing social arrangements within American society is the community of adults under age 70, to the detriment of those who are older. While Neugarten (1975), Pratt (1976), and Hudson (1978) are correct in suggesting that America's elderly as a group have made progress over the past fifty years in improving their standard of living and establishing legitimacy as an interest group, they fail to give adequate attention to the mechanisms of social control which have been evolving at the same time. To be sure, the elderly have achieved greater economic security; they have a national policy network in place, and they are growing in number. But these analysts have not adequately taken into consideration the growth of an elaborate system of social control by which the elderly are severely constrained. Furthermore, it is our contention that all of the helping and academic professions involved with elderly affairs are implicated in this tightening of controls.

We begin with an explication of the concept of "social control," exploring the forms it can take and noting that an increase in concern about proper social control of citizens was intimately linked with the rise of social casework and passage of Social Security. Because Social Security legislation was a harbinger of what was to come, we shall examine the causes of its enactment and outline some of the consequences for the elderly. Social Security led to an increase in autonomy with respect to intergenerational relationships; it became possible for millions of elderly Americans to remain economically independent of their middle-aged children. But this gain came at a cost: an increase in dependence on and control by the state and its representatives in various government bureaucracies. A case can be made that the bureaucratic structures established in connection with the Social Security program, and since expanded in response to legislation of the 1960s and 1970s, has increased the power and influence of the caretakers more than it has increased the power and influence of the elderly themselves.

For centuries humankind has debated the extent to which — if at all — individuals need to forego some liberties and exercise of free will so as to benefit from order and predictability within their environment (Hobbes, 1958; Rousseau, 1950). With the onset of industrialization and the social disruptions it triggered, this debate intensified in Europe and the United States.

Emile Durkheim (1958) in advancing the idea that the total community is greater than the sum of its parts or members was clearly suggesting that the balance of control is held by the group, not recalcitrant members. He went on to identify various means by which groups exert pressure on members to confine their behavior to acceptable boundaries. These include public opinion (reputation), law, belief systems, education, custom, religion, ceremony (rites of passage), and values — essentially all components of a social system. Indeed, the boundaries of acceptable behavior are often only defined through their violation. According to this argument, deviation from acceptable behavior may arouse group sentiment to the point where clear boundaries are identified or reaffirmed. Once a violator of norms is identified, he or she may be relegated to an "outgroup" status, and those not so-labeled can feel more strongly committed to the social order through their shared self-righteousness and conformity.[3]

Although Durkheim is credited with conceptualizing the magnitude of society's regulation of individual behavior, his analysis was not a justification for the status quo. His ideas are frequently contrasted with those of Marx (1964), but both in fact identified social stratification and the ensuing unequal distribution of resources and power as the major mechanism by which individuals' options are differentially limited and controlled.[4] Durkheim

---

[3]See Erikson (1964) for a discussion of how boundaries are frequently defined through activities that transgress them.

[4]See Davis (1975) for an elaboration of this argument.

assumed a certain normative consensus among community members about what constitutes appropriate behavior, but it was American social scientists who went so far as to depict society as an organism whose equilibrium is constantly being maintained. Deviants should change, not existing economic and social arrangements.[5]

The idea that society is an organism whose parts or institutions are in balance came to be known as *functionalism* (Spencer, 1896; Durkheim, 1958; Parsons, 1937, 1951). Early American social scientists lamented the loss of a "natural order" inherent in small rural communities (upheld by white, Anglo-Saxon, and male values) and saw deviation from social norms as individual pathology or sickness (Mills, 1943). According to this perspective, industrialism was the unavoidable wave of the future, and social selection of the fittest necessitated adjustment to this new order, assimilation (conformity) of immigrants, and amelioration of emerging social problems through correction of individual pathology. An order based on presumably shared sensibilities would be replaced with a legally based order. That which did not come "naturally" would be mandated through laws.

Concern among early social scientists about presumed animal drives within individuals and the desirability of social order has led to a dual approach in studying social control. On the one hand, efforts have been made to study and "rehabilitate" unadjusted individuals (i.e. deviants), and, on the other hand, some acknowledgement of structural strains within the social order has occurred. Theorists such as Merton (1957) have sometimes defined deviance as *adjustment* (not maladjustment) *to contradictions within the social system*. Thus, some roles, values, and goals that people are socialized to aspire to are structurally frustrated, and, therefore, behaviors must be adjusted.[6] Functionalists assume that the more effec-

---

[5]For a discussion of European and American differences in approaching the subjects of stratification and social control, see Horton (1964), as well as Pease, Form, and Rytina (1970).

[6]For example, within American society a structural tension can exist between the cultural goal of "success" and institutionalized means of attaining it, such as "working hard," "getting educated," etc. To the extent that the presumed means to the end do not work or are not available to all, individuals may find "innovative" ways of acquiring success or its symbols, that is, they may engage in criminal activities. Or in the case of some old persons who are denied access to the means, they may "retreat" from both the goals and the means.

tive the socialization process (informal control), the less need will exist for legal or formal means of social control.[7]

While functionalists focus on society and seek to study how individual deviance from norms can be contained or accommodated so as to enhance the system's survival, labeling theorists are interested in how people define one another and how these definitions constrain behavior. Because they reflect the symbolic interactionist perspective (Mead, 1934; Blumer, 1969), which stresses the importance of symbols in creating social reality, labeling theorists view social control as the successful manipulation of labels. According to this line of thought, elites, bosses, ruling classes, adults, men, Caucasians, and other dominant groups exercise power through controlling how people define the world and what is possible (Becker, 1973). Through the successful ascription of labels to people, a noncostly and *apparently* noncoercive type of oppression can be implemented and indeed eventually taken for granted.

Labeling theorists have traditionally studied deviant behavior in terms of legal definitions for creating social outgroups. Thus, deviance consists of (a) an act and (b) society's response to the act. Making certain behaviors "deviant" by law is a procedure by which a society literally creates its deviants (those who perform the outlawed act). And by labeling persons "deviant," a society sets up a process that can lead to further isolation and stigmatization of the offenders. With the deviant label society distributes stigma, and a self-fulfilling prophecy is set in motion—one which tightens the norm-breaker's outcaste status.

Unlike interactionist theorists who emphasize the part labeling or social control plays in *creating* deviant or disvalued careers, conflict theorists are more interested in locating the conditions under which official labeling occurs and in identifying high-level agents of social control, not middle-level ones (Davis, 1975). Rather than study how labeling can lead to a loss of autonomy and personal power, conflict theorists argue that the act of being labeled reflects *prior* powerlessness. According to this school of thought, the study of deviance is in itself an instrument of social control

---

[7]See Roucek (1947:17–27) for a discussion of this point.

because system victims are targeted for analysis, not the system or those benefiting from present resource arrangements (Liazos, 1972). Social control is thus an active control involving the regulation of powerless groups (Davis, 1975); economic stratification serves as the principal determinant of where power lies and what form laws will take. This emphasis upon structural inequalities underpinning social control is more derivative of early European social scientists (Durkheim and Marx), than early American ones who stressed individual pathologies.

Conflict theorists tend to believe that any political consensus that is reached is a manipulated consensus, not a communally based or pluralist one as functionalists imply. The state rather than being viewed as a neutral broker of interests is seen as using its legitimated authority to rationalize and supplement the exploitation of some groups by others. Market and political imperatives of elites determine the direction and scope of social changes, and the only reform proposals that are ever found acceptable to these elites involve technocratic solutions, such as creation of new bureaucracies, not redistributive ones (Davis, 1975). Conflict theorists assert that "reforms" enhance state power over controlled groups and that they invariably solidify the security of economic elites. This solidification occurs through the *appearance* that something is being done to redress a problem and a resultant diffusion of any challenge to existing economic arrangements.

Keeping in mind each of these theoretical perspectives on social control, we now turn to an examination of the changes in the status of the elderly that preceded the rise of the pension movement and followed enactment of Social Security legislation. We will consider whether the Social Security program tended to increase or decrease the power of the elderly. Did it result in more autonomy for the elderly or more social control of the elderly? It is our contention that it increased autonomy in certain spheres, but increased the extent of social control within others. The pension benefits have increased the economic well-being of the elderly and in so doing have increased their autonomy. But Social Security legislation has also created jobs for a wide variety of caretakers who have come to play an increasing role in the management and control of the lives of the elderly.

THE RISE OF THE PENSION MOVEMENT

Many political analysts and gerontologists cite both normative and economic changes within American society as the causes of a pension movement forming at the turn of this century. The old-age pension movement was part of a campaign to institute compulsory social insurance. Sponsors of the social insurance goal believed that neither the poor laws nor private social work enterprises were sufficient to provide "indemnity against financial losses from . . . ordinary contingencies in the workingman's life" (Brandeis, 1911:159).[8] These included accidents, sickness, maternity, disability, unemployment, old age, and death—risks that could bring an end to a worker's wage-earning capacity or opportunity. Now that so many Americans were wage-dependent, social insurance sponsors believed laborers needed income protection. Activists on behalf of an old-age pension were particularly concerned because forced retirement had become widespread in the absence of private pensions, and the elderly appeared to occupy an increasingly precarious financial and social position within the community.

Among those explanatory factors mentioned most often as indirect precipitators of the pension movement are an increase in secularism, an ethos of egalitarianism originally spawned by the American and French Revolutions, enlargement of the elderly population, Darwinism, industrialization, and eventually family difficulties in caring for senior members (Achenbaum, 1978*a;* Cowgill and Holmes, 1972; Burgess, 1960; Fischer, 1978). Concurrent with these various trends was the growth of "gerontophobia."[9] According to these accounts, early colonists—particularly Puritans—were heavily steeped in age hierarchy, and age was one indicator of being among God's elect (Fischer, 1978). The rarity of living till old age no doubt underscored its godly overtones.

By the late eighteenth century, the authority of age was already being challenged on several fronts. With the French and American

---

[8]See Graebner (1980) and Lubove (1968) for excellent discussions of the drive for Social Security and the various obstacles that were imposed.

[9]The term *gerontophobia* as commonly used refers to a fear of or aversion to old people and aging.

revolutions, values such as independence, liberty, and equality began to filter through society. Young people and transcendentalists in particular began to challenge the familial and communal control held by their elders and claimed that liberty was a "prior condition" and equality at odds with age having preference over youth.[10]

In the mid-nineteenth century, the decline in status of the elderly got markedly worse with the appearance of social Darwinism and accelerating industrialization. As technology developed and medical advances occurred, old age became much more commonplace and increasingly linked with death. While social Darwinism was siring descriptions of society as continually "progressing" with time and age, this assumption was not extended to individuals. Progress had a decisively dualistic nature (Achenbaum, 1978*b*).

Indeed human development was finite, and society's evolutionary progress portended brutal problems for those older persons who could not hold their own in the struggle for existence. When this emphasis upon progress was reinterpreted by the managers of industrial facilities to mean higher and higher productivity, society's "best" came to be depicted as those who were in the prime of their productive powers. In a world where human mastery over every aspect of nature became a goal, youth was designated the most vital and creative source for accomplishing this mastery. As the age of workers went up, the age of the most valued workers went down; as education level rose, the relative education of the elderly declined. Employment problems among the elderly resulted in a rapid increase in poverty within their ranks, but the presumably productive younger family members who were living in congested urban areas and expected to be geographically mobile were not in a good position to lend assistance.

While old persons were increasingly portrayed as unfit for the "productive" world of work and frequently ejected, they were also being labeled with characteristics that had formerly been applied to other economically deprived and nonmasterful groups. Specifi-

---

[10]Transcendentalism was a nineteenth century school of philosophy whose proponents argued that knowledge comes from intuition rather than objective experience. When this viewpoint caught on in America, it helped undermine the status of the elderly by minimizing the importance of experience (age). Both Emerson and Thoreau reflected this perspective.

cally, old age during the Puritan era was pictured as good when it was associated with other virtues (such as a manly life), and patriarchs were portrayed as "commanding masculine figures" (Fischer, 1978:114). But the poor elderly carried the stigma of poverty, not the virtue of age, and impoverished older widows were treated with a contempt so strong that they were sometimes ostracized by entire communities. As older male workers were portrayed as not being up to the requirements of industrial "progress," they were increasingly ascribed with the characteristics of weakness — dependence, passivity, and femininity. Thus they joined the ranks of other stigmatized groups, and the most gracious version presented the Victorian patriarch as a "dummy figure . . . stowed away in the rocking chair, a male softened by the kindly touch of time" (Fischer, 1978:226). Stereotypes mirrored economic exigencies.

Assuming that all these normative and economically based pressures contributed to a drop in the elderly's fortunes, we might ask whether proposed corrective measures were as equally broad-based. As it turned out, pension plans proposed by protest activists were forcefully resisted by elites within all institutions, and claims of adherence to "American" values were invoked by proponents and opponents.

Functional theorists argue that "deviants" who want a change in economic and political order can be used to help stabilize the social order, if successfully managed. They do this by identifying problem areas that need some attention and by organizing into political groups. By forming some kind of secondary group, such as a protest movement, which allows some expression of alienated feelings, political deviants are easily located and can be insulated from the rest of society.

In American society, mere use of the word "radical" in describing a political group is a potent weapon among elites in repelling alternative claims to legitimacy and tends to insulate a group's impact. While the deviant or protesting group is being put on the defensive by elites for being "un-American," its members are often found asserting that they represent America's *real* values. For example, economic elites frequently invoke the "American" value of free enterprise to prevent any redistribution of income, while proponents of redistribution often speak of Americans' traditional concern for fair play, justice, and a decent life for all. This claim among organized political deviants of being the true defenders of American values establishes a "bridge" whereby the group can be coopted (Parsons, 1951). By saying they are more American than elite defenders of the status quo, protesters are tacitly accepting the social order on the whole and are "set up" to settle for whatever minor accommodation to legitimacy their goals eventually receive. In this way, vested interests are not seriously threatened, and social order is strengthened through cooptation of alternative visions or ideologies. In the case of pension activists whose goals were eventually whittled down to social security legislation, this cooptation process of social control was followed to a tee.

SOCIAL SECURITY

By 1908, forced retirement was common, and since the net savings of most Americans approached zero, old age and poverty were unavoidably linked.[11] Even though most European nations had adopted a system of compulsory old-age insurance, the concept was perceived by America's institutional leaders as a repudiation of the American system of "volunteerism" and "individual liberty." Resistance to pensions came from elites of all major institutions, and each claimed that such a program would be a threat to American values. Religious leaders, economists, business persons, and union officers agreed that compulsory old-age insurance would be the corrupter of America's morals. Not only did such a plan represent socialist intentions and deferred wages, but it threatened the very underpinnings of national character. As one opponent summed up the situation, the prospect of old-age dependency is a "most powerful incentive which makes for character and growth in a democracy." Without such a threat we might revert to the behavior of our "barbarian ancestors" (Hoffman, 1909).

Even though the United States had a major public pension system already in operation for Civil War veterans, compulsory

---

[11]The distribution of assets has changed very little over the past seventy years in America, and this negligible savings level for all but the top economic stratum in 1908 has remained a characteristic feature. See Vanfossen (1979), Miller (1966), and Kolko (1962).

old-age pensions were described as "un-American." One Congress-person, in trying to reconcile this anomaly in thinking, proposed an "Old-Age Home Guard of the United States Army" in which all individuals 65 and above could "enlist" if their incomes were below $20 per month; their official responsibility would be to inform the War Department annually on the level of patriotism within their neighborhoods (Fischer, 1978).

Opponents of pensions did not stop with attacking the concept as un-American; they also denounced those who supported com-pulsory old-age insurance as un-American. To the extent that many early proponents were immigrants or first-generation Amer-icans from Eastern European countries and urban, they were not a part of the "natural order" frequently associated with Anglo-rural communities at that time. It was not until the 1920s when poverty among the elderly had become even more obvious that traditional or "American" institutions, such as the Fraternal Order of Eagles, promoted old-age insurance that proponents began to make any headway in their claims to legitimacy. Roosevelt and other New Deal architects nonetheless kept the first social insurance advo-cates, "un-American" upstarts that they were, at arm's length right through passage of the Social Security Act. These political "devi-ants" or "radicals" were never officially credited with the legisla-tion, and indeed other than its establishment of the right—as opposed to privilege—of benefits for certain categories of workers, it bore no resemblance to their visions.[12]

While goals of political deviants were being successfully contained by the boundaries acceptable to elites, pension movement leaders themselves contributed to this eventual cooptation by relying heav-ily upon the appeal that sending elderly persons to almshouses violated American values and sentiments of justice. Rather than

---

[12]Roosevelt was careful to keep control of the drafting of the Social Security legislation in conservative hands. Persons such as Isaac Rubinow and Abraham Epstein were kept at arm's length despite the major role they had played as activists in the old-age pension movement. Upton Sinclair organized the "EPIC" movement (End Poverty in California), which origi-nally proposed a modest $50 per month pension (which was eventually raised to $400 per month). More influential was the Townsend Plan, which called for a pension of $200 per month. In contrast, the old-age pension enacted by the Social Security Act of 1935 called for a pension of less than $25 per month. This is a far cry from what the old-age pension activists had in mind. See Fischer (1978:178–187) and Pratt (1976:11–25) for further elaboration.

labor was most needed. The discontent being expressed by poor families about the costs of caring for their unproductive members could be diffused without altering their wage rates. In addition, by making residence in these institutions most unpleasant and stigmatizing, those who were not contributing to the system would be properly punished, and those "poorer classes" who might be tempted to feign insanity or poverty to avoid work would be deterred from doing so. Furthermore, the concept of "outdoor relief" could be kept off the political agenda altogether.[15] Social participation within the community was thus prohibited in the absence of economic participation.

This use of institutions to isolate nonproductive members of society only gave way to outdoor relief in the form of social insurance programs, such as Unemployment Compensation and Social Security, when the needs of capital changed. Accordingly, as the costs of labor increased due to rises in required skill and education levels for many jobs, industrialists became interested in maintaining the capacity and willingness to work among these costly employees. Social insurance programs constituted an investment in human capital, and with their passage the state got even more deeply committed to subsidizing production costs (maintaining workers in body and spirit).

In order to attract an ambitious, proficient, and fit workforce, industrialists deemed it necessary to show "good faith" by assuring some continuity in income during workers' less "fit" period (Achenbaum, 1978*b*). It was presumed that removing "less efficient" old people from the labor force would boost morale, not to mention employment opportunities, for younger workers and enhance their commitment to work.[16] Retirement became a new

---

[15]The term *outdoor relief* refers to assistance that is provided without the requirement that the recipient be confined to an almshouse or a workhouse.

[16]These types of rationales were given by those employers who supported industrial pensions. Pensions were seen by some as legitimate business expenditures that would reduce labor turnover, attract superior workers, and relieve employers of any obligation to keep individuals on the payroll in the absence of "real productivity." These inducements for enhanced worker cooperation and productivity were assumed to rest upon the worker's comprehension that a pension would be withheld if his output fell short of expectations. See Lubove (1968) and NICB (1925:101).

and more subtle form of segregation and social control. Whatever passage of Social Security legislation may say about how social control is exercised by elites through the government process, it unquestionably proved to be a "trump card" of social control over the elderly in many more ways than are commonly acknowledged. First, it is clear that Social Security was passed in order to "cool out" America's elderly without making any seriously distributive changes in the system and to regulate the labor market by removing older members. It is probably not accidental that political activity on behalf of and by the aged fell into what has been termed by one observer as the "dismal years" (Pratt, 1976). In this sense, Social Security can be compared with public assistance in that its stated purpose was humanitarian, but actually it helped stabilize the social order and thereby sustain the dominance of existent elites (Piven and Cloward, 1971).[17]

Although the state had been involved in the subsidized segregation of the elderly to a limited degree before 1935 through maintenance of almshouses and municipal old-age homes, its role was greatly expanded with passage of Social Security legislation. Mandatory retirement was implicitly condoned, and the elderly became an official "problem" or target group of government policies. This formal labeling of people as "old" through Social Security eligibility along with the increased social distance between America's old and everyone else that Social Security payments permitted are appropriate issues for theorists of the labeling school.

A question debated by labeling theorists is whether society's fear of an act leads to labeling it deviant or whether the act of deviance leads to fear from society. We might ask what *act* America's elderly committed in order to become stigmatized, and the answer would be none in the sense that the word "deviance" is used by labeling theorists. It is important to make a distinction between

---

[17]In the case of Social Security, America's old were "cooled off," and unemployment eased with payments and the expunging of the elderly from the work force that payments helped rationalize. With relief or public assistance, unemployed persons are "cooled" during periods of civil disorder resulting from severe economic decline with higher benefits and relaxed eligibility criteria. They are then expunged into the labor force during quiet periods through stringent eligibility requirements to assure an adequate supply of low-wage labor (Piven and Cloward, 1971).

occupying a "deviant" status in the legal order and a "devalued" one in the social order, although the labeling dynamics can be identical. As Cohen (1966) notes, all deviant roles are devalued—they are usually low-status and undesirable roles—but not all devalued roles (such as being an old person) are deviant in terms of being illegal. While the deviant is usually assumed to choose violation of a norm, those occupants of a devalued role are seen as "unfortunate" and not "reprehensible." But once they are labeled or identified in some kind of segregating and stigmatizing way, their attempts to maneuver around the label or their failure to do so are similar to those of deviants.

The question raised about whether fear leads to the dispensing of stigma or vice-versa is relevant to the elderly. Just about the time that being old was labeled a "problem" to be dealt with legislatively, the elderly were becoming more numerous, and anxieties about how they were to be employed were growing. Thus, according to labeling theory, the "act" of being old—at least in large numbers—led to fear. Concurrently, medical scientists were busy studying senescence and turning out reports on the physical hardships of aging (Achenbaum, 1978b). Negative descriptions of the aging process contributed to fear and to the devaluing of the older person role.

This dual aspect of society's fear of the elderly continues today. America's old are feared because their numbers are growing and because the process of aging is presumed to involve loss of highly valued attributes such as activity, productivity, and independence—attributes made ever more elusive through our constraints on the elderly. Whereas earlier generations feared the physical aspects of aging, we have created a situation where social aspects are to be feared too. This straitjacketing of the elderly can best be examined by tracing the "career" of an old person. A process that begins with the labeling of someone as "old," and reflects an expression of power by those who do the labeling, results in a loss of power for the elderly, particularly with respect to personal autonomy and choice.

THE CAREER OF AN OLD PERSON

The concept of a career path has been ascribed to deviant behavior by Goffman (1961) and Becker (1973).[18] Just as the term refers to a sequence of movements from one position to another within the world of work, with one step often predisposing another, Becker uses the term to describe a sequence of events which can follow the act of being labeled deviant or devalued. This sequential approach presupposes an interaction process between the labeled person and society whereby the deviant's career path is determined by both objective facts of social structure (e.g. discrimination) and subjective changes in his or her perceptions, motivations, and goals (Becker, 1973).

This process model of cause-effect is very different from the multivariate-type explanations offered by functionalist thought, and although functionalists and labeling theorists both assume a normative basis for the dispensation of stigma, labeling theorists emphasize its oppressive rather than system-sustaining properties. From this perspective a deviant career is often characterized by labeling, segregation, and ever-increasing constraints on individual options, autonomy, and power. To some degree most theories of aging to date can be seen as theories on how people adjust to the career of being an old person—how the self and perceptions of what is possible respond to predictable, though not inevitable, changes in their objective milieu.[19]

From the moment a person is publicly "caught" in the status "old," her career has begun. This labeling in terms of social consequences can first be manifest in different ways. She may have physical signs of age, such as wrinkles, a physical limitation, or the mere inclusion of chronological age on a required document or application. More frequently, reaching the age of eligibility for

---

[18]Goffman (1961) first wrote of the "moral career" of a mental patient to denote the public and private sides of an individual's identity transition pre-, mid-, and post-incarceration. Becker (1973) uses the career concept when analyzing deviance to allow for the various contingencies involved and to underscore the chain-event aspect of labeling whereby a series of steps are set up, each partly anticipated by the previous event.

[19]For an attempt to integrate exchange theory and symbolic interactionism in explaining the impact of elderly resources upon their social leverage, see Dowd (1980a).

some elderly oriented service such as housing or Social Security payments can trigger the public labeling and certainly being retired does. To the extent that this public identification of being old results in a constriction of options, the person has moved into the second stage of her career. Or, in other words, she is beginning to have difficulties carrying on the routines of everyday life valued by the idealized community of nonelderly adults. Direct discrimination in gaining or keeping employment is one sanction; the requirement that wages not exceed a certain amount for those collecting Social Security pension benefits is a more indirect but potent exercise of social control at this stage.

Now that the old person can no longer work and has experienced a sizable drop in income, she may find that she has few social contacts, is engaging in less activity, and even has some new health problems. Thus, she might be exhibiting evermore socially expected signs of being an old person. At the point when the original public labeling and ensuing limitation of options lead to the acquisition of additional characteristics of the old-age stereotype, the person is in the third stage of her career path. Society is beginning to get the behaviors its structures promote.

If the elderly person manages to avoid succumbing to expected age-related behaviors, various familial and media-enforced weapons of social control will assist her career "development." She can for example indulge her recently acquired penchant for passivity and need for cheap entertainment by watching television. There she will view "a rather gloomy picture of aging"—one where old persons are practically invisible (2.2% of prime-time characters) and where women such as herself are "quite likely to be hurt or killed and to fail" (Brown, 1979). And if these women are not hurt or killed, they along with their male counterparts are treated with disrespect and portrayed as stubborn, eccentric, or foolish. Our viewer will also notice a double standard of aging on television whereby male characters sixty-five and above play settled adult roles with romantic possibilities more often than women characters of the same age. Women are invariably cast as "old"—meaning inactive, nonproductive, and sexless—in case our elderly viewer had not gotten the message yet of what it means to be labeled old.

If older people need to move in with adult children or have

frequent contact with them, they may experience certain costs for this relational dependence. Because most persons have needs for acceptance and nurturance, they often gear their behavior toward the expectations of others. Thus to the extent that an older person's relatives subscribe to age norms and try to get "appropriate" behavior from older family members, the elder's options may be constrained. For example, grandmother might be chastized for having a gentleman caller who is younger than herself, particularly if he is not as financially well-off and therefore automatically suspected of taking advantage of poor grandmother who must be feeling desperate or a little "crazy" to date a younger ne'er-do-well. Although age norms are restrictive for both men and women, they tend to be more confining for women — a form of social control which underscores the stereotype on television that older women have romantic adult roles less often than do older men. The stereotype both reflects reality and helps to sustain it.

If older individuals seek acceptance from their age peers, they may be confronted with equally strong age norms since many older Americans have internalized age as a reasonable criterion for evaluating behavior (Neugarten et al., 1965). As labeling theorists suggest, when a stigmatized or oppressed group censors its own members, there is no need for dominant groups to resort to more openly coercive social control mechanisms.

Sometimes the costs for dependence on relatives are stronger than mere ridicule or ostracism. Reports of physical abuse of older members have begun to surface (Steinmetz and Straus, 1974; Steinmetz, 1978). Elderly abuse like child abuse involves someone who is dependent upon a caretaker, lives in a *presumably* loving environment, and can be a source of financial, physical, or emotional stress to the caretaker. Along with some wife abuse victims, the elderly often have such low self-concepts that they either think they deserve such abuse or fear the unknown outside the family (including nursing homes) more than the known within (Block and Sinnott, 1979). The mere existence of nursing homes and mental institutions can exert pressure on fearful old persons to put up with the alternatives, no matter what their form or personal cost.

Without a doubt the most coercive structural control mechanism that can be encountered by old persons relate to labels suggesting incompetence, mental illness, or incontinence. Short of institutionalization, it is possible for the elderly to lose the legal right to oversee their own affairs and to be assigned to the protective custody of a social worker or court appointee. The availability of such an alternative as a threat can augment the power of some family members over their elderly, and it clearly elevates the caretaker role of the state to an impressive level. With institutionalization in either a nursing home or a mental institution, the old person loses the last vestiges of personal autonomy or power.

Functionalists, labeling theorists, and conflict proponents all perceive medicalization as a primary mode of formal social control in American society today, and all argue that while such control is rationalized as humane, it results in the political castration of the deviant or devalued person (Parsons, 1955; Szasz, 1963; Scull, 1977). As Goffman (1961) points out, when medicalization ends in confinement to a "total institution," the patient is exposed to a closed and rigidly administered life-style that reduces the individual to the symbolic antithesis of what is presumed to constitute "adulthood." Self-determination and freedom of action disappear as options, and for all practical purposes the old person drops through to the bottom of the age-grading system.

As confining as age norms can be for the elderly, being treated as a child at the age of seventy-five facilitates a complete degradation of self. Forced communal living, regimentation, infantilism, segregation from the outside world, staff impersonalism, and task orientation all conspire to stigmatize the identity to the point of nonpersonhood. If the resident does not submit to this institutional routine, he or she may encounter the use of chemical or mechanical constraints.

One of the most insidious aspects of the medicalization mode of social control is the disciplinary use of medicine under the guise of the medical service model (Goffman, 1961). Just as drugs have been employed to manage hyperactive school children, so are they used as a means of deterring potentially "disruptive behavior" within total institutions such as nursing homes and mental institutions. Also, to the extent that such drugs are used on an outpatient basis with the elderly so as to help them "adjust" or cope with any isolation, hostility, or alienation they are feeling, they are coercive on two levels. First, they focus corrective measures on the victim rather than the system, and second, even though the older person is still in the community, he or she is being managed or controlled. Tranquilizers used in any setting tend to "dampen, sedate, diminish, and dehumanize social interaction" and thus reduce personal autonomy (Bernstein and Lennard, 1981:182).

So far we have focused on the structural or objective aspects of the control edifice experienced by the elderly as they assume their careers as old persons. As we have seen, these range from material sanctions—unemployment or reduction in income—through media, family, and peer pressures to act as an old person and can take on visibly coercive proportions with institutionalization. Chronological age serves as a triggering mechanism for inclusion in any and all of these transitions, and it is not surprising that many older Americans try to avoid being "caught" and labeled as an old person. The gerontophobia that accompanies these structural controls may originate as a prejudice against others but often ends up as a hating of oneself.[20] Thus the career of an old person is embued with subjective dimensions as well.

Unlike individuals who are labeled deviant due to homosexual or delinquent behavior and who may possibly shed the label (though with much difficulty after it is publicly afixed), persons labeled "old" are usually stabilized in that role, and this is due to its castelike properties. People respond differently to the ascription of a role they did not actively seek.

Some older persons react as though they have what Goffman calls "a spoiled identity" and maneuver their presentation of self so as to play down this undesirable role. Typical of this response is the older individual who goes to great lengths to participate in activities with middle-aged or younger cohorts and avoid association with aged peers. Older politicians who never identify themselves with elderly constituents reflect one form this avoidance can take. Such persons tend to be hypersensitive to any reference to age by

---

[20]There is evidence that this loathing and fear is an extension of individuals' attitudes toward disabled people. This link exists among geriatric workers as well as the general public. See Drevenstedt and Banziger (1977) and McCourt (1963).

others and feel on the defensive. Shame of being old is implied, and sometimes those affected engage in "secret deviance" (Becker, 1973); that is, they try to avoid being publicly labeled as old by falsifying documents or consistently misrepresenting their age.

Others view their age as a hard-earned medal of survival and make no attempts to maneuver around any labeling as old. By and large though, studies indicate a reluctance among America's elderly to identify with being "old," even when they are seventy or more years of age (Riley and Foner, 1968; Cutler, 1974).[21] Gerontophobia does indeed have an impressive and controlling effect upon the elderly's self-concepts and identities.

A second subjective component in the career of an old person can be withdrawal into a subculture based on age. Although Rose's (1965a) theory of the old as a subculture has positive overtones for eventual political activity among the elderly, the concept of subculture connotes negative dynamics as well. When a person joins an organized group (subculture) of similarly labeled and devalued individuals, he or she has taken the final step in the career path. The negative part of this step is the assumption that it was forced. After labeling the person as old, setting a series of structural changes in motion (e.g. retirement, reduced income) and thereby limiting the older person's options within the community, the social control network has maneuvered the older person into a situation where he or she only feels free to be "old" among other old persons. Within the elderly subculture, the devalued role of being old can be carried out with a "minimum of trouble" (Becker, 1973).

In addition to factors mentioned earlier, fear of criminal victimization or familial abandonment could contribute to participation in an aged subculture to the extent that it takes the form of a retirement community. After being singled out as different by the larger community on the basis of age, those so-labeled can reach the point where this label becomes their superordinate basis for identity and behavior. Thus there is nowhere further to go in

---

[21]In a study based on a national sample, Cutler (1974) found that only 38 percent of persons over age 60 identified as being old as opposed to young or middle aged. Ward (1979) reports that in another study only 61 percent of those age 71 to 79 identified as being old.

the career of being old, and that which society originally labeled important (being old) has fulfilled the prophecy and become the ultimate source of identity to the labeled victim as well.

Labeling theorists implicate all social levels in the stigmatizing process and stress *people*, not abstract institutions, as the principal agents of social control. As Hughes (1964) puts it, "good people" allow others to do their "dirty work," and the greater social distance they want to place between themselves and the stigmatized, the more they allocate their handling to "caretakers." Degrees of segregation from the economic mainstream and social isolation reflect degrees of stigma tolerated by the community toward the labeled group.

According to this perspective, those performing society's "dirty work" with respect to the elderly would include legislators, social workers, Social Security administrators, nursing home entrepreneurs, psychiatrists, and interpreters of pension guidelines, to name just a few categories. These specialists in elderly care are akin to undertakers who protect Americans from their dead, only in this case the "loved one" is conscious. If Hughes is correct about the relationship between relegation of care and social distance, then this evidence of an increase in the number and types of specialists dealing with the elderly suggests an increase in gerontophobia in contemporary society. The act of these older members against the social order seems to have been growing old in the land of the young.

There have been at least two additional results of Social Security legislation that have had a tremendously constraining effect upon the well-being of the elderly. One is the deinstitutionalization of many state inmates of late, and the other is the huge network of caretakers and gerontologists which has flowered to deal with the "problem" group identified by Social Security. We not only increased old people's economic resources with enactment of Social Security, but we also created huge bureaucracies and what conflict theorists call "regimes of experts" to assess, regulate, advise, and ultimately control the elderly. We shall now examine each trend for its relevance to containment of the elderly within our society today.

DECARCERATION: A CHEAP WAY
TO PROTECT SOCIETY FROM ITS OLD?

The connections made earlier between the changing needs of capital and passage of Social Security legislation are important because we are witnessing repercussions today. As the state has absorbed more and more costs of production through subsidizing the employed and unemployed work forces, it has gotten into a fiscal bind so great that dismantling an earlier means of social control—institutionalization of deviants—has become politically desirable. Decarceration, as the dismantling process is called, is possible *only* because social insurance and welfare payments exist. In many ways this decarceration trend parallels the decentralization approach to the provision of social services that has evolved over the past ten years, and in both cases social control of deviant or devalued populations at lower costs is the goal, if not the outcome. The elderly in particular have been adversely affected by these changes.

The most striking feature of institutionalized care of the elderly during the 1960s was enactment of the Medicare and Medicaid programs in 1965 and the subsequent mushrooming of the nursing home industry. Because of the form in which this legislation passed—conforming to the entrepreneurial concerns of physicians, the drug industry, and nursing home operators—it quickly led to an avalanche of abuse, scandal, and fraud. Profiteering was manifest in various ways, ranging from skimping on food, charging privately paying patients extra fees for "bedsore," "incontinent," and "senile" care, to billing Medicaid patients after discharge and sometimes death (Mendelson, 1974; Percy, 1974; Williamson, Evans, and Munley, 1980; Vladeck, 1980).

After hearings on abuse were held and reforms instituted, the elderly joined other categories of the population being victimized by a wave of decarceration. Although this decarceration trend, which began in the 1960s for mental hospital and penal populations, was hailed at the time as a reform that would lead to more integrated life-styles and quality community care for deviant populations, it has resulted in a number of serious problems. Hundreds of thousands of persons—including many elderly—have been discharged from state mental facilities, for example, into communities where resources have never been allocated for their care. Screening procedures for identifying the best candidates for release have been nonexistent in numerous instances (Herman, 1979), and many of the released elderly have ended up in nursing homes. Further, when the Supplementary Security Income was introduced and the definition of "long-term" care was loosened to include boarding houses, these sprang up everywhere; in one case even taking the form of a converted chicken coop (U.S. Senate, 1976).

Some have charged that this "dumping" of stigmatized populations into the community is a new type of social control intended to cost less than institutionalization; and the recently decarcerated who lack adequate incomes, work, and in many cases basic coping mechanisms comprise "deviant ghettos" right in the heart of cities (Scull, 1977). Many cannot move or travel, and thus their whereabouts can be known. Also they tend to be dangerous only to one another. Essentially, older individuals are easy marks for crimes committed by other outcasts and for profiteering by adult home operators. Originally, adult homes in the community were intended for the frail elderly, but in states such as New York they have been opened to released mental patients who are eligible for Supplemental Security Income (SSI) funds. Because psychiatric hospitals are eager to release these persons and cut costs (with the guise that local communities will pick them up), they do not always mention a releasee's propensity for violent behavior if it exists, and the frail elderly have sometimes been criminally victimized by the mentally ill (Herman, 1979).

The reason nursing homes are still relied upon for elderly care in an era of decarceration is that they are privately run operations and do not constitute the same fiscal drain on the state that other total care facilities do.[22] The elderly in mental hospitals are finding themselves on the streets along with other devalued groups, sometimes with nothing more than a piece of paper inscribed with the name of a half-way house. Not only do many old persons never

---

[22]Because of the way nursing home legislation was passed, numerous inflated costs do exist as well as many remaining questions about the quality of care delivered. For a thorough examination of nursing homes, see Vladeck (1980).

locate such residences, but also some never collect their Supplementary Security Income payments—their "ticket" to the streets—because they do not know (or do not remember having been told) about them.

The state is subsidizing care providers by contracting out work to them, but it is also having enormous difficulties assuring any kind of quality for its investment. For example, in Massachusetts many private providers who "came to the state's rescue" with alternative treatment models for the deinstitutionalized populations now resist state "interference" with their operations. This has been a dilemma with physicians and nursing home operators since the introduction of Medicare and Medicaid. As one provider put it, "I could be running a zoo here, and they wouldn't care as long as I filled in the little blocks on the form" (Dietz, 1980). By the time the states hire enough persons to enforce quality guidelines for their contracted work, they may well spend as much money as they did when incarcerating most deviants, particularly where entrepreneurs resist their "interference."

Although the elderly who are unloaded from mental institutions onto the streets are a minority, the fact that such situations have been made possible by "reforms" authorized by the state raises serious questions about what the past fifty years of legislation have meant for older Americans. Whether we speak of social control as the exercise of legitimized authority in the form of laws (functionalism), constraint of personal autonomy (labeling theory), or dominance of one group by another (conflict theory), the elderly are a heavily controlled segment of the population. With enactment of Social Security and official recognition of the elderly as a dependent population, an "aging enterprise" (Estes, 1979) has evolved to service this group. Social Security not only helped to stabilize the social order and ensure the positions of elites, it also created the conditions whereby legions of "experts" would come to speak on behalf of the elderly; technocratic rather than redistributive policies were found. Indeed, if the number of specialists in caretaker roles for the elderly connotes social distance from the rest of society, ageism is worse today than it was one hundred years ago. If regimes of experts (researchers and policymakers) help control the claims of the nonexpert by advising them

of what is "good" for them, the elderly are in serious trouble on
two fronts.

CARETAKERS AND GERONTOLOGISTS
AS AGENTS OF SOCIAL CONTROL

One indication of the elderly's controlled position is the "legitimized" status of the aging network that is now in place. This
network is accepted by political elites and delimited as well. Goals
are incremental and *never* seriously challenge the existing distribution of income and wealth. Leaders of senior organizations want
to be "respected" and accepted by Washington's insiders and pride
themselves on "playing the game." The more these individuals
move in and out of private and public positions as other clientele
group leaders do, the more vested their interest will become in
being accepted by Washington peers and invoking these "working
relationships" to justify not rocking the boat (Pratt, 1976). Just as
union leaders have at times been charged with aligning with the
objective interests of business at the expense of rank and file
members in order to enhance their own respectability, so too are
senior organization leaders similarly suspect as they become politically entrenched.

Evidence of their coopted status comes from supposed victories
which have been claimed for the elderly. The Older Americans
Act of 1965 established the Administration on Aging, which was to
herald a new era in advocacy for the elderly; nonetheless, many
observers describe this administration as virtually impotent. Some
of its problems stem from having to deal with aged-related divisions of other federal departments and agencies rather than being
authorized to center all elderly services within the Administration
on Aging. Another problem is in funding. Despite substantial
expansion since its inception, present funding levels severely
restrict the scope of the social service programs supported by the
Administration on Aging.

National elderly advocates have been constrained by the New
Federalism put into effect in the 1970s to cut costs and put control
of elderly services in the hands of local authorities (Estes, 1979).
As was noted earlier, this decentralization of planning and resource

control paralleled the decarceration movement, and in both instances money was the bottom line. Not only does this decentralized strategy limit potential coordinating faculties of the Administration on Aging (as it was no doubt intended to do), but it has also fostered a situation where providers of indirect services for the elderly have increased, while direct services have received low priority. Thus Congress has made aging affairs so decentralized that some say almost everyone but the elderly is benefitting; and this occurred either in spite of or because of the regime of experts standing by in Washington to represent the interests of the elderly. Older persons may speak at public hearings or serve as consultants to local agencies, but their actual input is usually held to "technical matters"—not anything that would threaten agencies' bureaucratic rationales or the control of staff (Estes, 1979).

America's elderly are not only contained within the political arena by Congress and advocates on their behalf (including organizational leaders, entrepreneurs, and service providers), but they are also kept under close tabs by their benefactors in the local community as well. The elderly have been set aside as a "problem" group in need, and their resource deprivation must be maintained in order for their caretakers to justify their own continued existence. This may be a reason why so much money and effort is going toward indirect services such as referral agencies at the local level rather than into direct services, such as housing or adequate income maintenance—either of which requires a limited number of bureaucrats to operate. Amelioration of the elderly's difficulties is possible, it would seem, as long as their dependency as a group is not seriously dissipated.

It is important to note that gerontologists—including academically based ones—are implicated in the social control of the elderly. As a group that studies and services a social category called "the elderly," they are by their very existence underscoring the *separateness* of older Americans and prolonging their definition (label) as a problem group. The trouble with being a "special topic" or "problem group" in American society is that the group tends to be done to, is discouraged from doing, and becomes increasingly dependent through its separateness. To be a problem category is to carry a stigma whether the label is delinquent, welfare recipient, poor person, or old person. Also, to study the aging process so as to try and control it, as some researchers do, implies that the process is intrinsically negative and to be avoided. Gerontologists thus reflect the very values which they criticize at times.[23]

Second, although it is fashionable among social gerontologists to lament how policies to date have been piecemeal and of least assistance to the most disadvantaged elderly,[24] these observers do not tend to be in the vanguard of efforts to disassociate Social Security eligibility and funding from employment. Clearly those who are most socially devalued and therefore disadvantaged in the work world (e.g. women and nonwhites) are going to remain that way into old age. It would seem that gerontologists, just like most Americans, do not want to get caught on the side of an issue that is opposed by elites, who might label them "radicals" or withhold research funding.

Also, the incremental approach of Congress in subsidizing elderly well-being has been paralleled by a piecemeal and individualistic orientation among gerontologists themselves. For the most part, theories on aging have focused upon individual adjustment (called pathology in earlier days) to problems associated with aging, not on the structural creation of the problems.[25] Gerontologists have shown even more reticence in aggressively investigating, analyzing, and unmasking the insidious social control elements involved with medicalization, institutionalization, and decarceration of the elderly and in asking and exposing who ultimately benefits from these trends. The most critical analyses of "reforms" applicable to the elderly have by and large not been

---

[23]In this regard they are like poverty theorists, who argue that no such thing as a culture of poverty exists, and then proceed to study "the poor" as though they constituted a special or unique group.

[24]Reference has been made to the most disadvantaged elderly being excluded from many policies by several contributors to the July/August, 1978 issue of *Society* devoted to political gerontology and before that by Hudson and Binstock (1976) in their overview of the politics of aging.

[25]Even the recent work of Dowd (1980a) speaks of the need for elderly persons to manage their interaction processes with others so they are not perceived as victims. This solution does not address the problem of limited exchange resources available to the elderly, which Dowd himself goes to great lengths to delineate earlier in his analysis.

done by gerontologists,[26] nor directed at mass audiences. To the extent that gerontologists are conducting research funded by the government, are read by policymakers, or serve as advisors to the government, they are part of the regime of experts who presumably know more about the elderly than do the elderly. When their research, commentary, or advice deals with predicting future behavior of the elderly, particularly in the political realm as this book does, complicity in the political containment and control of older Americans is undeniable. Other forms this social control has taken among gerontologists include downplaying the potential of the elderly to bloc vote (Ragan and Davis, 1978), predicting a political backlash against the elderly if they pursue further age-based gains (Hudson, 1978b), and suggesting that incremental goals are the only feasible ones (Pratt, 1976). All of these ideas underpin the status quo and the existing distribution of society's resources. In fact, taken collectively, they promote defeatism about the desirability or possibility of significant change occurring — a situation that presumably would necessitate the continued services of the growing cadre of gerontologists on behalf of that special, segregated, and controlled group know as "the aged."

In this chapter we have highlighted the social control aspects of a variety of welfare programs for the aged. Many readers will, no doubt, question the propriety of being so openly critical of these programs, particularly in this era of welfare state retrenchment. Our goal has not been to suggest that today's elderly would be better off without these programs. To the contrary, they would most definitely be a great deal worse off without them. But if we are to design future programs in such a way as to minimize their most oppressive social control aspects, we must admit that a problem does exist, and only then will we begin to directly address this issue.

Similarly, it would be inappropriate to interpret our discussion of gerontologists as agents of social control as a call for gerontologists to fold up their tents and return whence they came, leaving the

---

[26]A major exception to the generally noncritical approach of gerontologists to the meaning of their work is Carroll Estes (1979). Although Estes does not speak in terms of social control, the events and dynamics she discloses do indeed reflect various aspects of the control apparatus.

elderly alone. Gerontologists are presently performing a wide range of valuable services to those who are elderly. We would hardly argue that the elderly would be better off if professional gerontologists did not exist. Rather, our goal is to sensitize gerontologists to the social control aspects inherent in many of their activities. Those who are aware of these ramifications will be in a better position to do something about it.

EPILOGUE

Chapter 9

PROSPECTS FOR THE FUTURE

One of the most distinctive aspects of research and commentary on the politics of aging is the emphasis given to the analysis of future trends. Given the perils of long-term social forecasting (Douglas, 1979), a strong case can be made for restricting one's analysis to the past and present. But political gerontology has as one of its major concerns the analysis of possible future trends in the political influence of the aged. Any comprehensive treatment of the politics of aging must address this issue.

In the present chapter we deal with the work of those who attempt to forecast trends for about the next fifty years. Were we to select a significantly shorter time frame of say twenty-five years, we could not reasonably expect much change from existing patterns. Were we to select a substantially longer period of say one hundred years, there would be too many imponderables; the result would be described with some justification as a form of science fiction.

Some gerontologists contend that the next fifty years will bring a marked increase in the political influence of the aged and the emergence of a significant "aging vote" (Rose, 1965a; Butler, 1974; Peterson et al., 1976). Others argue to the contrary that the elderly are not a significant force today and that they are unlikely to become a significant influence at any time in the foreseeable future (Hudson and Binstock, 1976; Campbell, 1971; Maddox, 1978). We will want to analyze the evidence with respect to each of these commonly held positions.

As should be evident from the analysis presented in previous chapters, we do not feel entirely comfortable with either of these positions. An alternative formulation that is more consistent with our interpretation of the available evidence will be outlined in the present chapter. We will argue that during the next fifty years there will be a marked increase in the *political resources* of the elderly. This trend may well lead to an actual increase in political influence, but such an outcome is by no means inevitable. We also see a number of counterbalancing factors, some of which are triggered by the aged's gains in resources; this suggests a dialectical model. The greater the gains of the elderly, the greater the resistance from other age groups to further gains.

INCREASING POLITICAL RESOURCES

There are a few analysts, particularly journalists, who believe that the elderly have already become a major political constituency (Roberts, 1981). More common is the view that the elderly will eventually become much more influential *if present trends continue* (Rose, 1965a; Ragan and Dowd, 1974; Cutler and Schmidhauser, 1975; Peterson et al., 1976). Such analysts have done a good job of uncovering the various factors that are likely to increase the political resources of the aged in years to come. But we part company with them in their conclusion that this anticipated increase in resources will necessarily (or very likely) lead to an actual increase in political power and influence. We will elaborate on this point in some detail later in the chapter, but it will be useful to first review some of the political resources to which we are referring.

Gerontologists and demographers generally agree that there will be a substantial increase in the number of old people during the next fifty years. By 1980, the elderly constituted 11 percent of the population, and if present trends continue they will constitute 17 percent or 18 percent of the population by 2025 (U.S. Bureau of the Census, 1979b).[1] With this demographic change will come an increase in the number of older voters. Today the elderly make up approximately 15 percent of the voting-age population and a similar percentage of votes cast. A reasonable estimate is that in 50 years they will account for 20 percent of votes cast (Hudson and Binstock, 1976). This change is seen as contributing to an increase in the influence of the elderly and in the degree of support for

---

[1]Estimates vary between 17 percent aged for 2030 (U.S. Bureau of the Census, 1975) to 18 percent for 2025 (U.S. Bureau of the Census, 1979b). The proportion over age 65 would be less than 18 percent if there were a sharp increase in birth rates.

legislation supporting their interests (Peterson et al., 1976). This increase in the number of old people is central to the thinking of those who forecast a marked increase in the strength of the so-called "senior movement," but it is not the only relevant segment of the population. There are an increasing number of people in their middle years who can identify with the elderly on many issues because of similar life circumstances (Neugarten, 1974; Binstock, 1976). One factor contributing to this is the trend toward earlier retirement. In 1900, 63 percent of men over age 65 were still in the labor force, but by 1977 the figure had decreased to 20 percent (Atchley, 1976; Schulz, 1980). There has been a similar trend with respect to persons aged 55 to 64 (those in late middle-age); in 1950, 87 percent were in the labor force, but the projected figure for 1990 is 70 percent (U.S. Bureau of the Census, 1976; Williamson, Evans, and Munley, 1980).[2] Both the retired elderly and retired persons in late middle-age are living on reduced and relatively fixed incomes; both share a concern with the consequences of inflation and tax increases; and both would find it difficult to reenter the labor force. Similarly, neither group continues to have the social roles and social status that work provides.[3]

Middle-aged persons with elderly parents are likely to support the interests of the elderly on many issues in part because they feel burdened by responsibilities toward their parents. They are likely to support efforts to increase Social Security, SSI, and other such benefits that help their parents maintain independent households. Some of these people are seeking relief from the present burden of providing economic support and various support services to their aging parents; others are looking to the future and hoping to minimize the burdens they see coming (Riley and Waring, 1976). Still others, no doubt, are seeking relief from guilt felt because they are not providing needed economic and service support.

---

[2] For men between the ages of 60 and 64, labor force participation rates declined from 82 percent in 1957 to 63 percent in 1977 (Rones, 1978). However, there are some who anticipate that the trend toward early retirement may be soon ending because of severe inflation (Cuniff, 1980).

[3] For a classic, but now somewhat dated, discussion of the social roles and social status associated with work, see Friedmann and Havighurst (1954).

Those who are employed in industries providing services to the elderly have a direct economic interest in government spending on various programs for the aged. This includes those who work in nursing homes and other such long-term care facilities. It includes the administrators who work in the various federal, state, and local agencies that provide services for the aged, as well as the various Area Agencies on Aging. These agencies are sometimes referred to as the "aging network" (Estes, 1978). It includes those who administer nutrition programs as well as those who provide transportation services, homemaker services, protective services, legal services, counseling, and home-health-aid services, to name only a few of the service programs involved.

In absolute numbers this segment of the senior movement is small by comparison with the others considered so far, but it is a strategically placed group of advocates on behalf of programs for the elderly. Some of these people are in a position to influence those who shape old-age policy and programs. This group tends to be very active in the interest group process by which so much government policy is formulated and modified (Estes, 1979). This service sector expanded rapidly during the late 1960s and early 1970s, but it will probably decrease in size during the 1980s given the trend toward cutting back social programs. However, even in the face of limited economic growth and austerity in government spending on social programs, it is reasonable to expect some expansion in this sector *over the long run*. If for no other reason than the marked increase in the number of the elderly who depend on such services, one would expect at least some expansion in the number of service providers. With this expansion will come an increase in the strength of the group and its influence on the share of government resources allocated to programs for the aged.

During the past twenty years organized labor has become increasingly concerned with old-age issues (Marmor, 1973; Pratt, 1976). As the number of union members who are retired increases and as retirement age declines, old-age issues become increasingly relevant to unions. Particularly relevant in this context are Social Security and health-care benefits. To the extent that organized labor's support for aging programs increases, there should be a corresponding increase in the ability of the aged to realize their political objectives.[4]

To this point we have considered trends that will contribute to an increase in the size of the elderly population as well as other groups likely to support elderly interests. These trends will increase the political resources of the elderly, and the impact will be particularly significant if there is at the same time a tendency for rates of political participation to increase.

When people get into their seventies and particularly their eighties there appears to be a drop in voter participation, especially among women (Wolfinger and Rosenstone, 1980; Brotman, 1977). Among the factors cited to explain this drop are poor health (Milbrath and Goel, 1977) and problems with transportation; however, there is reason to expect improvements on both of these counts in coming years. There has been a modest but steady improvement in the health status of the elderly since the turn of the century, a trend that is likely to continue. While life expectancy is unlikely to increase at the same rate during the next fifty years as it has since 1900, it is reasonable to expect the increase to continue; and there are some who point to the possibility of a dramatic increase in life expectancy during the next fifty years (Rosenfeld, 1976).[5] If life expectancy were extended to age 100, there could be a very profound impact on voter turnout rates among those presently considered elderly.

The issue of transportation is more difficult to forecast, and it is a bit harder to specify what the long-term trend has been. In the future, a higher proportion of the elderly will know how to drive and a higher proportion will be sufficiently healthy to drive. In addition, we can expect an increase in special public transporta-

---

[4]If the Social Security tax burden continues to increase, a point may be reached before long at which organized labor begins to support efforts to cut back on the economic commitment to the aged.

[5]In 1900, life expectancy at birth in the United States was 47 years; by 1980 it had increased to 73 years. However, most of this increase was due to reductions in mortality during the early years. During this period of time life expectancy at birth increased by 26 years, but life expectancy at age 45 increased by only 5 years. One projection is that life expectancy will increase to its upper limit of 85 years by the middle of the next century (Fries, 1980). However, some, such as Rosenfeld (1976), argue that it may be possible through advances in biological science to substantially increase the human life span. Were this to prove possible, life expectancy might increase to something well above 85 years.

tion tailored to the needs of the elderly. It is likely that transportation will be less of a problem rather than more of a problem for elderly voters in years ahead. This would be particularly true if some voting procedure were developed that did not require that a person be physically present at a specified voting place, possibly using some form of computer/telephone combination.

Even more significant than the trends toward improved health, increased life expectancy, and improvements in public transportation is the trend toward a more highly educated elderly electorate. Given the evidence that there is very little decline in voter participation among the elderly who are highly educated (Wolfinger and Rosenstone, 1980), this trend should contribute to an increase in voter participation among the elderly. A parallel argument can also be made with respect to other forms of political participation.

Since the late 1940s the absolute economic status of the elderly has been improving (U.S. Bureau of the Census, 1976; Johnson and Williamson, 1980). Looking to the future, it is reasonable to expect continued improvement in the economic status of the elderly (Schulz, 1980). There is no clear long-term trend in economic status relative to other age groups (U.S. Bureau of the Census, 1976), but during the 1970s there was marked improvement in the relative status of the elderly (Williamson, 1979). It is risky to speculate about long-term economic trends and thus about the economic status of the aged in coming years relative to the present. However, given the automatic cost of living adjustment that is written into existing Social Security legislation, the 1974 pension reform legislation, the increasing proportion of the population eligible for private pensions, and the increasing labor force participation among women, it is reasonable to project at least a modest increase in the economic status of the aged in the years ahead. Since people with higher incomes show higher political participation rates (Verba and Nie, 1972), these economic trends should contribute to an increase in political participation among the elderly.[6]

There is reason to believe that the stigma associated with being

---

[6]One study does, however, conclude that any impact of socioeconomic status on voter participation above and beyond the contribution of education is quite modest (Wolfinger and Rosenstone, 1980).

old may decline somewhat in coming years. Among the factors that could contribute to such a decline are increases in the elderly's level of education; changes in mass media old-age stereotyping; improvements in the economic and health status of the aged; the trend away from mandatory retirement and the trend toward voluntary early retirement; and the growth of various organizations committed to improving the image and influence of the aged. To the extent that there is a reduction in the stigma associated with being old, we should expect a corresponding increase in willingness to assume the identity as an elderly person. Since there is a tendency for those who identify as being elderly to be more supportive of programs on behalf of the elderly (Cutler and Schmidhauser, 1975; Bengtson and Cutler, 1976), any reduction in stigma could well contribute to an increase in the political participation and influence of the elderly.

During the past thirty years there has been a marked shift in the labor force participation of women; more women are spending more of their lives at work (Schulz, 1980). This trend along with the more general changes in traditional sex roles is likely to reduce the gap in political participation among elderly men and women. Today, elderly women show lower voter turnout rates than do elderly men (Wolfinger and Rosenstone, 1980). In addition, the decline in voter participation starts at an earlier age for elderly women. However, with increased labor force participation (Bednarzik and Klein, 1977) and changing sex roles, it is quite likely that in years to come voter participation rates for women will more nearly approximate those for men (Andersen, 1975).[7] This would contribute to an overall increase in voting rates for the elderly.

In recent years there has been a dramatic decline in the proportion of voters who identify as being either Democratic or Republican, and there has been a corresponding upswing in the proportion who identify as being independents (Nie et al., 1976). To the extent that voters of any population subgroup including the elderly identify as independents, they cannot be taken for granted by those running for elective office. This trend will give the elderly

---

[7]Wolfinger and Rosenstone (1980) take issue with Andersen; they find no evidence of greater voter participation among women in the paid labor force.

more political leverage than they presently have. In the past, the
elderly have been viewed as a very stable voting group (Campbell
et al., 1960). For this reason politicians have generally been hesi-
tant to focus too directly on the aging vote (Riemer and Binstock,
1978). If elderly voters have been supporting a particular party
over the years, they have been more likely than other age groups
to continue to do so (Hudson and Binstock, 1976). If a party can
assume that it is going to get the votes of a particular constituency,
this reduces the bargaining power of that constituency; in recent
years this has been a problem for black voters, who have traditionally
voted heavily Democratic. If the trend for the elderly to identify
as independents continues, it is likely that this will increase their
bargaining power in the political arena.

One of the most consistent findings to come out of gerontological
research over the years is that the elderly are not a homogeneous
group of people. In fact, they tend to be one of the most heterogeneous age groups with respect to a wide range of characteristics,
and it is often argued that this heterogeneity tends to reduce the
political power of the elderly (Harootyan, 1981; Binstock, 1972;
Campbell, 1971). However, there is reason to believe that the
elderly are becoming more homogeneous in certain respects and
that this trend may contribute to an increase in political influence
in the future.

One relevant factor in this context is the change in immigration
rates (U.S. Bureau of the Census, 1979b). There was a lot more
immigration into the United States during the first part of the
century than there is today.[8] As a result, fifty years from now a smaller
proportion of the aged will be first-generation immigrants, and there
will be a smaller proportion who do not speak English as their first
language. In addition, they will have been exposed to the homogenizing influence of television and other mass media for a longer period of time. All of these factors are likely to reduce the heterogeneity

---

[8]The average yearly immigration rate per 1000 U.S. population was 10.4 between 1901 and
1910, 5.7 between 1911 and 1920, 3.5 between 1921 and 1930, and 2.1 in 1977 (U.S. Bureau of
the Census, 1979b). However, such estimates do not take into consideration the number of
illegal immigrants, which seems to be increasing. Between 1930 and 1950 the immigration
rates were below 1.0, but since 1950 the rates have been increasing. In 1900, some 34 percent
of those age 60 to 64 were foreign born, and by 1970, only 10 percent of those in this age
group were foreign born (Uhlenberg, 1977).

among the elderly, and this could increase their political influence. To this point, our focus has been on factors likely to contribute to an increase in the political resources of the elderly in years ahead. Many analysts mention these same factors in connection with the argument that the political power and influence of the aged will be substantially greater in the future than it is today. A major reason that we take issue with the conclusion that the preceding trends will inevitably lead to a significant increase in the political influence of the aged is our recognition that there are a number of other factors that will also affect the magnitude of any shift in the relative influence of the elderly. Here we are referring to the factors that will tend to neutralize and counterbalance those mentioned to this point. In some cases there is a dialectical relationship between these counterbalancing forces and the trends considered above. The more powerful and successful the aged become in advancing their own interests, the stronger will be the incentive for other interest groups to organize to oppose further gains. These counterbalancing factors, to which we now turn, are often mentioned by those analysts who take the position that there will be little if any increase in the political influence of the aged in years ahead.

NEUTRALIZING AND COUNTERBALANCING FACTORS

The demographic evidence of a changing age structure is at the core of the arguments of many who expect an increase in the political influence of the elderly in coming years. No one can deny that the number of elderly people in this country has dramatically increased since the turn of the century, and it is also quite safe to project a continuing increase well into the next century. This argument makes the implicit assumption that the size of a population subgroup is a major source of political power. But if we look around, we are confronted with a great deal of evidence that numbers do not always translate into influence. There are many more poor people than there are rich people in this country (Williamson et al., 1975), but few would argue that the poor have more political influence than do the rich. Similarly, there are more women in the nation than there are men, but again the size of this segment of the population does not translate in any direct way into political influence. Since women have many sources of identity and ideological commitment, they are not politically united as an interest group and they do not have the political influence they would otherwise have.

Reasoning along similar lines the argument is made that an increase in the proportion of the population who are elderly will not necessarily translate into an increase in political influence. To the extent that the aged remain divided by their allegiance to a variety of other sources of identity such as social class, occupational background, race, religion, and ethnic background, any increase in numbers may be neutralized (Binstock, 1972). If an increase in the size of the elderly population is to translate into an increase in political influence, it would help if there were some increase in "age consciousness," but such a shift may not occur. The elderly have a variety of sources of identity other than age, and many of these other sources of identity are much more long standing and more highly valued (Campbell, 1971). For this reason some analysts argue that the elderly are a relatively weak political force today and are likely to remain so into the foreseeable future (Binstock, 1976; Maddox, 1978).

The heterogeneity of the elderly will continue to inhibit the development of a strong elderly voting block and the evolution of the elderly as a highly organized interest group. While there are trends discussed earlier in the chapter that may reduce the degree of heterogeneity among the elderly in coming years, there is no credible authority who argues that the heterogeneity will be eliminated. To the contrary, most would agree that the crosscutting sources of identity, loyality, and perceived self-interest such as social class, race, and ethnicity will remain and continue to affect political attitudes and behavior (Binstock, 1972; Campbell, 1971). Because some of these cleavages, such as social class, reflect very real differences in self-interest, it is going to be difficult to politically unify older people around aging issues and candidates committed to the interests of the elderly (Ragan and Davis, 1978).

One of the consequences of the demographic shift we have described is an increase in the "elderly dependency ratio" (the ratio of persons over age 65 to persons age 18 to 64). This ratio has been increasing since the turn of the century and most likely will continue to increase during the next fifty years (Cutler and Schmidhauser, 1975).[9] It reflects the increasing economic burden that the dependent elderly will be placing on the nonelderly. Some analysts argue that the burden could reach a point at which the nonelderly are unwilling to bear the burden (Hudson, 1978a). One reaction might be a major taxpayer's revolt. It is possible that the "Proposition 13 Movement" of the 1970s will turn out to have been just the opening round for a much more comprehensive revolt. The increasing tax burden on the nonelderly due in part to the cost of programs for the aged could serve to unify this segment of the population against continued government efforts to improve or even maintain the elderly's living standard.

Such a tax revolt would represent a major threat to the economic well-being of many who are elderly, and it could serve as a catalyst for political unity among the elderly (Weaver, 1981). But if this unity were to occur in response to a substantial anti-aging backlash in the general population, any potential increase in power among the elderly might well be neutralized. It is possible that the backlash would be sufficiently strong that the power and influence of the elderly *relative* to that of other age groups would actually decline.

Some analysts argue that there might in the not too distant future be a marked increase in age consciousness among the elderly in response to certain kinds of polarizing events. The most often cited example in this context is an actual or threatened reduction in standard of living available to the elderly (Wilson, 1973). If the nation were faced with a no-growth economy and marked inflation, the standard of living the elderly experience might be undercut. This could produce a strong political reaction on the part of the elderly and lead to an increase in "aging consciousness." To the extent that the elderly have a clear economic self-interest in common, an increase in age consciousness would be quite possible. This in turn could lead to more political unity and possibly to an "aging vote."

---

[9]The dependency ratio was 18/100 in 1980, and a recent projection puts the ratio at 31/100 for 2030. Looked at in another way, in 1940 there were 9 persons age 20 to 64 for every person age 65 and over; today the ratio is 6 to 1 and, by the year 2030, it will be 3 to 1 (Califano, 1981:283).

But there is a very important argument that the preceding scenario fails to deal with. It is entirely possible that the conditions that would be necessary to create a marked increase in age consciousness among the elderly would also tend to increase sentiments against the elderly. Age consciousness would probably increase in response to an economic collapse on the magnitude of the Great Depression, but such a collapse would not just impact the elderly, it would have profound effects on all age groups. In this situation there would be a great deal of competition from other age groups with their own needs. These other groups would not sit idly by watching their incomes fall relative to those of the elderly. The severe economic conditions necessary to produce a marked increase in solidarity among the aged would at the same time increase the resistance from other and more powerful segments of the population to any increase in the aged's share of the national budget. It is not at all clear that severe economic deprivation would lead to a net increase in the relative power and influence of the elderly.

Many who anticipate an increase in the elderly's political power in the future point to an increasing age consciousness, as exemplified by such organizations as the Gray Panthers. Critics point out that the number of older persons who identify as being "old" or "elderly" is surprisingly small (Riley and Foner, 1968). In one study based on a national sample, only 38 percent of those over age 60 identified as old (Cutler, 1974), and in another, only 61 percent of those aged 71 to 79 identified as being elderly or old as opposed to young or middle aged (Ward, 1979). Furthermore, those who are in the best health and who have the most education are the least likely to identify as being old (Binstock, 1976). With this evidence in mind it is reasonable to conclude that as education levels increase and the economic position of the elderly improves, we may find fewer rather than more of the elderly willing to identify as being elderly. This could make it difficult for those attempting to organize an old-age voting block based on age consciousness. Those who do not identify as being elderly are less likely to support efforts to improve the welfare of the elderly than are persons of comparable age who do identify as being old (Cutler and Schmidhauser, 1975; Cutler, 1974).

Implicit in much of our discussion to this point has been a model of government decision-making commonly referred to as *interest group pluralism.* It is one of the most frequently used models in discussions of aging policy (Estes, 1979; Binstock, 1972; Rose, 1965a). In the arena of interest group politics, *economic clout* is an important source of influence. Large corporations, unions, and other such well-financed interest groups are in a position to employ highly paid lobbyists to make sure the interests of their constituencies are well represented. In this process, the interest of the poor, the elderly, and other vulnerable groups are also represented, but less adequately than more well-organized and more highly financed groups. In this process there is no one-to-one correspondence between the size of a constituency and the amount of influence it is able to exert. All other things being equal, the larger a constituency the greater its clout; however, most typically all other things are not equal. The strength of the AMA lobby is certainly out of proportion to the actual size of its constituency, as is also the case with the lobby for the National Rifle Association and many other such well-financed and highly specialized special interest groups. To the extent that the model of interest group pluralism describes the way in which major governmental decisions are made in this country, there is reason to doubt that even a substantial increase in the number of elderly voters will significantly change the political influence of this segment of the population.

There are a variety of alternatives for assessing the relative power of different interest groups and population subgroups. We have already considered the problem with one of these by simply counting up the number of voters in the specified constituency. Another alternative is to look at the outcome of the political process. In this context one might consider the proportion of the federal budget in recent years that has gone to programs for the elderly.[10] A trend favorable to the elderly was particularly evident during the late 1960s and the 1970s. In 1967, approximately 16 percent of the federal budget was allocated to various programs for

---

[10]Another spending-related indicator is the amount that political parties spend in their efforts to obtain the vote of a specific interest group. In the 1976 presidential campaign, Carter allocated much less to the so-called "senior desk" than to desks for other special interest groups such as Jews, labor, and minorities (Riemer and Binstock, 1978).

the aging (U.S. Dept. of H.E.W., 1971). By 1980, it had increased to 25 percent, and some were projecting it would increase to 40 percent within the next 60 years (Rabushka and Jacobs, 1980). However, there are a number of criticisms that can be made of arguments based on these statistics. One is to question how much of the spending actually reaches the elderly in a form that significantly contributes to an increase in standard of living or quality of life. Another argument is that this trend seems to be changing. In recent years there has been a lot more talk about the need to increase defense spending than the need for increases in programs for the elderly; this change of mood and priorities will soon be reflected in the relative share of the national budget allocated to social programs including programs for the elderly.[11]

If we look at the legislation relevant to aging interests, we see evidence that a wide variety of new programs and government agencies have been created in recent years to look after the interests of the aged. Of particular relevance in this context are: the Older Americans Act (1965), the creation of the Administration on Aging (1965), enactment of Medicare and Medicaid legislation (1965), the 1972 amendments to the Social Security Act making cost of living increments in pension benefits automatic, the creation of the National Institute on Aging (1974), the 1974 pension reform legislation, and the legislation in 1978 increasing the minimum age of mandatory retirement from 65 to 70. It is clear that in terms of government programs the elderly did quite well between the mid-1960s and the late 1970s. However, there are some who contend that the easing of mandatory retirement rules represents the first step in an effort to keep the elderly in the labor force,

---

[11]For demographic reasons it is likely that the fraction of the federal budget going to Social Security benefits will continue to increase, even if there is no real increase in benefit levels to individual recipients. Because Social Security is such a big program, it is possible that the overall proportion of the federal budget going to programs for the aged will continue to increase, even if there are sharp reductions in programs other than Social Security. The economic burden of a "mature" Social Security system is not unique to the United States; the same problems are being faced in most other western industrial nations (Ross, 1979). In the popular press there are some who argue that the elderly have emerged as the only constituency of needy Americans that continues to command widespread support in Congress (Roberts, 1981), but more common are the reports of sentiments that the elderly are already getting more than their share (Chapman, 1981).

eventually against the will of many, through probable increases in the eligibility age for Social Security pension benefits (Graebner, 1980). There are others who argue that the amount of pro-elderly legislation seen during this span of years is not indicative of what we will be seeing in years to come. The argument is that all this legislative activity has transformed the elderly from a constituency generally viewed as neglected, to one that many believe is getting more than its fair share and more than the rest of the population can afford to pay for in an era of slow economic growth (Rabushka and Jacobs, 1980). Some analysts predict that it will become evident before too long that support for efforts to improve the elderly's welfare and relative standard of living peaked during the 1970s (Hudson, 1978a).

While some emphasize social programs and legislation in their analysis of outcomes of the political process, others prefer to emphasize trends in income distribution and relative economic status. If we look at the economic status of the elderly relative to other age groups, we see very little by way of movement over the years (U.S. Bureau of the Census, 1976). While the economic status of the elderly has improved and the poverty rate has declined significantly (U.S. Bureau of the Census, 1979a, 1980a), when we look at the median income of the elderly relative to other age groups, we do not see evidence of a dramatic improvement in the status of the elderly (U.S. Bureau of the Census, 1976). There were some gains for the elderly during the 1970s, but they did little more than compensate for the losses in relative economic status during the 1960s. This evidence, coupled with the sense among many analysts that efforts to improve the relative economic position of the aged probably peaked in the 1970s, leads some to conclude that there is little reason to expect a significant shift in favor of the elderly with respect to income distribution in the foreseeable future.[12]

---

[12]A reply to this argument is that there has been a substantial increase in in-kind benefits to the elderly during the past twenty years in the form of health insurance, housing subsidy, food stamps, and other sources (Schulz, 1980). If these contributions to standard of living are taken into consideration, a case can be made that there has been significant improvement in the relative economic position of the elderly during this period of time (Johnson and Williamson, 1980).

For many gerontologists, income distribution is the bottom line with respect to power (Binstock, 1972). To the extent that the elderly have been unable to obtain an increase in their income share, it can be argued that they have not obtained the results one would expect if in fact their relative power had increased (Hudson and Binstock, 1976). That is, the lack of gains in relative income is an indicator of little if any increase in political power. Alternatively, it can be argued that if the elderly do not increase their relative income share, they are unlikely to increase their political influence. This argument is based in part on the relevance of economic clout in the context of interest group bargaining.

The mass organizations of the elderly such as the National Retired Teachers Association/American Association of Retired Persons (NRTA/AARP) and the National Council of Senior Citizens (NCSC) are unwilling to press for changes in federal programs and policies that would significantly increase the elderly's share of the federal budget or significantly affect the distribution of income. These organizations always support modest incremental proposals. They must keep their demand in a range that is acceptable to the political officials with whom they deal. As long as their demands are modest, it is easy for politicians to support these demands without hard evidence that the organization is in a position to deliver substantial numbers of votes (Binstock, 1974). If, on the other hand, the organization were to make demands for a major increase in the elderly's share of federal resources, the politicians would be unwilling to support them. This would constitute a call of their "electoral bluff" (Pratt, 1976; Hudson and Binstock, 1976). If in this situation the organization was unable to deliver votes to those who did offer support and was unable to withhold votes from those who did not, their claim to be speaking on behalf of the millions of elderly persons who are members of the organization would be seriously undercut (Binstock, 1972). What little power they presently have would be considerably diminished. This situation is unlikely to change at any time soon.

Age does not seem to be a significant variable in accounting for voting swings (Binstock, 1974). There is evidence of substantial swings from one party to another and from one election to the next. These swings show up for the aged, but there is no evidence that special appeals to the elderly get them to swing in a direction that differs from that for other age groups. If there were clear evidence that the elderly were willing to shift from one party or candidate to another on the basis of specific aging issues, the elderly as a group would have considerably more political influence than they presently do.

One of the factors typically mentioned by those predicting a marked increase in the political influence of the aged is the growing government bureaucracy responsible for administering aging programs and the expanding network of agencies responsible for providing various services. These agencies constitute a significant interest group lobbying on behalf of programs for the aged. But some critics have begun to raise questions as to whose interests are being served by this lobby (Estes, 1979). While some elderly persons do benefit from such programs, the great majority do not benefit, or benefit in only minor ways. Most of the money spent goes to middle-class, nonelderly administrators and service providers. Some question the cash value to the elderly of the services provided. It has been argued that many who are elderly would get better value for the money spent were it instead used to increase Social Security pensions or SSI benefits.

POWER, POLITICS, AND POLICY: A SYNTHESIS

In any effort to forecast trends in the political influence of the aged, it is important to distinguish between the short run (5–10 years) and the long run (40–50 years). Considering first the short run — the decade of the 1980s — there is little reason at this time to expect a significant increase in the influence of the aged. It is likely that the elderly will be faced with program cuts, and it is unlikely that major new programs will be enacted that would tend to enhance their standard of living. It is possible that poverty rates among the aged will increase, and that the overall standard of living for the aged will decline somewhat.[13]

---

[13]By the late 1970s there was evidence of an increase in the size of the elderly poverty population, reversing a twenty-year trend. Between 1978 and 1979 the proportion of the elderly who were poor increased from 14 percent to 15 percent (U.S. Bureau of the Census, 1980b).

During the decade of the 1980s the test of the power of the aged as an interest group will more likely be reflected in the ability to resist substantial reductions in program benefits than in the ability to get new programs enacted. If the aged are more successful than other interest groups in resisting funding cutbacks, it is possible that by the end of the decade analysts will be attributing more power to the elderly than they do today, even if they have made no new programmatic gains.

Our forecasts for trends in the power and political influence of the elderly fifty years hence are quite different than those for the decade of the 1980s. Considering this more extended time horizon, we anticipate an increase in the political resources of the aged. It is likely that this increase in resources will translate into increases in autonomy and political influence, but such an outcome is by no means inevitable. It is possible that any increase in political influence will be so modest that those who today are forecasting no change in political influence will be able to claim that their predictions were essentially correct, but it is also possible that the increase will be much more substantial than even the most optimistic of today's pro-aging advocates anticipate.

We do not believe the evidence supports the conclusion that there will *necessarily* be an increase in power and influence, even if there are substantial increases in such political resources as size of the elderly population, level of education among the aged, and elderly voter turnout rates, and reduced party loyalty, group consciousness, and social homogeneity among the aged. As we have pointed out earlier, these and other resources will to some degree be neutralized by a number of other factors. It is particularly relevant to bear in mind that in some instances the counterbalancing factor is triggered in response to political and economic gains by the elderly. The more successful the aged are in their competition with the other interest groups for federal monies, the greater the risk of a loss of legitimacy as a constituency that is deserving of further increases in benefits. This illustrates the dialectical relationship between the gains of the elderly and the resistance from other interest groups to further gains.

During the past thirty years an increasing proportion of the federal budget has been allocated to programs for the elderly.

While it is quite possible that there will be a pause in this trend during all or most of the 1980s, it is likely that the trend will continue if we consider the longer time frame of the next fifty years. This can be expected on the basis of the demographic shift that will be increasing the proportion of the adult population who are eligible for Social Security pension benefits. Thus there would be an increase in the fraction of the federal budget spent on the elderly, even if there were no real increase in the size of benefits to individual Social Security recipients. While the Social Security program could by itself account for a continuation of the trend, it will not be the only source of the increase. The shift in age structure is also going to call for an increase in the proportion of federal health-care dollars spent on the elderly. With the increase in the number of old people there will be increases in spending on Medicare, Medicaid, and other health-related programs.

Increases in spending on programs for the aged can be interpreted as gains for the elderly, but these programmatic gains have not been without their costs. They have made it possible for a greater proportion of the elderly to avoid dependency on their children. This increase in autonomy and reduction in social control by one's children has been welcomed and has contributed to an improvement in quality of life for many who are elderly. But it is now becoming evident that for many of the elderly the cost of independence from one's children has been an increase in dependence on impersonal public bureaucratic structures and functionaries. The administrators and professional service providers associated with these various programs become agents of social control. The elderly now have Medicaid that pays much of the nursing home bill, but the limit on the amount the program allows for such benefits has implications for the quality of care such institutions can provide. As a result, life in these institutions is organized more around the goal of cost efficiency than patient autonomy. Many who in the past would have been taken care of at home in an environment over which they could exert considerable control find themselves recipients of government benefits, but at the cost of subjugation to a great deal of social control.

In efforts to assess trends in the power of the elderly it is possible to come to different conclusions, depending on what

arena we are considering. Most of our attention to this point has
been on federal government decision-making, particularly that
related to the allocation of federal monies. Trends in local communities will not always parallel the nation as a whole. This is
particularly likely to be true of sunbelt retirement communities.
In certain communities, including some large cities such as Miami
and St. Petersburg, the elderly have come to exercise considerable
influence on local government decision-making (Gustaitis, 1980;
Anderson and Anderson, 1981); as we look to the future we can
expect this trend to continue. In selected retirement communities
the elderly will constitute such a large fraction of the population
that they will exercise a great deal more influence than is the case
at the national level.

If we look at trends in power within families considering
intergenerational and marital relationships, we come up with
some very different conclusions than when we look at the power of
the elderly in the political arena. Let us first consider the
intergenerational relationships between elderly parents and their
adult children. The trend away from multigenerational households (Kobrin, 1976; U.S. Bureau of the Census, 1979b) and the
trend from rural to urban residence (Weber, 1963) have both tended
to decrease the control of the elderly over their children relative
to what it was one hundred years ago. As we look toward the future
it seems that the trend is for more, not less, independence. More of
the elderly will be living in their own households, and more will
be moving into retirement communities or other such age homogeneous living situations. These trends will reduce involvement
with children and lead to less influence over them. However, most
of the elderly will continue to live in their community of residence prior to old age, and most will continue to have frequent
contact with at least one of their children.

To this point we have focused on the prospects for the influence
of the elderly in the aggregate. Such an emphasis presupposes
that the elderly can be treated as a relatively homogeneous aggregate, but this is clearly not the case (Binstock, 1974; Campbell,
1971; Ragan and Davis, 1978). There are going to be significant
variations in the extent of any change in influence for different
subgroups of the elderly, and the trend may be quite different for

the elderly rich than for the elderly poor. There will probably be no increase in the political influence of the elderly rich, but there could be a significant increase in the political influence of the less-affluent elderly.

To the extent that relative power is reflected in the allocation of federal monies, one might argue that during the past fifty years there have been substantial relative gains by the elderly poor. However, it can be misleading to put too much emphasis on government expenditures. If we take into consideration the opportunities for tax avoidance that Congress has created for the rich of all ages, including the elderly, we are led to a different conclusion with respect to the trend in relative power and influence. Stanley Surrey (1973) points out that federal tax benefits are in many ways equivalent to government expenditures. In this context some have described these opportunities for tax avoidance as "welfare for the rich" (Stern, 1972). If we take these tax benefits into consideration, the value of federal benefits on a per capita basis are far greater for the elderly rich than for the elderly poor, and it is entirely possible that the value of these tax benefits has increased at a greater rate over the years than have Social Security pensions, SSI payments, and other social program benefits.

The American welfare state has been expanding during the past fifty years, and with this expansion has come at least a modest improvement in the position of the elderly poor. But if we take into consideration tax benefits as well as program benefits, a case can be made that the *relative* gains have been modest. During the next fifty years we can expect some additional growth in the welfare state, although the rate of expansion may be far below that of the past thirty years. However, given the historical evidence with respect to stability in the distribution of income in this country (U.S. Bureau of the Census, 1979*a*, 1980*a*; Pechman and Okner, 1974; Kolko, 1962), it is likely that the relative economic position of the elderly poor will remain similar to what it is today; any drift in a direction favorable to the elderly poor will be modest.

There may also be significant sex differences in the extent of any trend in influence over the next fifty years. We may find that there will be a substantial increase in the influence of elderly women relative to elderly men as the elderly female population becomes more educated and more economically self-sufficient. In the family sphere it is likely that there will be more of an increase in autonomy for women than for men. Women may come to have increasing influence over certain family decisions that have traditionally been considered as the male prerogative, such as when and where to retire. Similarly, women may take a more active part in family financial planning, with an eye to their future economic needs as widows.

This increase in the relative influence of women is also likely to be reflected in the realm of electoral politics. There is good reason to expect that over the next fifty years there will be a marked reduction in the gap between men and women with respect to electoral participation. Increased labor force participation will contribute to this trend, but an even more important factor will be the increase in level of education for elderly women relative to elderly men.

Elderly women, many of whom are widows, face a different set of life contingencies than do most elderly men. Related to these contingencies are special needs, such as those relating to living alone and the quality of life in nursing homes. Given the disproportionate representation of women among the elderly, it is possible that gains in influence for the aged will focus increasingly on the needs of elderly women.

Our analysis has implicitly assumed that during the next fifty years there will be no significant change in the definition of what it means to be elderly. However, it is possible that over the next few decades there may be a change in the age at which old age is seen as starting (Dowd, 1980*b*). Conceptions of old age have changed in the past and could change in the future.[14] The change could go in either of two directions with quite different implications. The most likely trend would be an upward shift with respect to when old age begins. The shift in mandatory retirement for the private

---

[14]Anthropologists report that old age often begins at an earlier age in a primitive tribe than in contemporary industrial societies. Among the Igorot tribe a person was considered old at age 45 (Simmons, 1945). Hippocrates asserted that old age begins at 56 (de Beauvoir, 1972). For Romans (Fischer, 1978), old age seems to have begun at age 60; the same was also true in colonial America (Demos, 1978).

sector from age sixty-five to seventy might contribute to such a trend. There has been much discussion about increasing the incentive to put off the start of Social Security benefits; if the incentive for a delay becomes substantial, this too could contribute to a trend toward later retirement.[15]

It is likely that 65 will continue to be the most frequently used age to indicate the point at which a person moves from the status of being middle-aged to being old, but there is by no means universal agreement on this. When people aged 65 are asked whether they consider themselves old or elderly (Cutler, 1974), a majority say they do not. With improvements in health status and economic status, it is possible that an increasing proportion of those who are 65, 70, and even 75 will consider themselves middle aged rather than old. Such a trend would be particularly likely as a consequence of medical breakthroughs that significantly extend life expectancy. If a shift were to occur and the shift were significant, we would have to qualify many of our projected trends with respect to the political power and influence of the elderly. For example, we have projected an increase in the proportion of voters who are elderly from 15 percent in 1980 to 20 percent in 2030. But if the definition of who the elderly are shifts during this time from age 65 and over to age 75 and over, there may be a *decrease* in the proportion of elderly voters.

Alternatively, it is possible that the definition of elderly might go in the opposite direction. As the health and economic status of the elderly improve, the stigma associated with old age may decline. This could lead to an increase in the number of people who are willing to identify as elderly and to a lowering of the age at which they are ready to assume this identity. It is even possible that some who are not yet age 65 will assume the identity of older persons because they are retired and in most respects share a life-style and a set of life concerns with those who are over age 65. The trend toward retirement at a younger age (U.S. Bureau of the Census, 1976) could lead to a substantial lowering of the age at which

---

[15]At present, there is a 3 percent per year increase for each year between age 65 and 72 that a person elects not to collect Social Security pension benefits, but this is a very weak incentive that has relatively little impact on retirement decisions for most people.

people perceive old age to begin. The term *elderly* could come to be synonymous with *retiree* and designate a segment of the population that in the future is younger than it is today.

If any such shift in the definition of who the elderly are were to occur, there would be a number of implications for the projections we have made. One of the most obvious is that it would contribute to a marked increase in the number of elderly voters, because a larger segment of the population would be included and because those added would be from the age group with the highest voter participation rate (Wolfinger and Rosenstone, 1980).

Our discussion of trends in the power and influence of the aged has to this point implicitly assumed that any changes in the social, political, and economic environment will be more or less comparable to those we have experienced during the past thirty years or so. This is a reasonable assumption when attempting to make statements about conditions five years in the future, but it is a risky assumption when attempting to look fifty years ahead. Clearly, we are in no position to specify what unexpected events or social changes will occur, but it is possible to explore a few alternative scenarios. This provides some idea of the kinds of modifications in our projections that may be called for.

Historically, the aged have done better during periods of social, political, and economic stability than during periods of rapid social change. In view of this, it is reasonable to ask whether this generalization is likely to hold during the next fifty years. We would argue that it depends on the source of any such rapid social change. For some sources, such as global nuclear war or a major worldwide depression, the standard of living, the quality of life, and the political influence of the aged would suffer. However, other possible changes such as those that might result from advances in biological science increasing life expectancy to something over age one hundred could substantially increase the political influence of those we now refer to as the aged.

A fundamental determinant of the political influence of the aged some fifty years hence will be the state of the economy between now and then. Alternative economic scenarios have profound implications for any changes in the influence of the aged. Consider first the case of a zero-growth or slow-growth economy during much of the next half century. If the economy continues to perform more or less at the level of the 1970s during the next fifty years, there will most likely be little by way of real gains in benefit levels for Social Security recipients and little if any expansion of existing social programs for the aged. For demographic reasons the actual level of government spending on programs for the aged might increase, but this would be to provide basically the same benefits presently being provided to a larger number of recipients. It would also be consistent with this economic scenario for there to be some modest overall reductions in average benefit levels while at the same time there was an overall increase in federal budget allocations for such programs. It is possible that there would be an increase in the political influence of the aged; however, this influence would more likely be reflected in the ability of the aged to defend their share of the federal budget than in the ability to get new programmatic initiatives enacted or benefit levels for existing programs increased.

In the event that the American economy turns out to be strong over much of the next fifty years, the resulting increase in productivity could lead to an increase in the funds available for social programs. Given that the elderly tend to be viewed as a deserving and legitimate constituency, it is possible that there would be significant programmatic gains. The social, health, and income support programs for the aged might well go beyond what is presently available in such advanced welfare state nations as Sweden.

There are some analysts who are forecasting an economic collapse on the order of the Great Depression of the 1930s at some point in the not too distant future. This would have a profound impact on the standard of living and the political influence of the elderly. One source of the strength of the aging lobby in recent years has been the support it has had from other segments of what is referred to as the *social welfare lobby.* In an extreme economic situation, it is possible that the elderly would be abandoned by their coalition partners; each segment of the social welfare lobby would be so involved in defending the interests of its specific constituency that there would be little time, money, or interest in supporting programs and legislation that primarily benefit other interest groups.

It is entirely possible that in fifty years the elderly will have considerably less political influence than they do today. This might occur if inflation were to be defined as a sufficient threat to the social order as to justify draconian measures to bring it under control—a response that would be much more likely in the United States than in Sweden given the influence of Lockean individualism extolling self-reliance in the American context. In such a situation there would be a great effort to minimize spending on social programs as part of the effort to bring inflation under control. One step, which appears already to be underway, would be to eliminate or drastically cut back on a variety of social service programs associated with the welfare state, including many that presently provide benefits to the elderly. If the inflation problem were viewed as sufficiently threatening, it is possible that the automatic cost of living provisions presently associated with the Social Security pension would be eliminated. We cannot say for sure that even so-called "hyper-inflation" would lead to efforts to strip the elderly of the benefits from the various social programs on which they have come to depend, but such an outcome is possible. Were such a situation to arise, there would be strong resistance from the elderly, but in any showdown with other segments of the population it is quite possible that the interests of the elderly would suffer.

Another event that could drastically alter the projections we have made would be a major war, particularly if it resulted in a loss of a substantial fraction of the population. If the United States were subjected to a loss of life comparable to that experienced by Germany or the Soviet Union during World War II, it is possible that in the aftermath there would be a great focus on the needs of the next generation at the expense of the elderly. There might be a marked increase in birth rates and a focus of national resources on building schools and pediatric health clinics; in short, an emphasis on providing for children at the expense of the elderly.[16] Today in many third-world nations there is little by way of govern-

---

[16]Basically, the same argument could be made if there were a substantial increase in fertility for any of a variety of other reasons. A sharp increase in fertility seems unlikely today, but then again, it also seemed very unlikely to those making demographic projections in the 1930s.

ment resources allocated to programs for the elderly; the focus is almost exclusively on the younger generation. This might also occur in the United States in the aftermath of a major war.

Alternatively, it is possible that under the right circumstances the increase in power and influence of the elderly could be far in excess of that which we have described as most plausible in light of existing evidence and present trends. A great deal of research is going on today in an effort to understand the process of cellular aging (Rosenfeld, 1976). It is possible that at some point during the next few decades this research will lead to a substantial increase in life expectancy. Some optimists assert that it may be possible to extend the human life expectancy to 150 years in the foreseeable future. If such advances were made, it might become common to remain politically active to well over age 100, and the elderly would constitute a much more substantial fraction of the electorate than our projection would suggest.

Other technological advances could contribute to an increase in the influence of the elderly, even in the absence of any significant increase in life expectancy. For example, advances in telecommunications and computer technology could make possible some form of "electronic democracy" through the use of a combination of television and interactive computers. With such a technology it would be possible for the voting public to be consulted on a regular basis, as opposed to the present policy of voting once every couple of years; it might be possible to significantly expand the range of issues on which the voting public is consulted.

Any such change in the electoral process could significantly change the relative political influence of different age groups. It would tend to increase the influence of those who have the time and interest to follow the issues and debates on television, possibly in the context of all-day televised hearings. It would also increase the influence of those who would otherwise find it difficult to make it to the polls to vote due to health problems and lack of adequate transportation. For these reasons, among others, we would expect an increase in the political influence of the elderly.[17]

The recent introduction of cable television is another innovation that could significantly affect the political influence of the elderly, as it offers the potential for age-specific programming. Eventually we may find an entire network devoted to concerns of older people, presenting an "elderly perspective" on world, national, and local issues. Such programming might lead to a significant increase in age consciousness among the elderly and provide a very effective tool for the political mobilization of the elderly around issues of common interest. Age-specific programming could be a particularly potent political tool if used in connection with interactive computer and telecommunication technology. It might be feasible for the elderly to hold video-political meetings with like-minded persons who were widely dispersed geographically.

An important objective of this book and particularly this chapter has been to forecast future trends in the power, autonomy, and political influence of the aged. We anticipate that our analysis of the factors likely to play an important role in determining these trends will prove to be of greater value than our specific projections based on what seem to be reasonable assumptions with respect to a number of these factors at this point in time. Thus, our major objective has been to describe the factors that will be important determinants of these trends. Given the uncertainties associated with a number of these factors, such as the state of the economy, any long-term projections of the political influence of the aged must remain tentative. Our analysis of alternative scenarios has been presented in an effort to make this discussion less speculative than it might otherwise have been.

Fifty years from today the elderly will, in all probability, have more by way of political resources than they have today. This will increase the potential for political influence, but the actual translation of these resources into real political influence is by no

---

[17]However, it is going to take more than technological advances for any form of electronic democracy to become a reality. There would undoubtedly be a great deal of resistance from Congress and various well-financed special interest groups to any proposal suggesting that political participation be broadened in this way.

means inevitable. A major reason for this is the dialectical relationship between these increasing resources and the efforts of those groups who oppose further increases in the power, influence, and autonomy of the elderly.

BIBLIOGRAPHY

Abramson, P. R.
1974   "Generational change in American electoral behavior." American
        Political Science Review 68:93–105.
Achenbaum, W. A.
1978a   Old Age in the New Land. Baltimore: Johns Hopkins University
        Press.
1978b   "The obsolescence of old age in America." Pp. 26–35 in M. M.
        Seltzer, S. L. Corbett, and R. C. Atchley (eds.), Social Problems of
        Aging. Belmont, California: Wadsworth.
Achenbaum, W. A., and P. N. Stearns
1978   "Old age and modernization." Gerontologist 18:307–312.
Adams, B. N.
1968   "The middle-class adult and his widowed or still-married mother."
        Social Problems 16:51–59.
1970   "Isolation, function, and beyond: American kinship in the 1960's."
        Journal of Marriage and the Family 32:575–597.
1975   The Family: A Sociological Interpretation. Chicago: Rand McNally.
Aging
1975   "Scandinavian experience in health and social services for the
        elderly." 246 (April):10–12.
Agnello, T. J.
1973   "Aging and the sense of political powerlessness." Public Opinion
        Quarterly 37:251–259.
Aldous, J.
1978   Family Careers: Developmental Change in Families. New York: Wiley.
Almond, G. A.
1958   "A comparative study of interest groups and the political process."
        American Political Science Review 52:270–282.
Almond, G. A., and S. Verba
1963   The Civic Culture: Political Attitudes and Democracy in Five
        Nations. Princeton, New Jersey: Princeton University Press.
Altmeyer, A. J.
1966   The Formative Years of Social Security. Madison, Wisconsin: Uni-
        versity of Wisconsin Press.
Andersen, K.
1975   "Working women and political participation, 1952–1972." Ameri-
        can Journal of Political Science 19:439–453.
Anderson, M.
1965   "Fiasco of urban renewal." Harvard Business Review 43(1):6–21.

Anderson, O. W.
1951   "Compulsory medical care insurance, 1910–1950." Annals of the
          American Academy of Political and Social Science 273:106–113.
Anderson, W. A., and N. D. Anderson
1981   "The politics of age exclusion: the adults only movement in Ari-
          zona." Pp. 86–97 in R. B. Hudson (ed.), The Aging in Politics.
          Springfield, Illinois: Charles C Thomas.
Andrus Gerontology Center
1978   Transportation and the Diverse Aged. Los Angeles: University of
          Southern California, Andrus Gerontology Center.
Anton, T. J.
1969   "Policy-making and political culture in Sweden." Scandinavian
          Political Studies 4:88–102.
Aristophanes
1961   The Birds. Translated by W. Arrowsmith. Ann Arbor, Michigan:
          University of Michigan Press.
1967   Ecclesiazusae. Translated by D. Parker. Ann Arbor, Michigan:
          University of Michigan Press.
Aristotle
1946   Politics. Translated by E. Baker. Oxford: Oxford University Press.
Armer, M., and A. Schnaiberg
1972   "Measuring individual modernity: a mere myth." American Soci-
          ological Review 37:301–316.
Aronoff, C.
1974   "Old age in prime time." Journal of Communication 24:86–87.
Arth, M. J.
1965   "The role of the aged in a West African village." Paper pre-
          sented at the Annual Meeting of the Gerontological Society, Los
          Angeles.
Atchley, R. C.
1976   The Sociology of Retirement. Cambridge, Massachusetts: Schenk-
          man.
Bahr, J.
1974   "Effects on power and division of labor in the family." Pp. 167–185
          in L. W. Hoffman and F. I. Nye (eds.), Working Mothers. San
          Francisco: Jossey-Bass.
Balbus, I. D.
1971   "The concept of interest in pluralist and Marxian analysis." Poli-
          tics and Society 1:151–177.
Baltes, P. B., and K. W. Shaie
1974   "Aging and IQ: the myth of the twilight years." Psychology Today
          7(March):35–40.
Barnet, R. J.
1980   The Lean Years: Politics in the Age of Scarcity. New York: Simon
          and Schuster.

Barnett, R., and G. Baruch
1979   "Women in the middle years: conceptions and misconceptions."
        Pp. 479–487 in J. H. Williams (ed.), Psychology of Women: Selected
        Readings. New York: Norton.
Bart, P. B.
1971   "Depression in middle-aged women." Pp. 163–186 in V. Gornick
        and B. Moran (eds.), Woman in Sexist Society: Studies in Power
        and Powerlessness. New York: Basic Books.
1975   "Emotional and social status of the older woman." Pp. 3–22 in No
        Longer Young: The Older Woman in America. Occasional Papers
        in Gerontology. Ann Arbor, Michigan: University of Michigan,
        Institute of Gerontology.
Beattie, W. M.
1976   "Aging and the social services." Pp. 619–642 in R. H. Binstock and
        E. Shanas (eds.), Handbook of Aging and the Social Sciences. New
        York: Van Nostrand Reinhold.
de Beauvoir, S.
1972   The Coming of Age. Translated by P. O'Brian. New York: G. P.
        Putnam's Sons.
Becker, H. S.
1964   (ed.), The Other Side. New York: Free Press.
1973   Outsiders. New York: Free Press.
Bednarzik, A. W., and D. P. Klein.
1977   "Labor force trends: a synthesis and analysis." Monthly Labor
        Review 100 (October):3–12.
Bell, D.
1974   The Coming of Post-Industrial Society. New York: Basic Books.
1976   The Cultural Contradictions of Capitalism. New York: Basic Books.
Bell, I. P.
1976   "The double standard." Pp. 150–162 in B. B. Hess (ed.), Growing
        Old in America. New Brunswick, New Jersey: Transaction.
Benet, S.
1971   "Why they live to be 100, or even older in Abkhasia." New York
        Times, December 26.
Bengtson, V. L., and N. E. Cutler
1976   "Generations and intergenerational relations: perspectives on age
        groups and social change." Pp. 130–159 in R. H. Binstock and E.
        Shanas (eds.), Handbook on Aging and the Social Sciences. New
        York: Van Nostrand Reinhold.
Bengtson, V. L., J. J. Dowd, D. H. Smith, and A. Inkeles
1975   "Modernization, modernity, and perceptions of aging: a cross-
        cultural study." Journal of Gerontology 30:688–695.
Bengtson, V. L., and J. A. Kuypers
1971   "Generational difference and the developmental stake." Aging and

Human Development 2:249–260.

Bentley, A. F.
1908   The Process of Government. Chicago: University of Chicago Press.

Berger, P. L.
1976   Pyramids of Sacrifice. Garden City. New York: Anchor/Doubleday.

Bernard, J.
1971   "The paradox of the happy marriage." Pp. 145–162 in V. Gornick
          and B. Moran (eds.), Woman in Sexist Society: Studies in Power
          and Powerlessness. New York: Basic Books.

Bernstein, A., and H. L. Lennard
1981   "Drugs, doctors, and junkies." Pp. 178–187 in J. B. Williamson, L.
          Evans, and A. Munley (eds.), Social Problems: The Contemporary
          Debates. Third edition. Boston: Little, Brown.

Bierstedt, R.
1974   Power and Progress: Essays on Sociological Theory. New York:
          McGraw-Hill.

Binstock, R. H.
1972   "Interest group liberalism and the politics of aging." Gerontologist
          12:265–280.
1974   "Aging and the future of American politics." Annals of the Ameri-
          can Academy of Political and Social Science 415:199–212.
1976   "The political economy of aging." Pp. 46–54 in Aging in America's
          Future. Somerville, New Jersey: Hoechst-Roussel Pharmaceuticals.

Binstock, R. H., and E. Shanas (eds.)
1976   Handbook of Aging and the Social Sciences. New York: Van
          Nostrand Reinhold.

Bird, C.
1979   The Two-Paycheck Marriage. New York: Rawson Wade.

Birren, J. E., and K. W. Schaie (eds.)
1977   Handbook of the Psychology of Aging. New York: Van Nostrand
          Reinhold.

Blackwell, R.
1974   "Political generation and attitude change among Soviet Obkom
          elites." Paper presented at the Annual Meeting of the American
          Political Science Association, Chicago.

Blau, P. M.
1964   Exchange and Power in Social Life. New York: Wiley.

Blau, Z. S.
1973   Old Age in a Changing Society. New York: New Viewpoints.

Block, M. R., and J. D. Sinnott
1979   The Battered Elder Syndrome: An Exploratory Study. College
          Park, Maryland: University of Maryland, Center on Aging.

Blood, R. O.
1963   "The husband-wife relationship." Pp. 282–305 in F. I. Nye and L.

W. Hoffman (eds.), The Employed Mother in America. Chicago: Rand McNally.

Blood, R. O., and R. L. Hamblin
1958   "The effect of the wife's employment in the family power structure." Social Forces 36:347–352.

Blood, R. O., and D. M. Wolfe
1960   Husbands and Wives. New York: Free Press.

Blumer, H.
1951   "Collective behavior." In A. M. Lee (ed.), New Outline of the Principles of Sociology. Second edition. New York: Barnes and Noble.
1969   Symbolic Interactionism: Perspective and Method. Englewood Cliffs, New Jersey: Prentice-Hall.
1971   "Social problems as collective behavior." Social Problems 18:298–306.

Board, J. B.
1970   The Government and Politics of Sweden. Boston: Houghton-Mifflin.

Boderman, A.
1964   Feelings of Powerlessness and Political and Religious Extremism. Unpublished doctoral dissertation. Minneapolis: University of Minnesota.

Bonjean, C. M.
1963   "Community leadership: a case study and conceptual refinement." American Journal of Sociology 68:672–681.

Booth, P.
1973   Social Security in America. Ann Arbor: University of Michigan—Wayne State University, Institute of Labor and Industrial Relations.

Bottomore, T.
1966   Classes in Modern Society. New York: Vintage.

Brandeis, L. D.
1911   "Workingmen's insurance—the road to social efficiency." Proceedings of the National Conference of Charities and Corrections.

Brim, O. G., H. E. Freeman, S. Levine, and N. A. Scotch (eds.)
1970   The Dying Patient. New York: Russell Sage.

Brinton, C.
1952   The Anatomy of Revolution. New York: Vintage.

Broder, D.
1973   "The old: benefits put a dangerous drain on U.S. funds." Los Angeles Times, February 1.

Broderick, C.
1975   "Power and governance of families." Pp. 117–128 in R. E. Cromwell and D. H. Olson (eds.), Power in Families. New York: Wiley.

Brotman, H. B.
1977   "Voter participation in November 1976." Gerontologist 17:157–159.
1978   "The aging of America: a demographic profile." National Journal

10:1622–1627.
Brown, L.
1979   "Study finds stereotyping in TV casts." New York Times, October
         30.
Brown, S.
1966   "We can't appease the younger generation." New York Times,
         November 27.
Burch, W., and F. Bormann (eds.)
1975   Beyond Growth—Essays on Alternative Futures. New Haven: Yale
         University Press.
Burgess, E. W.
1955   "Human aspects of social policy." Pp. 49–58 in Old Age in the
         Modern World. Edinburgh: E. and S. Livingston.
1960   (ed.), Aging in Western Society. Chicago: University of Chicago
         Press.
Burr, W. R., R. Hill, F. I. Nye, and I. L. Keiss (eds.)
1979   Contemporary Theories About the Family. New York: Free Press.
Busse, E. W., and E. Pfeiffer (eds.)
1977   Behavior and Adaptation in Late Life. Second edition. Boston:
         Little, Brown.
Butler, D., and D. Stokes
1971   Political Change in Britain. New York: St. Martin's Press.
Butler, R. N.
1974   "Pacification and the politics of aging." International Journal of
         Aging and Human Development 5:393–395.
1975   Why Survive? Being Old in America. New York: Harper and Row,
         1975.
1978   "Prospects for middle-aged women." Pp. 323–332 in Women in
         Midlife: Security and Fulfillment. Part I. A Compendium of Papers
         Submitted to the Select Committee on Aging and the Subcommit-
         tee on Retirement Income and Employment. U.S. House of Rep-
         resentatives, Ninety-Fifth Congress, Second Session. Washington,
         D.C.: U.S. Government Printing Office.
Butterfield, F.
1979   "Aging and leadership is worrying Peking." New York Times,
         November 26.
Cahn, A. F.
1977   "American women workers in a full employment economy: a sum-
         mary." Pp. 1–22 in American Women Workers in a Full Employ-
         ment Economy. A Compendium of Papers Submitted to the Com-
         mittee on Economic Growth and Stabilization of the Joint Com-
         mittee, Congress of the United States. Washington, D.C.: U.S.
         Government Printing Office.
1978   "Highlights of eighteen papers on problems of midlife women."
         Pp. 2–19 in Women in Midlife—Security and Fulfillment. Part I.

A Compendium of Papers submitted to the Select Committee on Aging and the Subcommittee on Retirement Income and Employment. U.S. House of Representatives, Ninety-Fifth Congress, Second Session. Washington, D.C.: U.S. Government Printing Office.

Calhoun, R. B.
1978   In Search of the New Old: Redefining Old Age in America, 1945–1970. New York: Elsevier.

Califano, J. A., Jr.
1981   "The aging of America and the four-generation society." Pp. 282–294 in R. B. Hudson (ed.), The Aging in Politics. Springfield, Illinois: Charles C Thomas.

Campbell, A.
1971   "Politics through the lifecycle." Gerontologist 11:112–117.
1976   "Subjective measures of well-being." American Psychologist 31: 117–124.

Campbell, A., and P. Converse (eds.)
1972   The Human Meaning of Social Change. New York: Russell Sage.

Campbell, A., P. Converse, W. Miller, and D. Stokes
1960   The American Voter. New York: Wiley.
1962   "Social and psychological determinants of voting behavior." Pp. 87–100 in W. Donahue and C. Tibbitts (eds.), Politics of Age. Ann Arbor: University of Michigan Press.

Cantril, H.
1951   Public Opinion, 1935–1946. Princeton: Princeton University Press.

Carlie, M. F.
1969   "The politics of age: interest group or social movement?" Gerontologist 9:259–263.

Carp, F.
1968   "Some components of disengagement." Journal of Gerontology 23:382–386.

Cartwright, D. (ed.)
1959   Studies in Social Power. Ann Arbor, Michigan: University of Michigan, Institute for Social Research.

Centers, R., B. Raven, and A. Rodrigues
1971   "Conjugal power structure: a re-examination." American Sociological Review 36:264–278.

Chandler, A.
1949   "The traditional Chinese attitude towards old age." Journal of Gerontology 4:239–247.

Chapman, S.
1981   "Goodies for oldies." New Republic (January 3/January 10):9–11.

Childs, M. W.
1980   Sweden: The Middle Way on Trial. New Haven: Yale University Press.

Clark, M.
1971   "Patterns of aging among the elderly poor of the inner city."
        Gerontologist 11:58–66.
Clark, M., and B. G. Anderson
1967   Culture and Aging. Springfield, Illinois: Charles C Thomas.
Clemente, F.
1975   "Age and the perception of national priorities." Gerontologist
        15:61–63.
Coffman, G. R.
1934   "Old age from Horace to Chaucer: some literary affinities and
        adventures of an idea." Speculum 9:249–277.
Cohen, A. K.
1966   Deviance and Control. Englewood Cliffs, New Jersey: Prentice-
        Hall.
Cohen, B.
1977   "Older Americans act funding inadequate to provide 'full range of
        services.'" Network (December):8.
Cohen, W.
1970   Social Security: The First Thirty Years. Ann Arbor: University of
        Michigan – Wayne State University, Institute of Gerontology.
Cohn, V.
1980   "Medicare now covering less." Boston Globe, December 17.
Coll, B.
1969   Perspectives in Public Welfare. Washington, D.C.: U.S. Govern-
        ment Printing Office.
1972   "Public assistance in the U.S.: Colonial times to 1860." Pp. 128–158
        in E. W. Martin (ed.), Comparative Development in Social Wel-
        fare. London: Allen and Unwin.
Comstock, G., S. Chaffee, N. Katzman, M. McCombs, and D. Roberts
1978   Television and Human Behavior. New York: Columbia University
        Press.
Connolly, W. E.
1969   "The challenge to pluralist theory." Pp. 3–34 in W. E. Connolly
        (ed.), The Bias of Pluralism. New York: Atherton.
Cook, F. L.
1979   Who Should be Helped? Public Support for Social Services. Beverly
        Hills: Sage.
Cooley, C. H.
1956   Two Major Works: Social Organization and Human Nature and the
        Social Order. Glencoe, Illinois: Free Press.
Corrales, R. G.
1975   "Power and satisfaction in early marriage." Pp. 197–216 in R. E. Crom-
        well and D. H. Olson (eds.), Power in Families. New York: Wiley.
Cottrell, F.
1960   "The technological and societal bases of aging." Pp. 92–119 in C.

Tibbitts (ed.), Handbook of Social Gerontology. Chicago: University of Chicago Press.

Cowgill, D. O.
1974a   "Aging and modernization: a revision of the theory." Pp. 123–146 in J. F. Gubrium (ed.), Late Life: Communities and Environmental Policy. Springfield, Illinois: Charles C Thomas.
1974b   "The aging of populations and societies." Annals of the American Academy of Political and Social Science 415:1–18.

Cowgill, D. O., and L. D. Holmes
1972   Aging and Modernization. New York: Appleton-Century-Crofts.

Crawford, M. P.
1971   "Retirement and disengagement." Human Relations 24:255–278.

Crittenden, J.
1962   "Aging and party affiliation." Public Opinion Quarterly 33:583–588.

Cromwell, R. E., and D. H. Olson
1975a   "Power in families." Pp. 3–11 in R. E. Cromwell and D. H. Olson (eds.), Power in Families. New York: Wiley.
1975b   "Multidisciplinary perspectives of power." Pp. 15–37 in R. E. Cromwell and D. H. Olson (eds.), Power in Families. New York: Wiley.

Cuniff, J.
1980   "Another dream is vanishing." Boston Globe, August 10.

Cutler, N. E.
1969   "Generation, maturation, and party affiliation: a cohort analysis." Public Opinion Quarterly 33:583–588.
1974   "The impact of subjective age identification on social and political attitudes." Paper presented at the Annual Meeting of the Gerontological Society, Portland, Oregon.
1976   "Resources for senior advocacy: political behavior and partisan flexibility." Pp. 23–40 in P. A. Kershner (ed.), Advocacy and Age: Issues, Experiences, and Strategies. Los Angeles: University of Southern California Press.

Cutler, N. E., and J. R. Schmidhauser
1975   "Age and political behavior." Pp. 374–406 in D. Woodruff and J. Birren (eds.), Aging: Scientific Perspectives and Social Issues. New York: Van Nostrand.

Dahl, R. A.
1961   Who Governs? New Haven: Yale University Press.
1971   Polyarchy: Participation and Opposition. New Haven: Yale University Press.

Daly, H. E.
1975   "A model for a steady-state economy." Pp. 127–145 in W. Burch and F. Bormann (eds.), Beyond Growth — Essays on Alternative Futures. New Haven: Yale University Press.

Davidson, L., and L. K. Gordon
1979   The Sociology of Gender. Chicago: Rand McNally.

Davies, D.
1975   The Centenarians of the Andes. New York: Anchor/Doubleday.
Davis, N. J.
1975   Sociological Constructions of Deviance: Perspectives and Issues in
            the Field. Dubuque, Iowa: W. C. Brown.
Davis, R. D.
1971   "Television and the older adult." Journal of Broadcasting 20:153–159.
1975   "Television communication and the elderly." Pp. 315–335 in D.
            Woodruff and J. Birren (eds.), Aging: Scientific Perspectives and
            Social Issues. New York: Van Nostrand.
Davis, R. D., A. E. Edwards, D. J. Bartel, and D. Martin
1976   "The assessment of television viewing behavior of older adults."
            Journal of Broadcasting 20:69–72.
Demos, J.
1970   "Underlying themes in the witchcraft of seventeenth century New
            England." American Historical Review 75:1311–1326.
1978   "Old age in early New England." Pp. 220–256 in M. Gordon (ed.),
            The American Family in Social-Historical Perspective. Second
            edition. New York: St. Martin's Press.
Derthick, M.
1979   "How easy votes on Social Security came to an end." The Public
            Interest 54(Winter):94–105.
Deutscher, I.
1964   "The postparental life: definitions of the situation." Journal of
            Marriage and the Family 26:52–59.
Dietz, J.
1980   "Social services: 'big business.' " Boston Globe, July 15.
Dimmick, J. W., T. A. McCain, and W. T. Bolton
1979   "Media use and the lifespan: notes on theory and method." Ameri-
            can Behavioral Scientist 23 (September/October): 7–31.
Dinkin, R. J.
1968   Provincial Massachusetts: A Deferential or a Democratic Society.
            Unpublished doctoral dissertation. New York: Columbia Universi-
            ty.
Donahue, W., and C. Tibbitts (eds.)
1962   Politics of Age. Ann Arbor: University of Michigan Press.
Dore, R. P.
1969   "The modernizer as a special case: Japanese factory legislation,
            1882–1911." Comparative Studies in Society and History 11:433–450.
Douglas, J. D.
1979   "Future perils." Society 16(July/August):57–63.
Dowd, J. J.
1975   "Aging as exchange: a preface to theory." Journal of Gerontology
            30:585–594.
1980a   Stratification Among the Aged. Monterey, California: Brooks/Cole.

1980*b*   "Exchange rates and old people." Journal of Gerontology 35:596–602.
Downs, A.
1957   An Economic Theory of Democracy. New York: Harper and Row.
Drevenstedt, J., and G. Banziger
1977   "Attitudes toward the elderly and toward the mentally ill." Psycho-
           logical Reports 41:347–353.
Durkheim, E.
1947   The Elementary Forms of Religious Life. Translated by J. W.
           Swain. New York: Free Press.
1958   The Rules of Sociological Method. Translated by S. A. Solovay
           and J. H. Mueller. New York: Free Press.
Easton, D.
1953   The Political System. New York: Knopf.
1965   A Framework for Political Analysis. Englewood Cliffs, New Jersey:
           Prentice-Hall.
The Economist
1977   "Can lifetime employment in Japan last?" 265(October):91–92.
Edinger, L. (ed.)
1967   Political Leadership in Industrialized Societies. New York: Wiley.
Eisdorfer, C., and F. L. Wilkie
1973   "Intellectual changes with advancing age." Pp. 21–29 in L. F.
           Jarvik, C. Eisdorfer, and J. E. Blum (eds.), Intellectual Functioning
           in Adults. New York: Springer.
Eisenstadt, S. N.
1966   Modernization: Protest and Change. Englewood Cliffs, New Jer-
           sey: Prentice-Hall.
Elder, G. H.
1963   "Parental power and its effect on the adolescent." Sociometry
           26:50–55.
Emerson, R. M.
1962   "Power-dependence relations." American Sociological Review
           27:31–41.
Epstein, A.
1931   "Facing old age." Pp. 77–82 in I. Rubinow (ed.), The Care of the
           Aged. Chicago: University of Chicago Press.
1938   Insecurity, a Challenge to America; a Study of Social Insurance in
           the United States and Abroad. New York: Random House.
Erikson, E. H.
1950   Childhood and Society. New York: Norton.
1968   "Generativity and ego integrity." Pp. 85–92 in B. Neugarten
           (ed.), Middle Age and Aging. Chicago: University of Chicago
           Press.
Erikson, K. T.
1964   "Notes on the sociology of deviance." Pp. 9–21 in H. S. Becker
           (ed.), The Other Side. New York: Free Press.

Erskine, H. G.
1961   "The polls." Public Opinion Quarterly 25:661.
1965   "The polls." Public Opinion Quarterly 29:332, 495.
Estes, C. L.
1978   "Political gerontology." Society 15(July/August): 43–49.
1979   The Aging Enterprise: A Critical Examination of Social Policies and Services for the Aged. San Francisco: Jossey-Bass.
Etheredge, L. S.
1976   The Case of the Unreturned Cafeteria Trays. Washington, D.C.: American Political Science Association.
Eysenck, H. J.
1954   The Psychology of Politics. London: Routledge and Kegan Paul.
Faramond, G.
1973   "Toward a happy old age." Current Sweden 5:1–7.
Faris, R. (ed.)
1964   Handbook of Modern Sociology. Chicago: Rand McNally.
Federal Reserve Bank of Saint Louis
1980   International Economic Conditions Annual Data 1960–1979. St. Louis: Federal Reserve Bank.
Fennell, V. I.
1977   "Age relations and rapid change in a small town." Gerontologist 17:405–411.
Fine, S.
1967   Laissez Faire and the General-Welfare State: A Study of Conflict in American Thought, 1865–1901. Ann Arbor: University of Michigan Press.
Fischer, D. H.
1978   Growing Old in America. Expanded edition. New York: Oxford University Press.
1979   "The politics of aging: a short history." Journal of the Institute for Socioeconomic Studies 4(2):51–66.
Fishel, J.
1969   "Party ideology and the congressional challenger." American Political Science Review 63:1213–1232.
Foner, A.
1974   "Age stratification and age conflict in political life." American Sociological Review 39:187–196.
Francher, J. S.
1973   " 'It's the Pepsi generation . . . ' accelerated aging and the television commercial." International Journal of Aging and Human Development 4:245–255.
Frank, L. K.
1943   "The older person in the changing social scene." Pp. 34–49 in G. Lawton (ed.), New Goals for Old Age. New York: Columbia University Press.

Freeman, J. (ed.)
1975   Women: A Feminist Perspective. Palo Alto: Mayfield.
Freuchen, P.
1931   Eskimo. New York: Liveright.
Friedan, B.
1963   The Feminine Mystique. New York: Dell.
Friedenberg, E. Z.
1969   "Current patterns of a generational conflict." Journal of Social
           Issues 25:21–48.
Friedmann, E., and R. Havighurst
1954   The Meaning of Work and Retirement. Chicago: University of
           Chicago Press.
Fries, J. F.
1980   "Aging, natural death, and the compression of morbidity." New
           England Journal of Medicine 303 (July 17):130–135.
Fuller, R., and R. Myers
1941a   "Some aspects of a theory of social problems." American Sociolog-
           ical Review 6:24–32.
1941b   "The natural history of a social problem." American Sociological
           Review 6:320–328.
Gans, H. J.
1966   "The failure of urban renewal." Pp. 537–557 in J. Q. Wilson (ed.),
           Urban Renewal: The Record and the Controversy. Cambridge,
           Massachusetts: M.I.T. Press.
Gerbner, G.
1977   "Speech to the American Medical Association." Miami Herald,
           June 23.
Gergen, K. G., and K. W. Back
1966   "Communication in the interview and the disengaged respond-
           ent." Public Opinion Quarterly 30:385–398.
Gerth, H., and C. W. Mills
1953   Character and Social Structure. New York: Harcourt, Brace.
Gillespie, D. L.
1975   "Who has the power? The marital struggle." Pp. 64–87 in J.
           Freeman (ed.), Women: A Feminist Perspective. Palo Alto: May-
           field.
Girshick, L. B., and J. B. Williamson
1982   "The politics of measuring poverty among the elderly." Policy
           Studies Journal, in press.
Glamser, F.
1974   "The importance of age to conservative opinions: a multivariate
           analysis." Journal of Gerontology 29:549–554.
Glasser, P. N., and L. Glasser
1962   "Role reversal and conflict between aged parents and their chil-
           dren." Marriage and Family Living 24:46–51.

Glazer, N., L. Majka, J. Acker, and C. Bose
1977   "The homemaker, the family and employment." Pp. 155-169 in
        American Women Workers in a Full Employment Economy. A
        Compendium of Papers Submitted to the Committee on Economic
        Growth and Stabilization of the Joint Committee of Congress of
        the United States. Washington, D.C.: U.S. Government Printing
        Office.
Glenn, N.
1969   "Aging, disengagement, and opinionation." Public Opinion Quar-
        terly 33:17-33.
1974   "Aging and conservatism." Annals of the American Academy of
        Political and Social Science 415:176-186.
Glenn, N., and M. Grimes
1968   "Aging, voting, and political interest." American Sociological Review
        33:563-575.
Glenn, N., and T. Hefner
1972   "Further evidence on aging and party identification." Public Opin-
        ion Quarterly 36:31-47.
Glick, P. C.
1977   "Updating the life cycle of the family." Journal of Marriage and
        the Family 39:5-13.
Goffman, E.
1959   The Presentation of Self in Everyday Life. Garden City, New York:
        Anchor/Doubleday.
1961   Asylums. Garden City, New York: Anchor/Doubleday.
Golembiewski, R. T.
1960   "The group basis of politics: notes on analysis and development."
        American Political Science Review 53:1117-1119.
Goody, J.
1976   "Aging in nonindustrial societies." Pp. 117-129 in R. H. Binstock
        and E. Shanas (eds.), Handbook of Aging and the Social Sciences.
        New York: Van Nostrand Reinhold.
Gordon, M. (ed.)
1978   The American Family in Social-Historical Perspective. Second
        edition. New York: St. Martin's Press.
Gornick, V., and B. Moran (eds.)
1971   Woman in Sexist Society: Studies in Power and Powerlessness.
        New York: Basic Books.
Gough, I.
1979   The Political Economy of the Welfare State. London: Macmillan
        Press.
Graebner, W.
1980   A History of Retirement. New Haven: Yale University Press.
Gray, J. H.
1878   China: A History of the Laws, Manners, and Customs of the

People. London: Macmillan.
Green, C. S., III
1975   "The equilibrium state and the other America." Pp. 175–211 in W.
          Burch and F. Bormann (eds.), Beyond Growth—Essays on Alterna-
          tive Futures. New Haven: Yale University Press.
Greenstein, F., and N. Polsby (eds.)
1975   Handbook of Political Science, Vol. II. Reading, Massachusetts:
          Addison-Wesley.
Greenstone, J. D.
1975   "Group theories." Pp. 243–318 in F. Greenstein and N. Polsby
          (eds.), Handbook of Political Science, Vol. II. Reading, Massachu-
          setts: Addison-Wesley.
Grew, R.
1977   "Modernization and its discontents." American Behavioral Scien-
          tist 21:289–312.
Grundmann, H.
1979   "Social Security beneficiaries receiving SSI payments." Social Secu-
          rity Bulletin 42(8):44.
Gubrium, J. F.
1974   (ed.), Late Life: Communities and Environmental Policy. Springfield,
          Illinois: Charles C Thomas.
1975   Living and Dying at Murray Manor. New York: St. Martin's Press.
Gustaitis, R.
1980   "Old vs. young in Florida." Saturday Review 7(February 16): 10–12.
Gutmann, D.
1977   "The cross-cultural perspective: notes toward a comparative psy-
          chology of aging." Pp. 302–326 in J. E. Birren and K. W. Schaie
          (eds.), Handbook of the Psychology of Aging. New York: Van
          Nostrand Reinhold.
Habermas, J.
1975   Legitimation Crisis. Boston: Beacon Press.
Hadley, A. T.
1978   The Empty Polling Booth. Englewood Cliffs, New Jersey: Prentice-
          Hall.
Hagan, C.
1958   "The group in political science." Pp. 38–51 in R. A. Young (ed.),
          Approaches to the Study of Politics. Evanston, Illinois: North-
          western University Press.
Hammerman, J.
1974   "Health services: their success and failure in reaching older adults."
          American Journal of Public Health 64:253–256.
Harlan, W.
1950   Isolation and Conduct in Later Life. Unpublished doctoral disser-
          tation. Chicago, Illinois: University of Chicago.
1964   "Social status of the aged in three Indian villages." Vita Humana

7:239–252.

Harootyan, R. A.
1981   "Interest groups and the development of federal legislation affecting older persons." Pp. 74–85 in R. B. Hudson (ed.), The Aging in Politics. Springfield, Illinois: Charles C Thomas.

Harris, C. S.
1978   Fact Book on Aging: A Profile of America's Older Population. Washington, D.C.: National Council on the Aging.

Harris, L.
1974   A Survey on Aging: Experiences of Older Americans vs. Public Expectations of Old Age. New York: Louis Harris and Associates.
1975   The Myth and Reality of Aging in America. Washington, D.C.: National Council on the Aging.

Hartz, L.
1955   The Liberal Tradition in America. New York: Harcourt, Brace.
1964   The Founding of New Societies. New York: Harcourt, Brace and World.

Hauser, P. M., and R. Vargas
1960   "Population structure and trends." In E. W. Burgess (ed.) Aging in Western Societies: A Comparative Survey. Chicago: University of Chicago Press.

Havighurst, R. J.
1963   "Successful aging." Pp. 299–320 in R. Williams, C. Tibbitts, and W. Donahue (eds.), Process of Aging. Volume 1. New York: Atherton.

Haynes, M. S.
1963   "The supposedly golden age for the aged in ancient Rome (a study of literary concepts of old age)." Gerontologist 3:26–35.

Heberle, R.
1951   Social Movements. New York: Appleton-Century-Crofts.

Heer, D.
1958   "Dominance and the working wife." Social Forces 36:341–347.
1963   "The measurement and bases of family power: an overview." Journal of Marriage and the Family 25:133–139.

Heidenheimer, A. J., H. Heclo, and C. T. Adams
1975   Comparative Public Policy: The Politics of Social Choice in Europe and America. New York: St. Martin's Press.

Heisler, M. O. (ed.)
1974   Politics in Europe: Structures and Processes in Some Post-Industrial Democracies. New York: David McKay.

Heisler, M. O., and R. B. Kvavik
1974   "Patterns of European politics: the 'European polity' model." Pp. 27–89 in M. O. Heisler (ed.), Politics in Europe: Structures and Processes in Some Post-industrial Democracies. New York: David McKay.

Hemming, R., and K. Ellis
1976   "How fair is T.V.'s image of older Americans?" Retirement Living

(April):21–24.

Herbst, P. G.
1952   "The measurement of family relationships." Human Relations 5:3–35.

Herman, R.
1979   "Mental patient release program leaves many to harsh fate." New York Times, November 18.

Hess, B. B.
1974   "Stereotypes of the aged." Journal of Communication 24:76–85.
1976   (ed.), Growing Old in America. New Brunswick, New Jersey: Transaction.
1978   "The politics of aging." Society 15(July/August): 22–23.

Hess, B. B., and J. M. Waring
1978   "Changing patterns of aging and family bonds in later life." Family Coordinator 27:303–314.

Hobbes, T.
1958
(1598)   Leviathan. New York: Liberal Arts Press.

Hoffer, E.
1951   The True Believer. New York: Harper and Row.

Hoffman, F. L.
1909   "State pensions and annuities in old age." American Statistical Association Quarterly Publications 11:367–390.

Hoffman, L. W., and F. I. Nye (eds.)
1974   Working Mothers. San Francisco: Jossey-Bass.

Hofstadter, R.
1945   Social Darwinism in American Thought 1860–1915. Philadelphia: University of Pennsylvania Press.

Holmberg, A. R.
1961   "Age in the Andes." Pp. 86–91 in R. W. Kleemeier (ed.), Aging and Leisure. New York: Oxford University Press.

Holmes, L. D.
1976   "Trends in anthropological gerontology: from Simmons to the seventies." International Journal of Aging and Human Development 7:211–220.

Holtzman, A.
1963   "Analysis of old age politics in the United States." In C. B. Vedder (ed.), Gerontology: A Book of Readings. Springfield, Illinois: Charles C Thomas.

Homans, G. C.
1961   Social Behavior: Its Elementary Forms. New York: Harcourt, Brace and World.

Homer
1950   The Iliad. Translated by W.H.D. Rouse, New York: Mentor.

Hopper, R. D.
1950   "The revolutionary process: a frame of reference for the study of revolutionary movements." Social Forces 28:270-279.
Horton, J.
1964   "The dehumanization of anomie and alienation." British Journal of Sociology 15:283-300.
Howard, J. B., K. E. Strong, and K. E. Strong, Jr.
1977   "Medication procedures in a nursing home: abuse of PRN orders." Journal of the American Geriatrics Society 12:83-85.
Howe, L. K.
1977   Pink Collar Workers. New York: Avon.
Hudson, R. B.
1978a   "The 'graying' of the federal budget and its consequences for old-age policy." Gerontologist 18:428-440.
1978b   "Emerging pressures on public policies for the aging." Society 15:30-33.
1981   (ed.), The Aging in Politics. Springfield, Illinois: Charles C Thomas.
Hudson, R. B., and R. H. Binstock
1976   "Political systems and aging." Pp. 369-400 in R. H. Binstock and E. Shanas (eds.), Handbook of Aging and the Social Sciences. New York: Van Nostrand Reinhold.
Hughes, E. C.
1964   "Good people and dirty work." Pp. 23-36 in H. S. Becker (ed.), The Other Side. New York: Free Press.
Hughes, H. S.
1958   Consciousness and Society: The Reorientation of European Social Thought 1890-1930. New York: Vintage.
Hunt, C.
1960   "Private integrated housing in a medium size Northern city." Social Problems 7:196-209.
Hunter, F.
1953   Community Power Structures. Chapel Hill, North Carolina: University of North Carolina Press.
Hunter, R.
1965
(1904) Poverty. New York. Torchbook/Harper and Row.
Hwang, J.
1974   "Aging and information." Communication 3:58-61.
Inkeles, A., and D. H. Smith
1974   Becoming Modern: Individual Change in Six Developing Countries. Cambridge, Massachusetts: Harvard University Press.
International Labour Office
1979   The Cost of Social Security: Ninth International Inquiry, 1972-1974.

Geneva: International Labour Organization.
International Monetary Fund
1980   International Financial Statistics, December 1980, Volume 33, No.
          12. Washington, D.C.: International Monetary Fund.
Johnson, E. S., and J. B. Williamson
1980   Growing Old. New York: Holt, Rinehart and Winston.
Jones, D.
1975   Geographic Mobility and Society in Eighteenth-Century Essex,
          Massachusetts. Unpublished doctoral dissertation. Waltham, Mas-
          sachusetts: Brandeis University.
de Jouvenel, B.
1958   "Authority: the efficient imperative." Pp. 159–169 in C. J. Friedrich
          (ed.), Authority. Cambridge, Massachusetts: Harvard University
          Press.
Kahn, A. J., and S. B. Kamerman
1975   Not for the Poor Alone: European Social Services. Philadelphia:
          Temple University Press.
Kariel, H. S.
1961   The Decline of American Pluralism. Stanford, California: Stanford
          University Press.
Karp, D. A., and W. C. Yoels
1979   Symbols, Selves and Society. New York: J. B. Lippincott.
Kastenbaum, R. (ed.)
1964   New Thoughts on Old Age. New York: Springer.
Keelor, R.
1976   "Physical fitness and health: part II." Aging (May/June):8–9.
Kellerman, B.
1979   "Is there life after adolescence and, if so, should political scientists
          care?" Paper presented at the Annual Meeting of the American
          Political Science Association, Washington, D.C.
Kenniston, K.
1965   The Uncommitted. New York: Dell.
Kerchoff, A. C.
1966   "Norm-value clusters and the strain toward consistency among
          older married couples." Pp. 138–159 in I. H. Simpson and J. C.
          McKinney (eds.), Social Aspects of Aging. Durham, North Carolina:
          Duke University Press.
Kershner, P. A. (ed.)
1976   Advocacy and Age: Issues, Experiences, and Strategies. Los Angeles:
          University of Southern California Press.
Key, V. O., Jr.
1964   Politics, Parties, and Pressure Groups. New York: Crowell.
Keyssar, A.
1974   "Widowhood in eighteenth century Massachusetts: a problem in
          the history of the family." Perspectives on American History

8:83–119.

Killian, L.
1964   "Social movements." Pp. 426–455 in R. Faris (ed.), Handbook of Modern Sociology. Chicago: Rand McNally.

Killian, L., and J. Haer
1958   "Variables related to attitudes regarding school desegregation among white Southerners." Sociometry 21:159–164.

King, C. W.
1956   Social Movements in the United States. New York: Random House.

Klebaner, B. J.
1952   "Public poor relief in America, 1790–1860." Unpublished doctoral dissertation. New York: Columbia University.

Kleemeier, R. W. (ed.)
1961   Aging and Leisure. New York: Oxford University Press.

Kluckhohn, C., and H. A. Murray (eds.)
1955   Personality in Nature, Society, and Culture. Second edition. New York: Knopf.

Koblik, S. (ed.)
1975   Sweden's Development from Poverty to Affluence: 1750–1970. Minneapolis: University of Minnesota Press.

Kobrin, F. E.
1976   "The fall in household size and the rise of the primary individual in the United States." Demography 13:127–138.

Kolko, G.
1962   Wealth and Power in America: An Analysis of Social Class and Income Distribution. New York: Praeger.

Komarovsky, M.
1962   Blue-Collar Marriage. New York: Random House.

Kreps, J.
1976a   "The economy and the aged." Pp. 272–285 in R. H. Binstock and E. Shanas (eds.), Handbook of Aging and the Social Sciences. New York: Van Nostrand Reinhold.
1976b   (ed.), Women and the American Economy: A Look to the 1980's. Englewood Cliffs, New Jersey: Prentice-Hall.

Kuypers, J. A., and V. L. Bengtson
1973   "Social breakdown and competence: a model of normal aging." Human Development 16:181–201.

Kvavik, R. B.
1974   "Interest groups in a 'cooptive' political system: the case of Norway." Pp. 93–116 in M. O. Heisler (ed.), Politics in Europe: Structures and Processes in Some Post-Industrial Democracies. New York: David McKay.

Labouvie-Vief, G. V.
1976   "Toward optimizing cognitive competence in later life." Educational Gerontology 1:75–91.

Lang, K., and G. Lang
    1961   Collective Dynamics. New York: Thomas Y. Crowell.
Laslett, P.
    1971   The World We Have Lost. Second edition. New York: Schriber.
    1976   "Societal development and aging." Pp. 87–116 in R. H. Binstock
              and E. Shanas (ed.), Handbook on Aging and the Social Sciences.
              New York: Van Nostrand Reinhold.
    1979   "The traditional English family and the aged in our society." Pp.
              97–113 in D. Van Tassel (ed.), Aging, Death and the Completion of
              Being. Philadelphia: University of Pennsylvania Press.
Lasswell, H., and A. Kaplan
    1950   Power and Society. New Haven: Yale University Press.
Lasswell, H., and D. Lerner (eds.)
    1966   World Revolutionary Elites: Studies in Coercive Ideological Move-
              ments. Cambridge, Massachusetts: M.I.T. Press.
Latham, E.
    1952   The Group Basis of Politics. Ithaca: Cornell University Press.
Lawton, G. (ed.)
    1943   New Goals for Old Age. New York: Columbia University Press.
Leaf, A.
    1973   "Getting old." Scientific American 229:45–52.
Learner, M.
    1970   "When, why and where people die." Pp. 5–29 in O. G. Brim, H. E.
              Freeman, S. Levine, and N. A. Scotch (eds.), The Dying Patient.
              New York: Russell Sage.
Lee, A. M. (ed.)
    1951   New Outline of the Principles of Sociology. Second edition. New
              York: Barnes and Noble.
Lefcourt, H. M.
    1976   Locus of Control: Current Trends in Theory and Research.
              Hillsdale, New Jersey: L. Erlbaum Associates.
Lehman, H. C.
    1953   Age and Achievement. Princeton, New Jersey: Princeton Univer-
              sity Press.
Lenski, G.
    1966   Power and Privilege: A Theory of Social Stratification. New York:
              McGraw-Hill.
Lenski, G., and J. Lenski
    1978   Human Societies: An Introduction to Macrosociology. New York:
              McGraw-Hill.
Lerner, D.
    1958   The Passing of Traditional Society. New York: Free Press.
    1968   "Modernization: social aspects." Pp. 386–395 in D. Sills (ed.),
              International Encyclopedia of the Social Sciences. New York: Mac-
              millan.

Lerner, D., I. Pool, and G. Schueller
1966   "The Nazi elite." Pp. 194–318 in H. Lasswell and D. Lerner (eds.), World Revolutionary Elites: Studies in Coercive Ideological Movements. Cambridge, Massachusetts: M.I.T. Press.
Leslie, G. R.
1973   The Family in Social Context. Second edition. New York: Oxford University Press.
Levine, R., and D. Campbell
1972   Ethnocentrism: Theories of Conflict, Ethnic Attitudes, and Group Behavior. New York: Wiley.
Levy, M. J.
1966   Modernization and the Structure of Societies. Princeton: Princeton University Press.
Lewin, L.
1975   "The debate on economic planning in Sweden." Pp. 282–302 in S. Koblik (ed.), Sweden's Development from Poverty to Affluence: 1750–1970. Minneapolis: University of Minnesota Press.
Liazos, A.
1972   "The poverty of the sociology of deviance: nuts, sluts, and preverts." Social Problems 20:103–120.
Lieberman, G. L.
1978   "Children of the elderly as natural helpers: some demographic differences." American Journal of Community Psychology 6: 489–498.
Lipman, A.
1970   "Prestige of the aged in Portugal: realistic appraisal and ritualistic deference." International Journal of Aging and Human Development 1:127–136.
Lipman-Blumen, J.
1975   "Toward a theory of sex roles: an explanation of the social institutions of sex segregation." Paper presented at the American Economics Association Committee on the Status of Women's Conference on Occupational Segregation of Women. Wellesley, Massachusetts: Wellesley College, Center for the Study of Women in Higher Education and the Professions.
Lipset, S. M.
1959   Political Man: The Social Bases of Politics. Garden City, New York: Doubleday
Litwak, E.
1960   "Occupational mobility and extended family cohesion." American Sociological Review 25:9–21.
Lodge, G. C.
1976   The New American Ideology. New York: Knopf.
Lowenthal, M. F.
1975   "Psychosocial variations across the adult life course: frontiers for

298   *The Politics of Aging*

research and policy." Gerontologist 15:6–12.

Lowi, T.
1964   "American business, public policy, and political theory." World Politics 16:676–715.
1969   The End of Liberalism: Ideology, Policy, and the Crisis of Public Authority. New York: Norton.
1971   The Politics of Disorder. New York: Basic Books

Lubove, R.
1968   The Struggle for Social Security 1900–1935. Cambridge, Massachusetts: Harvard University Press.

McConnell, G.
1966   Private Power and American Democracy. New York: Knopf.

McCourt, J. F.
1963   A Study of the Acceptance of the Geriatric Patient among Selected Groups of Hospital Personnel. Unpublished doctoral dissertation. Boston, Massachusetts: Boston University.

McKenzie, R., and A. Silver
1968   Angels in Marble: Working Class Conservatives in Urban England. Chicago: University of Chicago Press.

McKinlay, S. M., and M. Jeffreys
1974   "The menopausal syndrome." British Journal of Preventive and Social Medicine 28:108–115.

McRae, J.
1975   Elderly in the Environment: Northern Europe. Tallahassee: Florida Department of Health and Rehabilitative Services.

Maddox, G. L.
1970   "Themes and issues in sociological theories of human aging." Human Development 13:17–27.
1974   "Is senior power the wave of the future?" Paper presented at the Annual Meeting of the American Association for the Advancement of Science, San Francisco.
1978   "Will senior power become a reality?" Pp. 185–196 in L. F. Jarvik (ed.), Aging into the 21st Century: Middle-Agers Today. New York: Gardner Press.

Maddox, G. L., and E. B. Douglass
1974   "Aging and individual differences: a longitudinal analysis of social, psychological and physiological indicators." Journal of Gerontology 29:555–563.

Mansfield, H.
1970   "Disguised liberalism." Public Policy 18:605–628.

Marmor, T. R.
1969   "The Congress: Medicare politics and policy." Pp. 2–66 in A. D. Snidler (ed.), American Political Institutions and Public Policy: Five Contemporary Studies. Boston: Little, Brown.
1973   The Politics of Medicare. Chicago: Aldine.

1981   "The politics of Medicare." Pp. 105–134 in R. B. Hudson (ed.),
        The Aging in Politics. Springfield, Illinois: Charles C Thomas.
Martin, E. W. (ed.)
1972   Comparative Development in Social Welfare. London: Allen and
        Unwin.
Martin, W. C., V. L. Bengtson, and A. Acock
1974   "Alienation and age: a context-specific approach." Social Forces
        53:266–274.
Marx, K.
1964   Selected Writings in Sociology and Social Philosophy. Edited by T.
        B. Bottomore and M. Rubel. Baltimore, Maryland: Penguin.
Mason, P. A.
1957   The Ancient Civilizations of Peru. London: Penguin.
Matthews, S. H.
1978   The Social World of Old Women. Beverly Hills, California: Sage.
Mauss, A.
1971   "On being strangled by the stars and stripes: the New Left, the Old
        Left, and the natural history of American radical movements."
        Journal of Social Issues 27:185–202.
1975   Social Problems as Social Movements. Philadelphia: J. B. Lippincott.
Mead, G. H.
1934   Mind, Self, and Society: From the Standpoint of a Social Behaviorist.
        Edited by C. W. Morris. Chicago: University of Chicago Press.
Meadows, D. H., D. L. Meadows, J. Randers, and W. W. Behrens, III
1972   The Limits to Growth. New York: Potomac Associates.
Mendelson, M. A.
1974   Tender Loving Greed. New York: Knopf.
Merton, R. K.
1957   Social Theory and Social Structure. New York: Free Press.
Merton, R. K., and R. Nisbet (eds.)
1976   Contemporary Social Problems. Fourth edition. New York: Har-
        court, Brace, and Jovanovich.
Meyersohn, R.
1961   "An examination of commercial entertainment." Pp. 243–273 in R.
        W. Kleemeier (ed.), Aging and Leisure. New York: Oxford Univer-
        sity Press.
Milbrath, L. W., and M. L. Goel
1977   Political Participation. Second edition. Chicago: Rand McNally.
Miller, H. P.
1966   Income Distribution in the United States. Washington, D.C.: U.S.
        Government Printing Office.
Miller, K. E.
1968   Government and Politics in Denmark. Boston: Houghton-Mifflin.
Mills, C. W.
1943   "The professional ideology of social pathologists." American

Journal of Sociology 49:165–180.

Ministry of Economic Affairs and National Institute of Economic Research
1980a   The Swedish Economy, January 1980: Preliminary National Budg-
         et. Stockholm: Ministry of Economic Affairs.
1980b   The Swedish Economy, April 1980. Revised National Budget.
         Stockholm: Ministry of Economic Affairs.

Monk, A., A. Cryns, and K. Milbrath
1976   "Personal and social value concerns of Scandinavian elderly: a
         multivariate study." International Journal of Aging and Human
         Development 7:221–230.

Moore, K. A., and I. V. Sawhill
1976   "Implications of women's employment for home and family life."
         Pp. 102–122 in J. Kreps (ed.), Women and the American Economy:
         A Look to the 1980's. Englewood Cliffs, New Jersey: Prentice-Hall.

Morrison, P.
1979   "Beyond the baby boom: the depopulation of America." Futurist
         8(April): 131–139.

Murdock, G. P.
1934   Our Primitive Contemporaries. New York: Macmillan.

Myles, J. F.
1981   "The aged and the welfare state: an essay in political demography."
         Paper presented at the meetings of International Sociological
         Association, Research Committee on Aging, Paris.

National Industrial Conference Board (NICB)
1925   Industrial Pensions in the United States. New York: National
         Industrial Conference Board.

Nettl, J. P.
1968   International Systems and the Modernization of Societies. New
         York: Basic Books.

Neugarten, B. L.
1964   (ed.), Personality in Middle and Late Life. New York: Atherton.
1968   (ed.), Middle Age and Aging. Chicago: University of Chicago Press.
1974   "Age groups in American society and the rise of the young-old."
         Annals of the American Academy of Political and Social Science
         415(September):187–198.
1975   "The future and the young-old." Gerontologist 15:4–9.

Neugarten, B. L., and L. Brown–Rezanka
1978   "Midlife women in the 1980's." Pp. 23–38 in Women in Mid-
         life—Security and Fulfillment. Part I. A Compendium of Papers
         Submitted to the Select Committee on Aging and the Subcom-
         mittee on Retirement Income and Employment. U.S. House of
         Representatives, Ninety-Fifth Congress, Second Session. Wash-
         ington, D.C.: U.S. Government Printing Office.

Neugarten, B. L., J. W. Moore, and J. C. Lowe
1965   "Age norms, age constraints, and adult socialization." American

Journal of Sociology 70:710–717.
Neugarten, B. L., V. Wood, R. J. Kraines, and B. Loomis.
1968   "Women's attitudes toward the menopause. Pp. 195–200 in B. L. Neugarten (ed.), Middle Age and Aging. Chicago: University of Chicago Press.
New York Times
1979   "Poll finds public supports variety of moves in fight on inflation." November 8.
Newquist, D., and J. DiMento
1980   "Ask not how old the candidate is." New York Times. February 25.
Nie, N., S. Verba, and J. Kim
1974   "Political participation and the lifecycle." Comparative Politics 6:319–340.
Nie, N., S. Verba, and J. Petrocik
1976   The Changing American Voter. Cambridge, Massachusetts: Harvard University Press.
North, R., and I. Pool
1966   "Koumintang and Chinese communist elites." Pp. 319–455 in H. Lasswell and D. Lerner (eds.), World Revolutionary Elites: Studies in Coercive Ideological Movements. Cambridge, Massachusetts: M.I.T. Press.
Nye, F. I., and L. W. Hoffman (eds.)
1963   The Employed Mother in America. Chicago: Rand McNally.
O'Kelly, C. G.
1980   Women and Men in Society. New York: Van Nostrand.
Olson, D. H.
1969   "Measurement of family power by self-report and behavioral methods." Journal of Marriage and the Family 31:545–550.
Olson, D. H., and C. Rabunsky
1972   "Validity of four measures of family power." Journal of Marriage and the Family 34:224–234.
Olson, M.
1965   The Logic of Collective Action: Public Goods and the Theory of Groups. Cambridge, Massachusetts: Harvard University Press.
Ophuls, W.
1975   "The environmental crisis and the collapse of laissez-faire politics." Pp. 146–172 in W. Burch and F. Bormann (eds.), Beyond Growth-Essays on Alternative Futures. New Haven: Yale University Press.
Oppenheimer, V. K.
1974   "Life cycle squeeze: the interaction of men's occupational and family life cycles." Demography 11:227–245.
Organization for Economic Cooperation and Development
1980   OECD Economic Surveys: Sweden, April 1980. Paris: Organization for Economic Cooperation and Development.

Painton, F.
1981   "Reassessing the welfare state." Time 117 (January 12): 32–33.
Palmore, E.
1975   The Honorable Elders. Durham, North Carolina: Duke University Press.
1976   "The future status of the aged." Gerontologist 16:297–302.
Palmore, E., and G. L. Maddox
1977   "Sociological aspects of aging." Pp. 31–58 in E. W. Busse and E. Pfeiffer (eds.), Behavior and Adaptation in Late Life. Second edition. Boston: Little, Brown.
Palmore, E., and K. Manton
1974   "Modernization and status of the aged: international correlations." Journal of Gerontology 29:205–210.
Palmore, E., and F. Whittington
1971   "Trends in the relative status of the aged." Social Forces 50:84–91.
Parsons, T.
1937   The Structure of Social Action. New York: McGraw-Hill.
1951   The Social System. New York: Free Press.
1955   "Illness and the role of the physician: a sociological perspective." Pp. 609–617 in C. Kluckhohn and H. A. Murray (eds.), Personality in Nature, Society, and Culture. Second edition. New York: Knopf.
1964   "Evolutionary universals in society." American Sociological Review 29:339–357.
1969   Politics and Social Structure. New York: Free Press.
Pease, J., W. H. Form, and J. H. Rytina
1970   "Ideological currents in American stratification literature." American Sociologist 5:127–138.
Pechman, J. A., and B. A. Okner
1974   Who Bears the Tax Burden? Washington, D.C.: Brookings Institution.
Pepper, C.
1978   San Francisco Chronicle, November 30.
1980   "Older Americans are the poorest Americans." New York Times, February 29.
Percy, C. H.
1974   Growing Old in the Country of the Young. New York: McGraw-Hill.
Peterson, D. A., C. Powell, and L. Robertson
1976   "Aging in America: toward the year 2000." Gerontologist 16:264–270.
Piven, F. F., and R. A. Cloward
1971   Regulating the Poor: the Functions of Public Welfare. New York: Random House.
Plato
1941   The Republic. Translated by F. M. Cornford. New York: Oxford University Press.

Pomeroy, S.
1975   Goddesses, Whores, and Slaves: Women in Classical Antiquity. New York: Schocken.

Powell, L. A.
1980   "Causal attribution toward recipients of public aid: Americans' beliefs about others' success and failure and their implications for distributive justice." Paper presented at the third Annual Meeting of the International Society of Political Psychology, Boston.

Pratt, H. J.
1976   The Gray Lobby. Chicago: University of Chicago Press.
1981   "Old age groups and the enactment of the 1972 Social Security Amendments." Pp. 135–150 in R. B. Hudson (ed.), The Aging in Politics. Springfield, Illinois: Charles C Thomas.

Press, I., and M. McKool, Jr.
1972   "Social structure and the status of the aged: toward some valid cross-cultural generalizations." Aging and Human Development 3:297–306.

Price–Bonham, S.
1976   "A comparison of weighted and unweighted decision-making scores." Journal of Marriage and the Family 38:629–640.

Pye, L. W.
1968   The Spirit of Chinese Politics: A Psychocultural Study of the Authority Crisis in Political Development. Cambridge, Massachusetts: M.I.T. Press.
1972   China: An Introduction. Boston: Little, Brown.

Quarterly Economic Review
1980*a*   United States: Annual Supplement 1980. London: Economic Intelligence Unit.
1980*b*   Sweden: Annual Supplement 1980. London: Economic Intelligence Unit.
1980*c*   Germany: Annual Supplement 1980. London: Economic Intelligence Unit.

Rabushka, A., and B. Jacobs
1980   "Are old folks really poor? Herewith a look at some common views." New York Times, February 15.

Ragan, P. K., and W. J. Davis
1978   "The diversity of older voters." Society 15 (July–August):50–53.

Ragan, P. K., and J. J. Dowd
1974   "The emerging political consciousness of the aged: a generational interpretation." Journal of Social Issues 30:137–158.

Raven, B., R. Centers, and A. Rodrigues
1975   "The bases of conjugal power." Pp. 217–236 in R. E. Cromwell and D. H. Olson (eds.), Power in Families. New York: Wiley.

Reed, E.
1981   "Women: caste, class or oppressed sex?" Pp. 142–151 in J. B.

Williamson, L. Evans, and A. Munley (eds.), Social Problems: The Contemporary Debates. Third edition. Boston: Little, Brown.

Reissman, L.
1973   "The solution cycle of social problems." American Sociologist 7:7–9.

Renshon, S.
1974   Psychological Needs and Political Behavior: A Theory of Personality and Political Efficacy. New York: Free Press.

Rice, D. P., and L. A. Horowitz
1968   "Medical care price changes in Medicare's first two years." Social Security Bulletin 31(11):2–11.

Richardson, B.
1933   Old Age Among the Ancient Greeks. Baltimore: Johns Hopkins University Press.

Riemer, Y., and R. H. Binstock
1978   "Campaigning for the 'senior vote': a case study of Carter's 1976 campaign." Gerontologist 18:517–524.

Rigby, T. H.
1972   "The Soviet Politburo: a comparative profile, 1951–1971." Soviet Studies 24:3–23.

Riley, M. W., and A. Foner
1968   Aging and Society. Volume 1: An Inventory of Research Findings. New York: Russell Sage.

Riley, M. W., J. W. Riley, Jr., and M. E. Johnson (eds.)
1969   Aging and Society. Volume 2: Aging and the Professions. New York: Russell Sage.

Riley, M. W., and J. M. Waring
1976   "Age and aging." Pp. 355–410 in R. K. Merton and R. Nisbet (eds.), Contemporary Social Problems. Fourth edition. New York: Harcourt, Brace, and Jovanovich.

Rimlinger, G. V.
1971   Welfare and Industrialization in Europe, America, and Russia. New York: Wiley.

Roberts, S. V.
1981   "National mood helps shape Congress committees." New York Times, February 15.

Rodman, H.
1967   "Marital power in France, Greece and Yugoslavia, and the United States: a cross-national discussion." Journal of Marriage and the Family 29:320–324.
1972   "Marital power and the theory of resources in cultural context." Journal of Comparative Family Studies 3:50–67.

Rogers, C. J. and T. E. Gallion
1978   "Characteristics of elderly Pueblo Indians in New Mexico." Gerontologist 18:482–487.

Rones, P. L.
1978   "Older men — the choice between work and retirement." Monthly
        Labor Review 101 (November):3–10.
Rose, A. M.
1965a   "The subculture of aging: a framework for research in social
        gerontology." Pp. 3–16 in A. M. Rose and W. A. Peterson (eds.),
        Older People and Their Social World. Philadelphia: F. A. Davis.
1965b   "Group consciousness among the aging." Pp. 19–36 in A. M. Rose
        and W. A. Peterson (eds.), Older People and Their Social World.
        Philadelphia: F. A. Davis.
Rose, A. M., and W. A. Peterson (eds.)
1965   Older People and Their Social World. Philadelphia: F. A. Davis.
Rose, R.
1964   Politics in England. Boston: Little, Brown.
Rosen, B., and R. Salling
1971   "Political participation as a function of internal-external locus of
        control." Psychological Reports 29:880–882.
Rosenbaum, J. E.
1980   "Organizational careers and life-cycle stages." Paper presented at
        the Annual Meeting of the American Sociological Association,
        New York.
1981   Organizational Career Tracking and Individuals' Careers: The
        Internal Stratification of a Corporation. New York: Academic Press.
Rosenfeld, A.
1976   Prolongevity. New York: Avon.
1977   "Prolongevity: the extension of the human life span." Futurist 11
        (February):13–22.
Rosenthal, R., D. Archer, M. R. DiMatteo, J. H. Koivumaki, and P. L. Rogers
1974   "Body talk and tone of voice: the language without words." Psy-
        chology Today 8(September):64–68.
Rosow, I.
1967   Social Integration of the Aged. New York: Free Press.
1973   "The social context of the aging self." Gerontologist 13:82–87.
1974   Socialization to Old Age. Berkeley: University of California Press.
1976   "Status and role change through the life span." Pp. 457–482 in R.
        Binstock and E. Shanas (eds.), Handbook of Aging and the Social
        Sciences. New York: Van Nostrand Reinhold.
Ross, E. A.
1928   Social Control: A Survey of the Foundation of Order. New York:
        Macmillan.
Ross, S. G.
1979   "Social Security: a worldwide issue." Social Security Bulletin
        42(August):3–10.
Rostow, W. W.
1963   The Economics of Take-Off into Sustained Growth. New York: St.

Martin's Press.

Rothman, S.
1960   "Systematic political theory: observations on the group approach."
        American Political Science Review 54:15–33.

Rotter, J. B.
1966   "Generalized expectancies for internal vs. external control of rein-
        forcement." Psychological Monographs 80:1–28.

Roucek, J. S.
1947   Social Control. New York: Van Nostrand.

Rousseau, J. J.
1950
(1762) The Social Contract. New York: E. P. Dutton.

Rubin, J.
1970   Do It! New York: Simon and Schuster.

Rubin, J., and B. R. Brown
1975   The Social Psychology of Bargaining and Negotiation. New York:
        Academic Press.

Rubin, L.
1979   Women of a Certain Age: The Midlife Search for Self. New York:
        Harper and Row.

Rubinow, I. (ed.)
1931   The Care of the Aged. Chicago: University of Chicago Press.

Safilios-Rothschild, C.
1970   "Study of family power structure: 1960–1969." Journal of Marriage
        and the Family 32:539–552.
1976   "A macro and micro-examination of family power and love: an
        exchange model." Journal of Marriage and the Family 38:355–362.

Sahlins, M.
1972   Stone Age Economics. Chicago: Aldine-Atherton.

Salisbury, R. H.
1969   "An exchange theory of interest groups." Midwest Journal of Polit-
        ical Science 1:1–32.
1970   Interest Group Politics in America. New York: Harper and Row.

Samuelsson, K.
1975   "The philosophy of Swedish welfare policies." Pp. 335–346 in S.
        Koblik (ed.), Sweden's Development from Poverty to Affluence
        1750–1970. Minneapolis: University of Minnesota Press.

Samuelson, R. J.
1978   "The withering freedom to govern." Washington Post, March 5.

Sanders, D. S.
1973   The Impact of Reform Movements on Social Policy Change: The
        Case of Social Insurance. Fair Lawn, New Jersey: R. E. Burdick.

Scanzoni, J.
1970   Opportunity and the Family. New York: Free Press.
1972   Sexual Bargaining: Power Politics in American Marriage. Engle-

    wood Cliffs, New Jersey: Prentice-Hall.

1978   Sex Roles, Women's Work and Marital Conflict. Lexington, Massachusetts: D.C. Heath.

1979   "Social processes and power in families." Pp. 295–316 in W. R. Burr, R. Hill, F. I. Nye, and I. L. Keiss (eds.), Contemporary Theories about the Family. Volume I. New York: Free Press.

Schattschneider, E. E.

1960   The Semi-Sovereign People. New York: Holt, Rinehart and Winston.

Schlesinger, A., Jr.

1958   The Politics of Upheaval. Boston: Houghton-Mifflin.

Schlesinger, J. A.

1966   Ambition and Politics: Political Careers in the United States. Chicago: Rand McNally.

1967   "Political careers and party leadership." Pp. 266–293 in L. Edinger (ed.), Political Leadership in Industrialized Societies. New York: Wiley.

Schorr, A. L.

1960   Filial Responsibility in the Modern American Family. Social Security Administration, Division of Program Research. Washington, D.C.: U.S. Government Printing Office.

Schottland, C. I.

1970   The Social Security Program in the United States. Second edition. New York: Appleton-Century-Crofts.

Schram, R. W.

1979   "Marital satisfaction over the family life cycle: a critique and proposal." Journal of Marriage and the Family 41:7–12.

Schramm, W.

1954   (ed.), The Process and Effects of Mass Communications. Urbana, Illinois: University of Illinois Press.

1969   "Aging and mass communication." Pp. 352–375 in M. W. Riley, J. W. Riley, Jr., and M. E. Johnson (eds.), Aging and Society. Volume 2: Aging and the Professions. New York: Russell Sage.

Schramm, W., and D. White

1954   "Age, education, and economic status as factors in newspaper reading: conclusions." Pp. 71–73 in W. Schramm (ed.), The Process and Effects of Mass Communications. Urbana, Illinois: University of Illinois Press.

Schulz, J. H.

1980   The Economics of Aging. Second edition. Belmont, California: Wadsworth.

Scull, A. T.

1977   Decarceration: Community Treatment and the Deviant—A Radical View. Englewood Cliffs, New Jersey: Prentice-Hall.

Searing, D., G. Wright, and G. Rabinowitz

1975   "The primacy principle: attitude change and political socialization."

British Journal of Political Science 6:83–133.
Seelbach, W. C.
1978   "Correlates of aged parents' filial responsibility expectations and realizations." Family Coordinator 27:341–350.
Seeman, M.
1959   "On the meaning of alienation." American Sociological Review 24:783–791.
1972   "Alienation and engagement." In A. Campbell and P. Converse (eds.), The Human Meaning of Social Change. New York: Russell Sage.
1975   "Alienation studies." Annual Review of Sociology. Volume 1. Palo Alto, California: Annual Reviews.
Seligman, M. E. P.
1975   Helplessness: On Depression, Development, and Death. New York: W. H. Freeman.
Seltzer, M. M., S. L. Corbett, and R. C. Atchley (eds.)
1978   Social Problems of Aging. Belmont, California: Wadsworth.
Shanas, E., and R. Binstock (eds.)
1976   Handbook of Aging and the Social Sciences. New York: Van Nostrand Reinhold.
Shanas, E., and G. Streib (eds.)
1965   Social Structure and the Family: Generational Relations. Englewood Cliffs, New Jersey: Prentice-Hall.
Shanas, E., P. Townsend, D. Wedderburn, H. Friis, P. Milhoj, and J. Stehouwer
1968   Old People in Three Industrial Societies. New York: Atherton.
Sheehan, T.
1976   "Senior esteem as a factor of socioeconomic complexity." Gerontologist 16:433–440.
Sherfey, M. J.
1973   The Nature and Evolution of Female Sexuality. New York: Vintage.
Shichor, D., and S. Bergman
1979   "Patterns of suicide among the elderly of Israel." Gerontologist 19:487–495.
Sills, D. (ed.)
1968   International Encyclopedia of the Social Sciences. New York: Macmillan.
Silvern, L. E., and C. Y. Nakamura
1971   "Powerlessness, social-political action, and social-political views." Journal of Social Issues 27:137–157.
Simanis, J. G., and J. R. Coleman
1980   "Health care expenditures in nine industrialized countries, 1960–76." Social Security Bulletin 43(1):3–8.
Simmons, L. W.
1945   The Role of the Aged in Primitive Society. New Haven: Yale

University Press.
1952   "Social participation of the aged in different cultures." Annals of the American Academy of Political and Social Science 279:43–51.
1960   "Aging in preindustrial societies." Pp. 69–91 in C. Tibbitts (ed.), Handbook of Social Gerontology. Chicago: University of Chicago Press.
Simpson, I. H., and J. C. McKinney (eds.)
1966   Social Aspects of Aging. Durham, North Carolina: Duke University Press.
Slater, P.
1964   "Cross-cultural views of the aged." Pp. 229–236 in R. Kastenbaum (ed.), New Thoughts on Old Age. New York: Springer.
Smelser, N.
1962   Theory of Collective Behavior. New York: Free Press of Glencoe.
Smith, D. H., J. Macaulay, and Associates
1980   Participation in Social and Political Activities. San Francisco: Jossey-Bass.
Smith, D. S.
1978   "Old age and the 'great transformation': a New England case study." Pp. 285–302 in S. F. Spicker, K. M. Woodward, and D. Van Tassel (eds.), Aging and the Elderly. Atlantic Highlands, New Jersey: Humanities Press.
Snidler, A. D. (ed.)
1969   American Political Institutions and Public Policy: Five Contemporary Studies. Boston: Little, Brown.
Somers, H., and A. Somers
1967   Medicare and the Hospitals: Issues and Prospects. Washington, D.C.: Brookings Institution.
Sontag, S.
1972   "The double standard of aging." Saturday Review 55(September 23):29–38.
Spencer, H.
1896   The Principles of Sociology. New York: Appleton.
1969
(1851)   Social Statics. New York: Augustus M. Kelley, Publishers.
Spencer, P.
1965   The Samburu: A Study of Gerontocracy in a Nomadic Tribe. Berkeley, California: University of California Press.
Spicker, S. F., K. M. Woodward, and D. Van Tassel (eds.)
1978   Aging and the Elderly. Atlantic Highlands, New Jersey: Humanities Press.
Spiegel, J. P.
1971   Transactions: The Interplay Between Individual, Family and Society. New York: Science House.

Sprey, J.
1972   "Family power structure: a critical comment." Journal of Marriage
        and the Family 34:235–238.
1975   "Family power and process: toward a conceptual integration." Pp.
        61–79 in R. E. Cromwell and D. H. Olson (eds.), Power in Families.
        New York: Wiley.
Stannard, C. I.
1973   "Old folks and dirty work: the social conditions for patient abuse
        in a nursing home." Social Problems 20:329–342.
Steinmetz, S. K.
1978   "Battered parents." Society 15(5):54–55.
Steinmetz, S. K., and M. A. Straus (eds.)
1974   Violence in the Family. New York: Harper and Row.
Stephens, J. D.
1979   The Transition from Capitalism to Socialism. London: Macmillan
        Press.
Stephenson, J. B.
1968   "Is everyone going modern? A critique and a suggestion for meas-
        uring modernism." American Journal of Sociology 74:265–275.
Stern, P. A.
1972   The Rape of the Tax Payer. New York: Random House.
Stevens, R., and R. Stevens
1974   Welfare Medicine in America. New York: Free Press.
Stone, L.
1977   "Walking over grandma." New York Review of Books, May 12.
Storing, H. J. (ed.)
1962   Scientific Study of Politics. New York: Holt, Rinehart and Winston.
Stouffer, S. A.
1955   Communism, Conformity, and Civil Liberties. Garden City, New
        York: Doubleday.
Struyk, R. J., and B. J. Soldo
1980   Improving the Elderly's Housing: A Key to Preserving the Nation's
        Housing Stock and Neighborhoods. Cambridge, Massachusetts:
        Ballinger.
Sullivan, W.
1978   "Very old people in the Andes are found to be merely old." New
        York Times, March 17.
Sumner, W. G.
1911   "The absurd effort to make the world over." Pp. 195–210 in War
        and Other Essays. New Haven: Yale University Press.
1963
(1883) Social Darwinism: Selected Essays of William Graham Sumner.
        Edited by S. Persons. Englewood Cliffs, New Jersey: Prentice-Hall.
Sumner, W. G., and A. G. Keller
1927   The Science of Society. New Haven: Yale University Press.

Surrey, S. S.
1973   Pathways to Tax Reform—The Concept of Tax Expenditures. Cambridge, Massachusetts: Harvard University Press.
Survey Research Center
1965   Who Votes for Whom. Ann Arbor: University of Michigan.
Sussman, M. B.
1976   "The family life of old people." Pp. 218–243 in E. Shanas and R. Binstock (eds.), Handbook of Aging and the Social Sciences. New York: Van Nostrand Reinhold.
Szasz, T. S.
1963   Law, Liberty and Psychiatry: An Inquiry into the Social Uses of Mental Health Practices. New York: Macmillan.
Taber, G. M.
1980   "Capitalism: is it working?" Time 115(April 21):40–55.
Thomas, D., D. Franks, and J. M. Calanico
1972   "Role-taking and power in social psychology." American Sociological Review 37:605–615.
Thoreau, H. D.
1942   Walden. Edited by G. S. Haight. New York: Walter J. Black.
Thurow, L.
1980   The Zero-Sum Society: Distribution and Possibilities for Economic Change. New York: Basic Books.
Tibbitts, C. (ed.)
1960   Handbook of Social Gerontology. Chicago: University of Chicago Press.
Tingsten, H.
1937   Political Behavior: Studies in Election Statistics. London: P. S. King and Son.
Tipps, D. C.
1973   "Modernization theory and the comparative study of societies: a critical perspective." Comparative Studies in Society and History 15:199–266.
de Tocqueville, A.
1954   Democracy in America. New York: Vintage.
Tomasson, R. P. (ed.)
1979   Comparative Studies in Sociology. Greenwich, Connecticut: JAI Press.
Townsend, P.
1968a   "Medical services." Pp. 71–101 in E. Shanas et al., Old People in Three Industrial Societies. New York: Atherton.
1968b   "Summary and conclusion." Pp. 424–453 in E. Shanas et al., Three Industrial Societies. New York: Atherton.
1968c   "Welfare services and the family." Pp. 102–131 in E. Shanas et al., Old People in Three Industrial Societies. New York: Atherton.

Trattner, W. I.
1974   From Poor Law to Welfare State. New York: Free Press.
Treas, J.
1977   "Family support systems for the aged: some social and demographic consideration." Gerontologist 17:486–491.
1979   "Socialist organization and economic development in China: latent consequences for the aged." Gerontologist 19:34–43.
Troeltsch, E.
1931   The Social Teaching of Christian Churches. New York: Macmillan.
Troll, L. E., S. J. Miller, and R. C. Atchley
1979   Families in Later Life. Belmont, California: Wadsworth.
Truman, D. B.
1951   The Governmental Process. New York: Knopf.
Turk, H., J. Smith, and H. P. Meyers
1966   "Understanding local political behavior: the role of the older citizen." Pp. 254–276 in I. H. Simpson and J. C. McKinney (eds.), Social Aspects of Aging. Durham, North Carolina: Duke University Press.
Turk, J. L., and N. W. Bell
1972   "Measuring power in families." Journal of Marriage and the Family 34:215–223.
Uhlenberg, P.
1977   "Changing structure of the older population of the USA during the twentieth century." Gerontologist 17:197–202.
United Nations
1979a   Yearbook of National Accounts Statistics 1979: Volume I, Individual Country Data. New York: United Nations Publication Service.
1979b   Yearbook of National Accounts Statistics 1979: Volume II, International Tables. New York: United Nations Publication Service.
U.S. Bureau of the Census
1975   "Projection of the population in the United States, 1975–2050." Current Population Reports, Series P-25, No. 601. Washington, D.C.: U.S. Government Printing Office.
1976   "Demographic aspects of aging and the older population in the United States." Current Population Reports, Special Studies Series P-23, No. 59. Washington, D.C.: U.S. Government Printing Office.
1978   "Money income in 1976 of families and persons in the United States." Current Population Reports, Series P-60, No. 114. Washington, D.C.: U.S. Government Printing Office.
1979a   "Money income and poverty status of families and persons in the United States: 1978." Current Population Reports, Series P-60, No. 120. Washington, D.C.: U.S. Government Printing Office.
1979b   Statistical Abstract of the United States: 1979. Washington, D.C.: U.S. Government Printing Office.
1980a   "Money income in 1978 of households in the United States." Cur-

rent Population Reports, Series P-60, No. 121. Washington, D.C.: U.S. Government Printing Office.

1980*b*   "Money income and poverty status of families and persons in the United States: 1979." Current Population Reports, Series P-60, No. 125. Washington, D.C.: U.S. Government Printing Office.

1980*c*   "Characteristics of the population below the poverty level: 1978." Current Population Reports, Series P-60, No. 124. Washington, D.C.: U.S. Government Printing Office.

U.S. Department of Commerce, International Trade Administration
1980   National Economic Indicators, June 1980. Washington, D.C.: U.S. Government Printing Office.

U.S. Department of Health, Education, and Welfare
1971   "Federal outlays in aging, fiscal years 1967–1972." Facts and Figures on Older Americans, No. 4. Washington, D.C.: U.S. Government Printing Office.

U.S. Department of Health, Education, and Welfare, Social Security Administration
1973   "Supplemental Security Income for the aged: a comparison of five countries." Washington, D.C.: Office of Research Statistics.

U.S. Department of Health and Human Services, Social Security Administration
1980   Social Security Programs throughout the World 1979. Washington, D.C.: U.S. Government Printing Office.

U.S. House of Representatives
1977   Congressional Directory of the 95th Congress. Washington, D.C.: U.S. Government Printing Office.

U.S. House of Representatives Select Committee on Aging
1976   Senior Transportation: Ticket to Dignity. Washington, D.C.: U.S. Government Printing Office.

1977   "Age stereotyping and television." Washington, D.C.: U.S. Government Printing Office.

U.S. Senate Special Committee on Aging
1976   "The role of nursing homes in caring for discharged mental patients (and the birth of a for-profit boarding home industry)." Supporting Paper No. 7. Washington, D.C.: U.S. Government Printing Office.

Vaillant, G. C.
1950   The Aztecs of Mexico. London: Penguin.

Vanfossen, B. E.
1979   The Structure of Social Inequality. Boston: Little, Brown.

Van Tassel, D. (ed.)
1979   Aging, Death, and the Completion of Being. Philadelphia: University of Pennsylvania Press.

Vedder, C. B. (ed.)
1963   Gerontology: A Book of Readings. Springfield, Illinois: Charles C Thomas.

Veevers, J. E.
1974   "Voluntarily childless wives: an exploratory study." Sociology and
          Social Research 57:356–366.
Verba, S., and N. Nie
1972   Participation in America: Political Democracy and Social Equali-
          ty. New York: Harper and Row.
Vinocur, J.
1979   "Swedish socialists post early gain: conservative party also advances."
          New York Times, September 17.
Vladeck, B. C.
1980   Unloving Care: The Nursing Home Tragedy. New York: Basic
          Books.
Waller, W.
1937   "The rating and dating complex." American Sociological Review
          2:727–734.
Walum, L. R.
1977   The Dynamics of Sex and Gender: A Sociological Perspective.
          Chicago: Rand McNally.
Wang, H. S., W. D. Obrist, and E. W. Busse
1970   "Neurophysiological correlates of the intellectual function of eld-
          erly persons living in the community." American Journal of Psy-
          chiatry 126:1205–1212.
Ward, R. A.
1977   "Aging group consciousness: implication in an older sample."
          Sociology and Social Research 61:496–519.
1978   "Limitations of the family as a supportive institution in the lives of
          the aged." Family Coordinator 27:365–373.
1979   The Aging Experience. New York: J. B. Lippincott.
Watson, H. W., and R. J. Maxwell (eds.)
1977   Human Aging and Dying: A Study in Sociocultural Gerontology.
          New York: St. Martin's Press.
Weaver, J. L.
1981   "The elderly as a political community: the case of national health
          policy." Pp. 30–42 in R. B. Hudson (ed.), The Aging in Politics.
          Springfield, Illinois: Charles C Thomas.
Weber, A. L.
1963   Growth of the Cities in the Nineteenth Century. Ithaca, New York:
          Cornell University Press.
Weber, M.
1968   Economy and Society. Three Volumes. Translated and Edited
          by G. Roth and C. Wittich. Totowa, New Jersey: Bedminster
          Press.
Webster, H.
1932   Primitive Secret Societies: A Study in Early Politics and Religion.
          New York: Macmillan.

Wedderburn, D.
1968a   "The financial resources of older people: a general review." Pp.
        347–387 in E. Shanas et al., Old People in Three Industrial Socie-
        ties. New York: Atherton.
1968b   "The characteristics of low income receivers and the role of gov-
        ernment." Pp. 388–423 in E. Shanas et al., Old People in Three
        Industrial Societies. New York: Atherton.
Weiner, M.
1966   Modernization: The Dynamics of Growth. New York: Basic Books.
Weinstein, L.
1962   "The group approach: Arthur F. Bentley." Pp. 151–224 in H. J.
        Storing (ed.), Scientific Study of Politics. New York: Holt, Rinehart
        and Winston.
Wen, C.
1974   "Secular suicidal trend in postwar Japan and Taiwan: an examina-
        tion of hypotheses." International Journal of Social Psychiatry
        20:8–17.
White House Conference on Aging
1971   Toward a National Policy on Aging. Final Report, Volume II.
        Washington, D.C.: White House Conference on Aging.
Whittaker, D., and W. A. Watts
1969   "Personality characteristics of a non-conformist subculture." Jour-
        nal of Social Issues 25:65–89.
Wildavsky, A.
1964   Leadership in a Small Town, Totowa, New Jersey: Bedminster
        Press.
Wilensky, H. L.
1975   The Welfare State and Equality: Structural and Ideological Roots
        of Public Expenditures. Berkeley, California: University of Cali-
        fornia Press.
Williams, J. H. (ed.)
1979   Psychology of Women: Selected Readings. New York: Norton.
Williamson, J. B.
1969   Subjective Efficacy as an Aspect of Modernization in Six Develop-
        ing Nations. Unpublished doctoral dissertation. Cambridge, Mas-
        sachusetts: Harvard University.
1979   "The economic status of the elderly: is the problem low income?"
        Journal of Sociology and Social Welfare 6:673–700.
Williamson, J. B., et al.
1975   Strategies Against Poverty in America. Cambridge, Massachusetts:
        Schenkman.
Williamson, J. B., L. Evans, and A. Munley
1980   Aging and Society. New York: Holt, Rinehart, and Winston.
1981   (eds.), Social Problems: The Contemporary Debates. Third edi-
        tion. Boston: Little, Brown.

316 *The Politics of Aging*

analysis." International Journal of Comparative Sociology 18:
242–253.
Williamson, J. B., and J. W. Weiss
1979   "Egalitarian political movements, social welfare effort, and convergence theory: a cross-national analysis." Pp. 289–302 in R. P.
Tomasson (ed.), Comparative Studies in Sociology. Volume 2.
Greenwich, Connecticut: JAI Press.
Wilson, J. Q.
1966   (ed.), Urban Renewal: The Record and the Controversy. Cambridge, Massachusetts: M.I.T. Press.
1973   Political Organizations. New York: Basic Books.
Wolfe, D. M.
1959   "Power and authority in the family." Pp. 99–117 in D. Cartwright
(ed.), Studies in Social Power. Ann Arbor, Michigan: University of
Michigan, Institute for Social Research.
Wolfinger, R. E., and S. J. Rosenstone
1980   Who Votes? New Haven: Yale University Press.
Woodruff, D. S., and J. E. Birren (eds.)
1975   Aging: Scientific Perspectives and Social Issues. New York: Van
Nostrand.
Wrong, D. H.
1980   Power: Its Forms, Bases and Uses. New York: Harper and Row.
Young, F.
1965   Initiation Ceremonies: A Cross-Cultural Study of Status Dramati-
zation. New York: Bobbs-Merrill.
Young, R. A. (ed.)
1958   Approaches to the Study of Politics. Evanston, Illinois: North-
western University Press.
Young, T.
1979   "Use of the media by older adults." American Behavioral Scientist
23(September/October):119–136.
Zeigler, H.
1964   Interest Groups in American Society. Englewood Cliffs, New Jersey: Prentice-Hall.
Zetterberg, H.
1979   "Maturing of the Swedish Welfare State." Public Opinion 2(5):42–47.
Zisk, B. H. (ed.)
1969   American Political Interest Groups: Readings in Theory and
Research. Belmont, California: Wadsworth.

NAME INDEX

A

B

317

SUBJECT INDEX

A

Administration on Aging, 8, 75, 95, 97, 177, 240
AFL-CIO, 90, 93
Age consciousness, 10, 96, 100, 101, 256–258
Age of leadership and officeholders, 134–141
Ageism, 10–11, 105, 120, 138, 142, 231–232, 234, 236, 239
    discrimination, 55, 56, 105
    gerontophobia, 234, 236
    stereotyping, 10–11, 105, 120, 138, 142, 231–232, 253
Aging network, 102, 144, 240, 250
Aging vote, 11, 104, 247, 254, 256–257 (see also Senior vote; Senior power)
American Association of Labor Legislation, 80, 157
American Association of Retired Persons (AARP) (see National Retired Teachers Association/ American Association of Retired Persons)
American Medical Association (AMA), 92–93, 159, 259
Area Agencies on Aging, 177
Attitudes about the aged, 5–6, 32–33, 35, 40, 45, 49
    ambivalence, 5, 32–33, 35, 40, 45, 49
    veneration, 6, 39, 44, 58, 64, 139
    (see also Stereotyping; Ageism)
Attitudes of the aged, 9, 105–113, 125–128
    attitude stability, 9, 106–107
    conservatism, 105–113
    political alienation, 125–128
    political efficacy, 126–128
Australia, 156, 164, 173
Austria, 132–133, 156, 173
Authority, 20–24, 31, 38–42, 51, 194, 239
Autonomy, 8, 9, 24, 47, 176, 197, 213–214, 219, 229, 239, 274
Aztecs, 31

B

Belgium, 148, 156, 164, 173

C

Canada, 173
China, 27, 34, 38–42, 46–47, 112–113, 135, 139–141
Citizens Committee for Old-Age Pensions, 88
Class differences, 6, 44, 59, 67–68, 194, 196, 255, 267
    family decision making, 194
    impact of modernization, 68
    political influence, 255, 267
    power, 44, 59, 196
    response to parental dependency, 196
    status of elderly, 67
    veneration of the elderly, 6
    (see also Poverty; Wealth)
Coalition formation perspective, 12, 78, 93, 96, 100
Collective behavior, 12, 76
Colonial America, 6, 39, 43–45, 58
Command generation, 125–128
Committee on Economic Security, 93
Conflict theory, 218–219, 233, 236, 239
Conservatism with aging, 9, 105–113
    attitude stability, 9, 107
    elderly issues, 110
    inflexibility, 9
    moderation, 113
    party identification, 107–108
    slower response to cultural shift, 107
Cuba, 113, 140
Culture (see Political culture)

D

Decarceration, 238, 242
Deinstitutionalization, 236

327

Political interest, 9–10, 114–115
  level of information about politics,
    9–10, 115
Political participation, 128–142
  leadership and officeholding, 11, 134–
    141
  nonelectoral activities, 131
  voting, 11, 129–132, 247, 251–252
  (*see also* Senior power; Senior move-
    ment)
Political resources of the elderly, 4, 247–255,
  274–275
Poverty, 33, 34, 35, 58, 79, 82, 152, 153, 157,
  175, 180, 184, 197, 222, 255, 261, 263
  elderly poor, 6, 29, 44, 180, 222, 267
  poor laws, 152, 153
Power, definition, 14–24 (*see also* Political influence of the aged; Family relationships)
Powerlessness, 126 (*see also* Political alienation)
Property (*see* Wealth)

R

Religion, 5, 36, 43, 44, 49, 223
Resource theory, 191–194
Retirement, 48, 56, 156, 173, 201, 227–228,
  249
  mandatory retirement, 8, 253, 260
Ritual deference, 28, 30, 59, 62
Rome, ancient, 6, 27, 31, 32, 34, 38–42

S

Scandinavia, 150, 151, 156, 160, 170, 172, 175,
  185
Secret knowledge, 36, 37
Senate Special Committee on Aging, 8, 91
Senior Citizens for Kennedy, 91
Senior lobby, 92–93
Senior movement, 8, 11, 78–101, 249, 250
  coalescence, 89–95
  fragmentation and demise, 98–101
  incipiency, 81–89
  institutionalization, 95–98
Senior power, 4, 11, 75–101, 103, 104, 117, 119
Senior vote, 104, (*see also* Aging vote)
Sex differences, 196–204, 253, 267–268
  earnings, 13

marital power, 196, 197–204
modernization, impact of, 67–68
political influence, 267–268
power, 13, 34, 41, 44, 47, 197–201
status of elderly, 67
stereotypes of old age, 231
voter turnout rates, 253
Social change, 50–71, 78, 270 (*see also* Modernization)
Social control, 4, 16–18, 214–244
  age norms, 232, 233
  bureaucratic structures, 215, 236
  caretakers, 219, 233, 236, 239–244
  control by one's children, 8, 232
  drugs, 233, 234
  elderly as agents of control, 5, 8, 68
  gerontologists, 241–244
  institutionalization, 233
Social Darwinism, 154, 155, 156, 221
Social movement perspective, 12, 76, 77,
  81–101
Social Security, 86–90, 156–158, 164–168,
  223–229
  criticism of program, 86–89
  expenditures, 97
  Social Security Act, 7, 8, 11, 75, 86,
    156–162, 174, 260
  Social Security Administration, 75
  source of autonomy, 14, 215, 219
  source of control, 215, 219
  taxation, 87, 167, 168, 182
Social services, 3, 181, 182, 186
Soviet Union, 135, 140, 272
Stereotyping, 10, 11, 105, 120, 142, 231, 232,
  253 (*see also* Mass media)
Stigma, 222, 233, 234, 238, 252, 253
Subculture of the aged, 100, 144, 235
Supplemental Security Income (SSI), 174,
  176, 179, 197, 238, 239, 249, 263, 267
Surplus wealth, 28, 29
Sweden, 12, 147–148, 156, 160–168, 170–173,
  186, 187, 272
Switzerland, 173

T

Taxpayer backlash, 103, 147, 148, 168, 257
Telecommunications, 10, 120, 121, 122, 273,
  274